VOLUME 3

DAILY READINGS

from the Life of

CHRIST

GRACE FOR TODAY

VOLUME 3

DAILY READINGS

from the Life of

CHRIST

— JOHN —

MACARTHUR

MOODY PUBLISHERS
CHICAGO

Cover design and illustrator: Kirk DouPonce, DogEared Design
Interior design: Ragont Design

Published in association with the literary agency of Wolgemuth & Associates, Inc.

Library of Congress Cataloging-in-Publication Data

MacArthur, John,
 Daily readings from the life of Christ / John MacArthur.
    p. cm.
 Includes bibliographical references.
 ISBN 978-0-8024-5602-1
 1. Jesus Christ--Biography--Meditations. 2. Devotional calendars. I. Title.
 BT301.3.M33 2008
 232.9'5--dc22

2008025053

This book is printed on acid free recycled paper containing 30% PCW
(Post Consumer Waste) and manufactured in the United States of
America by Lake Books.

We hope you enjoy this book from Moody Publishers. Our goal is to provide high-quality, thought-provoking books and products that connect truth to your real needs and challenges. For more information on other books and products written and produced from a biblical perspective, go to www.moodypublishers.com or write to:

Moody Publishers
820 N. LaSalle Boulevard
Chicago, IL 60610

1 3 5 7 9 10 8 6 4 2

Printed in the United States of America

*To Bill and Kerry Fickett and their sons,
Campbell and Cooper. Bill's careful, diligent oversight
for more than twenty-three years has been vital to the
smooth daily operation of Grace to You. His love for the
people of God sets the tone for our ministry's service
to our listeners. The Ficketts are faithful servants of
Christ and part of the backbone of our church body.*

The rapid pace of twenty-first-century living is not very conducive to setting aside time to slow down, read the Bible, and pray and meditate on God's Word. Yet such activity ought to be the daily priority of every Christian—it is the primary way God leads us in our sanctification. Just as physical nourishment is essential to physical life, so spiritual nourishment is essential to spiritual life—your growth in Christ depends on it.

The frustration comes for many Christians when they're unable to find the time to study God's Word as they would like. I certainly understand that frustration. While I think you should be striving to carve out as much time as possible to spend with the Lord, which you can do by letting go of less important priorities, I do realize that's not easy to do.

That's why I offer you my latest book of daily readings from God's Word. Its goal is to help you develop a consistency in reading and meditating on the truths of the Bible—yet this does not mean a large time commitment on your part.

However, that doesn't mean this is like other devotional books that merely offer inspirational thoughts and meditations to help you feel good about your life. This book contains substantial, thought-provoking selections that come from my commentaries on the Gospels, which are products of my lifetime of study in God's Word.

The focus of this volume, as with the first two in this trilogy, is the life of our Lord and Savior, Jesus Christ. My greatest joy in the pulpit has been teaching from the Gospels and seeing how our Lord lived and interacted with all sorts of people, from the disciples who truly loved Him, yet were weak in their faith, to the masses of people who were mesmerized by His miraculous acts, yet many of whom never believed in Him, and to the religious hypocrites who pretended to want to know Him, yet always wanted to kill Him. In short, by observing how Christ interacted with people, you'll gain great insight into how you can live as He did.

In each of the selections that follow, you'll draw daily nourishment from a nugget of God's Word. In this volume I focus on the final Judean and Perean activities of Jesus' life and ministry, along with much focus on His final conflicts with the Jewish leaders and a fairly detailed look at His Olivet Discourse and His teachings and prayers from the upper room. I conclude this volume with a consideration of our Lord's final days on earth—His death, burial, resurrection, and ascension. Each entry will challenge you to meditate and act on significant truth. My desire for you as you conclude this third year of reading and meditating is a growing commitment to deeper, subsequent study, meditation, and prayer with our great heavenly Father.

THE PURPOSE OF ONE MAN'S BLINDNESS

*"It was neither that this man sinned, nor his parents; but it was so
that the works of God might be displayed in him."* —JOHN 9:3

There is not always a direct connection between suffering and personal sin, as Jesus' statement to the apostles asserts. At another time Christ instructed that neither those Galileans killed by Pilate nor those who died as the tower of Siloam fell (Luke 13:1–5) suffered because they were worse sinners than others, as His listeners had arrogantly assumed. Instead, our Lord pointed to those events as a warning that all sinners face death, and when it arrives they will perish unless they repent and trust Him.

Like Job, the real reason the blind man suffered his affliction was "so that the works of God might be displayed in him." In his commentary on John's gospel, F. F. Bruce gives this insight:

> This does not mean that God deliberately caused the [man] to be born blind in order that, after many years, his glory should be displayed in the removal of the blindness; to think so would again be an aspersion on the character of God. It does mean that God overruled the disaster of the [man's] blindness so that, when [he] grew to manhood, he might, by recovering his sight, see the glory of God in the face of Christ, and others, seeing this work of God, might turn to the true Light.

ASK YOURSELF

In looking for reasons and answers to your suffering, where does your mind usually run? Are most of your conclusions biblical, or are they shaped more by your feelings and others' opinions? How could you foresee God receiving glory from the situations you're facing right now?

JESUS' PRIORITY

"We must work the works of Him who sent Me as long as it is day; night is coming when no one can work. While I am in the world, I am the Light of the world."
—JOHN 9:4–5

Jesus' top priority was clearly to "work the works of Him who sent Me." Whereas the apostles wanted to look back and analyze why and how the man was born blind, the Lord looked ahead and eagerly desired to place God's power on display for the man's benefit. (Jesus' use of "we" includes the apostles and all Spirit-empowered believers in the divine mission.)

The phrase "as long as it is day" implies further urgency regarding ministry. It refers to the few months Jesus had left with the apostles on earth. After that the darkness of His departure (cf. John 12:35) would overtake them and they'd be unable to minister again until Pentecost.

During His earthly ministry, our Lord was most certainly "the Light of the world." And after His death He did not stop being that Light, because the apostles by His power continued His ministry (Matt. 28:18–20).

Christ's instructions to the apostles apply to all believers. They should serve God with a sense of urgency, "making the most of [their] time, because the days are evil" (Eph. 5:16). The Puritan Richard Baxter wrote, "I preached as never sure to preach again, and as a dying man to dying men."

ASK YOURSELF

What keeps you from sensing an urgency to live with deep conviction for Christ? What keeps you from making His priorities the same ones that drive your own daily schedule? Which of these hindrances to full surrender could stand to be completely eliminated from your life?

JESUS' POWER OVER BLINDNESS

When He had said this, He spat on the ground, and made clay of the spittle, and applied the clay to his eyes, and said to him, "Go, wash in the pool of Siloam"... So he went away and washed, and came back seeing. —JOHN 9:6–7

Jesus had previously used His saliva to heal a deaf and mute man (Mark 7:33) and a blind man (8:23); but here is the only time He made clay with His saliva. Ancient interpreters have said making clay symbolizes Christ's creating a new, functioning pair of eyes to replace the blind ones (cf. Gen. 2:7). But Leon Morris wisely comments, "Jesus performed His miracles with a sovereign hand and He cannot be limited by rules of procedure. He cured how He willed."

As well as representing water sent into the pool from the Gihon spring, "Siloam" symbolized the blessings God sent to Israel. Here it is the Father's ultimate blessing to the nation: Jesus Christ, God's Sent One (Mark 9:37; Luke 4:18; John 12:44–45, 49).

The blind man obediently heeded Jesus' command and washed in the pool, which gave him sight. His response represents the obedience of true saving faith (Rom. 16:26; Heb. 5:9), which the man would soon demonstrate. This healing is also a living parable, showing Christ's ministry as the Light shining into a spiritually dark world (see John 1:5).

ASK YOURSELF

Have you put limits on God's activity, expecting Him to work only in certain ways? What do you run the risk of missing when you try to erect fences and boundaries around God's plans for your life? How do you keep a careful, biblical mind-set without leaking over into rigid legalism?

Perplexity over the Larger Meaning

Therefore the neighbors, and those who previously saw him as a beggar, were saying, "Is not this the one who used to sit and beg?". . . So they were saying to him, "How then were your eyes opened?" —John 9:8, 10

The blind man's healing caused sensation and much confusion for the people. Some had to ask if it was really that man, whereas others were certain it was. But other skeptical people found it easier to believe in mistaken identity than in a miraculous healing.

The man himself tried to eliminate the people's confusion by briefly summarizing that Jesus placed saliva-moistened clay on his eyes, told him to wash at Siloam, after which he received his sight. This prompted the people to wonder where such an amazing miracle worker was; however, the man could not tell them, being unable to recognize Him (see vv. 11–12).

Our Lord's healing of this blind man wonderfully illustrates the salvation process. The man born blind would not have received sight (Rom. 8:7) had Jesus not reached out to him. And in salvation, God's Spirit must reach out and draw spiritually blind sinners to redemption (John 6:44, 65). Just as the man was healed only when he obeyed Jesus' order to wash at Siloam, so also God saves sinners only when they sincerely embrace the truth of the gospel (Rom. 1:5; cf. 2 Thess. 1:8; 1 Peter 4:17).

ASK YOURSELF

Who in your life continues to show many of the telltale signs of spiritual blindness, unable to see truth when it's staring them in the face? Commit to praying steadfastly for them throughout this coming year, asking God to open their eyes of faith so they can see what they've been missing.

UNBELIEF IS INCONSISTENT

Therefore some of the Pharisees were saying, "This man is not from God, because He does not keep the Sabbath." But others were saying, "How can a man who is a sinner perform such signs?" And there was a division among them.
—JOHN 9:16

The Pharisees' statement, "This man is not from God, because He does not keep the Sabbath," reveals their biased approach to the situation. They thought Jesus had broken the Sabbath, not because He had violated scriptural regulations but because He had ignored their extrabiblical legalisms.

Why did Jesus deliberately irritate the Jewish leaders by violating their Sabbath rules? Primarily He did so because of His divine authority as Lord of the Sabbath (Luke 6:5). Second, He wanted to show how unnecessary and burdensome such man-centered regulations were on the people. All the legalistic, trivial rules had perverted God's design for a weekly day of rest and gratitude to God. By contrast, Jesus noted, "The Sabbath was made for man, and not man for the Sabbath" (Mark 2:27).

It seemed obvious to the sabbatarian Pharisees that Jesus could not be Messiah if He did not strictly keep their kind of Sabbath (cf. Deut. 13:1–5). Other Jews, however, were not as easily convinced, countering the first group's logic with reasoning of their own: since Jesus opened blind eyes as only God can do, He must be from God. But there was still a division among the Jews (cf. John 7:40–43), revealing unbelief's faithless inconsistency.

ASK YOURSELF

How can you tell when a staunch stance for righteousness is more about controlling other people than defending God's Word? What are some of our other reasons and rationales for holding arbitrary standards over others' heads, equating compliance with our rules as Christian character?

UNBELIEF IS STUBBORN

The Jews then did not believe it of him, that he had been blind and had received sight, until they called the parents of the very one who had received his sight, and questioned them. —JOHN 9:17–19a

There was no doubt that Jesus had miraculously healed the blind man—he was the physical proof standing before the Pharisees. But they stubbornly refused to accept the evidence and purposely remained unconvinced of the truth. The Jews thus were like that "perverse generation, sons in whom is no faithfulness" (Deut. 32:20).

That the stubborn Pharisees would ask the man again what he thought of Jesus reveals their continued confusion and unbelieving scorn toward the beggar. The man's confident identification of Jesus, "He is a prophet," proves he believed the reality that the spiritually blind Pharisees refused to: Christ was sent from God.

The Jews essentially wanted the man to join them in their unbelief of Jesus' claims. They urged him to disingenuously "Give glory to God" (John 9:24) but not to Jesus, who was in fact God's Son and Himself worthy of glory. Such an incomplete confession would equal agreement with the Jewish leaders' obstinate conviction that Jesus was a sinner and not empowered by God (cf. 8:52), but such an attitude merely showed the stubbornness of unbelief.

ASK YOURSELF

How often are you accused of stubbornness—if not in unbelief, perhaps in other areas of life? Even if you don't see a stubborn streak in yourself, what of value could you likely learn from this rebuke?

UNBELIEF IS IRRATIONAL

They reviled him and said, "You are His disciple, but we are disciples of Moses.
We know that God has spoken to Moses, but as for this man, we do not know
*where He is from." —*JOHN 9:28–29

The healed man was undoubtedly frustrated by the Pharisees' irrational bias and repeated interrogation of him. Thus he "answered them, 'I told you already and you did not listen; why do you want to hear it again?'" (v. 27). Realizing their animosity toward Jesus, the formerly blind man sardonically asked the Jews if their repetitive questions concerning our Lord meant that they wanted to learn more and therefore also "become His disciples."

To the Pharisees, the man's courageous response was insolent, and they angrily and piously answered him by retreating to the safety of their alleged loyalty to Moses. After all, they asserted, "God has spoken to Moses, but as for this man, we do not know where He is from." The healed man's next rejoinder completely exposed the Pharisees' lack of faith: "Well, here is an amazing thing, that you do not know where He is from, and yet He opened my eyes." Christ did what only God's power would enable someone to do—He healed the man's congenital blindness and created eyes with vision—yet the Jewish leaders professed ignorance of His origin. Such irrational rejection of the obvious evidence has occurred ever since sinners have heard the gospel and still clung to their unbelief.

ASK YOURSELF

One of the grandest qualities of Christian virtue is being able to admit when you're wrong. Are there areas of life that you continue to defend, even when you know you're standing on shaky ground? What shape could your surrender from that position take?

UNBELIEF IS INSOLENT

They answered him, "You were born entirely in sins, and are you teaching us?"
*So they put him out. —*JOHN 9:34

They couldn't refute the healed man's logic about Jesus and His healing and, furious that he would lecture to them, therefore the Pharisees insolently piled personal abuse on him. They attacked him disdainfully and sarcastically implied that as one born blind, he or his parents must have committed some horrendous sin. Ironically, now through their insolent words they finally admitted that the man who received sight had indeed been born blind. But this admission did not prevent them from excommunicating him from the synagogue.

We learn from this account, as from other places in the Gospels, that when hardened doubters investigate Jesus' miracles or other supernatural biblical events, they reach only one conclusion. Unless the Holy Spirit opens their eyes, they deny the truth no matter what the evidence. Here the man healed of blindness was living proof of our Lord's divine power, yet the Pharisees tried to deny the undeniable and refute the irrefutable. As Paul later wrote to the Corinthians, "A natural man does not accept the things of the Spirit of God, for they are foolishness to him; and he cannot understand them, because they are spiritually appraised" (1 Cor. 2:14; cf. John 6:44).

ASK YOURSELF

What are some of the most common sources for a person's doubts and hardnesses? Is there much to be gained by getting to know someone well who persists in unbelief, seeing if you can detect the sources of their confusion and blindness? How have you seen a hard heart opened?

SPIRITUAL SIGHT COMES FROM GOD

Jesus heard that they had put him out, and finding him, He said,
"Do you believe in the Son of Man?" —JOHN 9:35

Just as the Lord Jesus did in bestowing physical sight to the blind beggar, He seized the initiative in opening the man's spiritual eyes. Rejected by the religious leaders, the man was sought out by the Savior.

If God did not sovereignly reach out to sinners, no one would be saved. Paul summarizes such total inability: "There is none righteous, not even one; there is none who understands, there is none who seeks for God; all have turned aside, together they have become useless; there is none who does good, there is not even one" (Rom. 3:10–12; cf. John 6:44, 65; 15:16). Even as the physically blind cannot restore their own sight, neither can the spiritually dead be reborn by their own strength (cf. John 1:12–13; 6:37).

When Jesus found the man, He asked the question "Do you believe in the Son of Man?" using the personal pronoun "you" to stress the man's need to respond. Our Lord confronted the healed man with his crucial need to trust the Messiah as his personal Lord and Savior. And the answer he wants everyone to give is a sincere and unqualified "Yes," which entails repenting of sin, accepting God's forgiveness, and resting by faith in His everlasting redemption.

ASK YOURSELF

How attuned are you to the spiritual needs in those you encounter on a regular basis? What are some of the things you would likely pick up if you were predisposed to listening for hunger and thirst in the hearts of your friends, your family members, even total strangers?

SPIRITUAL SIGHT RESPONDS IN FAITH

He answered, "Who is He, Lord, that I may believe in Him?" —JOHN 9:36

The healed man already considered the Lord as sent from God, and he had experienced directly His healing power. Now he implicitly trusted Jesus to lead him to the One in whom he was to place his faith. This clearly illustrates that salvation, though divinely initiated, never occurs apart from a faith response.

Early in His ministry Christ had declared that lost sinners must "repent and believe in the gospel" (Mark 1:15). The best known gospel verse promises us "that whoever believes in [Jesus] shall not perish, but have eternal life" (John 3:16; cf. 1:12; 5:24; 6:40). In His Bread of Life discourse, our Lord affirmed, "Truly, truly, I say to you, he who believes has eternal life" (6:47; cf. Acts 10:43). When the jailor at Philippi asked Paul and Silas, "'Sirs, what must I do to be saved?' they said, 'Believe in the Lord Jesus, and you will be saved, you and your household'" (Acts 16:30–31).

What happened at Antioch applies to the healed man: "When the Gentiles heard [see Isa. 49:6], they began rejoicing and glorifying the word of the Lord; and as many as had been appointed to eternal life believed" (Acts 13:48). God sovereignly chooses those who will be awakened, empowered, and enabled to respond in faith (cf. Eph. 2:8–9).

ASK YOURSELF

How have you responded to the Lord in faith—not merely in receiving His gift of salvation but also in appropriating His authority in your life, or in making a certain decision, or in choosing an unpopular path? Are you continuing to sense the necessity of faith as a requirement for daily life?

SPIRITUAL SIGHT BELIEVES IN JESUS CHRIST

Jesus said to him, "You have both seen Him, and He is the one who is talking with you." And he said, "Lord, I believe." And he worshiped Him.
—JOHN 9:37–38

Jesus presented Himself to the man as the object of saving faith, just as He did earlier to the people at Capernaum: "This is the work of God, that you believe in Him whom He has sent" (John 6:29; cf. 3:36; 6:40; 11:25–26).

The Holy Spirit opened his heart to the gospel ("Lord, I believe") and revealed Jesus' true identity to him. He who was blind from birth exemplified this divine principle: "If anyone is willing to do His will, he will know of the teaching, whether it is of God or whether I speak from Myself" (7:17).

As the Spirit dispelled the final vestiges of spiritual darkness from the man's heart, he clearly wanted to worship Jesus. Spurgeon summarizes that moment:

> Then, further, *he acted as a believer:* for "he worshipped him." This proves how his faith had grown. I should like to ask you who are the people of God when you are happiest. . . . My happiest moments are when I am worshipping God, really adoring the Lord Jesus Christ. . . . It is the nearest approach to what it will be in heaven, where, day without night, they offer perpetual adoration unto him that sitteth upon the throne, and unto the Lamb. Hence, what a memorable moment it was for this man when he worshipped Christ! (emphasis in original)

ASK YOURSELF

What do you miss by not turning your thoughts more often to praise and thanksgiving of God? How has worship produced some of the most exciting experiences and seasons of your life?

SPIRITUAL BLINDNESS RECEIVES JUDGMENT

And Jesus said, "For judgment I came into this world, so that those who do not see may see, and that those who see may become blind." —JOHN 9:39

Although Christ came to save, not to condemn (Luke 19:10; John 12:47), sinners who reject His gospel condemn themselves and place themselves under judgment (John 3:18, 36). To reject the Lord's peace is to receive His punishment; to reject His grace is to receive His justice; to reject His mercy is to receive His wrath; to reject His love is to receive His righteous anger. Spiritual sight comes only to those who confess their spiritual blindness and their need for the Light of the world. But contrariwise, sinners outside of the Savior who think their own sight is enough deceive themselves and remain spiritually blind.

The danger for those who think their carnal sight is sufficient is that their rejection of Jesus and refusal to embrace His gospel is irreversible, and their spiritual blindness may well become permanent. In other words, they can find themselves divinely fixed in their position (cf. Ex. 8:15; 10:1; Isa. 6:10; Acts 28:26–27; Rom. 11:8–10). Many of the Pharisees reached that point when they rejected the Father's light of His Son (Matt. 12:24–32). And that is a most precarious spiritual posture for any needy sinner to take.

ASK YOURSELF

What are some of the implications in your own life of this principle: that decisions build on each other, making future changes and corrections even harder to make? What are some of the slippages you need to catch early, while you can, while they're still small enough to tackle?

SPIRITUAL BLINDNESS REJECTS THE NEED OF SIGHT

Those of the Pharisees who were with Him heard these things and said to Him, "We are not blind too, are we?" Jesus said to them, "If you were blind, you would have no sin." —JOHN 9:40–41a

Could Jesus really be saying the Pharisees were spiritually blind like the masses who didn't know the Law (John 7:49)? As the elite religious leaders of the Jews, they were certain they did not lack spiritual perception. But the reality was they were blind to spiritual truth and refused to admit it. In so doing they simply intensified the darkened condition of their hearts and increased their hatred for the true Messiah.

Our Lord's answer to the Pharisees probably surprised them because they were expecting a more direct reply to their question. Nonetheless, Jesus' point for the leaders was that if they would only confess their spiritual blindness and thus admit their need for Him, the true Light, they "would have no sin." Instead, it would be divinely forgiven (Ps. 32:5; 1 John 1:9).

As John Calvin comments, "[Christ] only means that the disease may easily be cured, when it is truly felt; because, when a *blind* man is desirous to obtain deliverance, God is ready to assist him; but they who, insensible to their diseases, despise the grace of God, are incurable." Many, like the Pharisees, have stubbornly refused to admit their spiritual blindness and therefore doomed themselves to eternal darkness.

ASK YOURSELF

What was Jesus' reason for so often answering questions with another question, or (in this case) with a response that took the matter deeper than expected? When people ask you questions about the Christian faith, what might they really be asking? When is a straight answer not always best?

SPIRITUAL BLINDNESS RESULTS IN DOOM

"But since you say, 'We see,' your sin remains." —JOHN 9:41*b*

The always-damning sin of unbelief is in view here. Jesus' pronouncement that the Pharisees' "sin remains" (cf. Heb. 6:4–6; 10:29–31) conveys a sense of finality. It parallels His confirmation of others in their willful unbelief: "Every plant which My heavenly Father did not plant shall be uprooted. Let them alone; they are blind guides of the blind. And if a blind man guides a blind man, both will fall into a pit" (Matt. 15:13–14). The sobering words, "Let them alone," show that the Father sometimes directly judges unrepentant sinners by abandoning them, or even hardening them in their unbelief (cf. Rom. 1:18, 24, 26, 28).

As the sovereign Redeemer (Rev. 19:16), Christ is the divine determiner of a sinner's destiny. Simeon prophesied in the presence of the infant Jesus, "Behold, this Child is appointed for the fall and rise of many in Israel" (Luke 2:34). People who follow the healed man's example, confess their spiritual blindness, and turn to the Light "will not walk in the darkness, but will have the Light of life" (John 8:12). But those who follow the Pharisees' pattern and persist in the darkness (3:19) will likely stay in that spiritual gloom (12:35; 1 John 2:11), absent any saving sight (Matt. 6:23). The first group will spend eternity in heaven (Rev. 22:5); the others will spend it in hell (Matt. 8:12; 25:30).

ASK YOURSELF

Since God alone possesses knowledge about who will "walk in darkness" and who will receive the "Light of life," how are we to treat the various individuals in our path who do not now profess Christ as Savior and Lord? How can we unwisely let this doctrine lead us into unconcern?

JESUS THE GOOD SHEPHERD, PART 1

"He who enters by the door is a shepherd of the sheep. To him the doorkeeper opens, and the sheep hear his voice, and he calls his own sheep by name and leads them out." —JOHN 10:2–3

Perhaps Jesus' most precious title is that of Shepherd. Centuries before Messiah came, Micah prophesied that He would "arise and shepherd His flock in the strength of the Lord, in the majesty of the name of the Lord His God" (Mic. 5:4; cf. Ezek. 34:23; Matt. 2:6 [quoting Mic. 5:2]).

The New Testament also portrays Jesus as the Shepherd. Peter describes Him as the Shepherd of believers' souls (1 Peter 2:25) and as the Chief Shepherd of the church (5:4). But here Christ most vividly depicts Himself as the Shepherd of His flock. And this presentation flows directly from Jesus' dealings with the blind man, the Pharisees, and all who witnessed what occurred.

Because He's the Good Shepherd, the sheep hear Jesus' voice when He calls them out of Israel and into His messianic fold. The imagery pictures the human response to the divine call of salvation (John 6:44, 65; Rom. 8:28–30). The Lord "calls his own sheep by name" because they *are* His. Their names were divinely "written from the foundation of the world in the book of life of the Lamb who has been slain" (Rev. 13:8), and the Father has sovereignly given them to the Son (John 6:37).

ASK YOURSELF

As you meditate on Jesus as Shepherd, what are some blessings that come to mind? How has He proven Himself the Good Shepherd in your life? How could you express this to someone as both an encouragement to them and a gift of worship to God?

JESUS THE GOOD SHEPHERD, PART 2

"When he puts forth all his own, he goes ahead of them, and the sheep follow him because they know his voice. A stranger they simply will not follow, but will flee from him, because they do not know the voice of strangers." —JOHN 10:4–5

The reason the Good Shepherd's sheep follow Him is "because they know his voice"—and true saints will not abandon Christ, the Good Shepherd, to follow false shepherds, "the voice of strangers." John expresses this truth, in part, in his first letter:

> But you have an anointing from the Holy One, and you all know. I have not written to you because you do not know the truth, but because you do know it, and because no lie is of the truth. Who is the liar but the one who denies that Jesus is the Christ? This is the antichrist, the one who denies the Father and the Son. Whoever denies the Son does not have the Father; the one who confesses the Son has the Father also. As for you, let that abide in you which you heard from the beginning. If what you heard from the beginning abides in you, you also will abide in the Son and in the Father. (1 John 2:20–24; cf. 4:1–6)

Those who belong to the Good Shepherd never leave Him to follow false shepherds who deny the truth and seek to lead saints astray.

ASK YOURSELF

Can you identify the false shepherds who parade in our culture today? What do they pretend to offer those who follow them? Which of their appeals and attractions are the easiest for you to be tempted by? How do we keep ourselves reminded that theirs is the voice of "strangers"?

JESUS IS THE ONLY DOOR

So Jesus said to them again, "Truly, truly, I say to you,
*I am the door of the sheep." —*JOHN 10:7

In this metaphor, Jesus is the only door through which the sheep can enter God's fold and enjoy the blessing of His pasture. Only through Him can sinners approach God and receive the salvation He provides (see John 14:6; 1 Tim. 2:5).

Christ's declaration, "All who came before Me are thieves and robbers" (v. 8) excludes Israel's true spiritual leaders prior to Him—Moses, Samuel, David, Nehemiah, the prophets, and others. He is referring to false shepherds—Israel's wicked rulers, corrupt priests, and false prophets. But again, true believers "did not hear them" or go astray because of them.

Jesus then repeats the truth, "I am the door," and adds the certain promise, "If anyone enters through Me, he will be saved" (v. 9). The sheep of the Good Shepherd experience God's love, forgiveness, and salvation. They never need to fear any spiritual harm, and they will discover satisfying pasture from their Lord (cf. Ps. 23:1–3) and His Word (cf. Acts 20:32).

The contrast between the false shepherds and the Good Shepherd is striking: the false ones come to ruin the sheep, but the Good Shepherd comes "that they may have life, and have it abundantly" (v. 10). The unparalleled gift of eternal life far exceeds all other expectations (cf. Rom. 8:32).

ASK YOURSELF

What does abundant life look, sound, and feel like? How does a person know when he or she is experiencing it? What are the gaps and hindrances standing between you and the full enjoyment of all that the Lord Jesus has promised to provide you? What will you do today in light of this?

THE GOOD SHEPHERD DIES FOR THE SHEEP

"I am the good shepherd; the good shepherd lays down His life for the sheep."
—JOHN 10:11

The expression "good shepherd" sets Jesus the Good Shepherd completely apart from all other kinds of shepherds. He has the noble character (cf. 1 Tim. 3:7; 1 Peter 4:10) that identifies Him as the perfect Shepherd, preeminent above all pretenders.

A faithful shepherd will be willing to give up his life to protect the flock. (In the first-century Middle East, robbers and wild animals were a constant threat; see 1 Sam. 17:34; Isa. 31:4.) But the Good Shepherd went far beyond a mere willingness to risk His life for the sheep, or even actually putting it at risk; He in fact sacrificed His life for them (John 6:51; 18:14). Jesus died for His sheep because His Father chose them to become part of the divine flock (cf. Rom. 5:6, 8; 2 Cor. 5:14–15; 1 Peter 3:18). This beautifully illustrates the doctrine of election: His atoning death provided propitiation for the sins of all who believe, as the Holy Spirit called and regenerated them, and the Father chose them.

What a comfort for Christians that their Shepherd has savingly died for them, in contrast to the hired hands and wolves of Jesus' illustration—mercenaries doing ministry not for the love of people and the truth but for money (Titus 1:10–11; 1 Peter 5:2).

ASK YOURSELF

We've known for so long of Jesus' dying for us that the full impact of His saving act can easily be lost in familiarity. But think of the love required for you to actually sacrifice your own life that another might live. How do you begin to worship Him for what He suffered in your place?

The Good Shepherd
Loves and Unites the Sheep

"I have other sheep, which are not of this fold; I must bring them also, and
they will hear My voice; and they will become one flock with one shepherd."
—John 10:16

Jesus uses "know" (John 10:14) to denote the sacrificial love relationship He has with His own. God said of Israel, "You only have I known of all the families of the earth" (Amos 3:2 NKJV). He was aware of other nations, but He had a unique love relationship with His people. One day the Lord will in judgment send away unbelievers because He doesn't know them—He has no love relationship with them (Matt. 7:23). Christians are forever caught up in the strong and intimate affection shared between the Father and the Son (John 15:10; 17:25–26).

The "other sheep" are the Gentiles whom Jesus calls to salvation (Isa. 49:6; Rom. 1:16). Believing Jews and Gentiles "will become one flock with one shepherd." Because Jews and Gentiles had a mutual animosity for one another, such unity was a revolutionary concept:

> In Christ Jesus you who formerly were far off have been brought near by the blood of Christ. For He Himself is our peace, who made both groups into one and broke down the barrier of the dividing wall, by abolishing in His flesh the enmity . . . so that in Himself He might make the two into one new man, thus establishing peace. (Eph. 2:13–15)

Because they both know the Shepherd, believing Jews and Gentiles enjoy true unity.

ASK YOURSELF

How open and adept are you at experiencing unity with your other brothers and sisters in Christ? What could you do to enhance your desire for it and your practice of it?

THE GOOD SHEPHERD COMPLIES WITH THE FATHER'S WILL

"For this reason the Father loves Me, because I lay down My life so that I may take it again. . . . This commandment I received from My Father."
—JOHN 10:17, 18*b*

Because it's impossible to love God without obeying Him (John 15:9; 1 John 5:3), the key attitudes of love and obedience are inseparably linked. God loves the Shepherd because the Shepherd willingly died for the sheep, the sinners God chose in eternity past and gave to the Son in time. Jesus manifested His love for the Father "by becoming obedient to the point of death, even death on a cross" (Phil. 2:8). No one took Christ's life from Him—He surrendered it by His own initiative. Our Lord told Pontius Pilate, "You would have no authority over Me, unless it had been given you from above" (John 19:11). What transpired with the Savior's death and resurrection above all reveals His compliance with and loving obedience to the will of His Father. And by the power of His resurrection, He will raise all believers to everlasting glory (6:39–40, 44).

In spite of the Jews' biases, Jesus' words and deeds prompted many witnesses to say, "These are not the sayings of one demon-possessed. A demon cannot open the eyes of the blind, can he?" (10:21). Like the healed blind man, they concluded that Jesus' works proved He was indeed the Good Shepherd sent from God (cf. 7:31).

ASK YOURSELF

In what areas of your life has obedience been the hardest to maintain? In identifying these sins, what do they seem to provide that your relationship with God does not? How could developing a deeper love for God weaken your desire to get your needs met in sinful, insufficient ways?

A CONFRONTATION WITH CHRIST

The Jews then gathered around Him, and were saying to Him, "How long will You keep us in suspense? If You are the Christ, tell us plainly." —JOHN 10:24

John's reference to winter (10:23) probably symbolizes the Jews' spiritual coldness at that time. Commentator Gerald Borchert notes, "The thoughtful reader of the Gospel understands that time and temperature notations . . . are reflections of the spiritual condition of the persons in the stories."

By confronting Jesus and asking if He was the Christ (Messiah), the leaders were asking the most important question (cf. Matt. 16:15–16). But given their hostility to what Jesus had already revealed, their motive was suspect. Theirs was not a sincere request for information but a desperate attempt to find some reason to discredit and destroy Him. They hated His miracles, were tired of the divisions He'd caused, were resentful of His threat to their status, and were outraged by His claim to be God. Instead of being thankful and joyful to receive Him as their Messiah, as genuine believers always are, they simply showed themselves as reprobates who wanted to use a public declaration by Jesus of messiahship only to arrest Him rather than worship Him. This is the kind of behavior and attitude that always derives from hardened unbelievers.

ASK YOURSELF

Have you experienced wintry seasons in your life with Christ? What are some of the circumstances and events that led to them? How did Jesus eventually thaw the coldness in your heart and draw you back to the warmth of fellowship? Are you as warm now as you want to be?

CHRIST'S CERTAIN CLAIM, PART 1

"My sheep hear My voice, and I know them, and they follow Me; and I give eternal life to them, and they will never perish; and no one will snatch them out of My hand." —JOHN 10:27–28

From the vantage point of human responsibility, the antagonistic Jews did not believe because they had purposely rejected the truth. But from the divine sovereignty perspective, they failed to believe in Jesus because they were not His sheep. A complete understanding of how these two perspectives work together is beyond our comprehension; but the omniscience of God perfectly grasps the relationship. Peter preached that Christ was "delivered over [to the cross] by the predetermined plan and foreknowledge of God." Yet Israel was responsible for having "nailed [Jesus] to a cross by the hands of godless men" who "put Him to death" (Acts 2:23). Divine sovereignty never excuses human sin.

Here Jesus also confidently articulated wonderful claims of eternal security for true believers. After He grants them eternal life, they can never perish and no one can take them out of His hand or His Father's. This is the strongest biblical affirmation of the absolute eternal security for all genuine believers. Christ's certain claim clearly teaches that salvation security doesn't depend on human effort but solidly rests in the sovereign election, promise, and power of a gracious Father.

ASK YOURSELF

What are the everyday implications of Jesus' statement about our eternal security as believers? How would you respond to those who claim that this doctrine takes all the motivation and urgency out of following Christ? Why should it instead have the exact opposite effect?

CHRIST'S CERTAIN CLAIM, PART 2

"My sheep hear My voice, and I know them, and they follow Me; and I give eternal life to them, and they will never perish; and no one will snatch them out of My hand." —JOHN 10:27–28

Our Lord's words here proclaim seven truths that forever ensure the lasting salvation of believers. First, Christians are His sheep, and the Good Shepherd will protect His flock. "This is the will of Him who sent Me, that of all that He has given Me I lose nothing, but raise it up on the last day" (John 6:39).

Second, the sheep hear only Christ's voice and follow only Him, so they can't possibly listen to a stranger and wander away after him.

Third, true sheep have eternal life, and to speak of it ending is a contradiction in terms.

Fourth, God's sheep did nothing to earn eternal life, and they can do nothing to lose it.

Fifth, Jesus promised believers would never spiritually perish. If even one did so, our Lord would become a liar.

Sixth, no one—not false shepherds, false prophets, or even Satan— is strong enough to snatch Christ's sheep out of His hand.

Lastly, the Son's hand holds His sheep, and the Father's hand also holds them so that no one can take them away. Therefore, the believer's "life is hidden with Christ in God" (Col. 3:3).

ASK YOURSELF

How do you handle those times when you may doubt that the hand of Christ is strong enough to hold you firmly? Where do these doubts tend to take you? May the Holy Spirit flood your heart today with the assurance that His Word is true and the power of His love is unending.

The Jews' Charge against Jesus

The Jews answered Him, "For a good work we do not stone You, but for
blasphemy; and because You, being a man, make Yourself out to be God."
—John 10:33

Jesus did not water down or retract His claim to be equal with the Father. Instead, He forced His opponents to deal with the miraculous good works He did with the Father's approval. Those works offered tangible, inescapable proof of Christ's oneness with God (cf. John 5:36). Thus they proved He was not the blasphemer His enemies claimed—in fact, His critics showed themselves to be the real blasphemers.

Christ's foes refused to consider the possibility that His claim to be God might be true. In their twisted thinking, Jesus was the ultimate blasphemer because, as they charged Him, "You, being a man, make Yourself out to be God." As with such episodes before (5:16–18; 8:58–59), the Jewish leaders ardently wanted to kill the Lord. But their accusations of blasphemy could not have been further from the truth. He was not just a deranged teacher arrogantly promoting himself to be God. Our Lord was actually the only begotten Son of the heavenly Father who had selflessly condescended to become a man (1:14; cf. Phil. 2:5–11) who so loved the world that He died to save sinners (John 3:13–16).

ASK YOURSELF

Other people may challenge or question your belief in the teachings of Jesus. But what are some of the works He has done in your life—proofs that His presence in you and His love for you are more than words on a page? What do His actions continue to tell you about Him?

The Results of the Lord's Challenge

Many came to Him and were saying, "While John performed no sign, yet
everything John said about this man was true." Many believed in Him there.
—John 10:41–42

As always, some people believed and embraced Jesus as Savior and
Lord (e.g., 7:12, 43; 11:45), even if the scribes, Pharisees, and lawyers did
not—this time at Bethany beyond the Jordan. The people there remembered Him and turned out to see Him, as they had earlier streamed out to
encounter John the Baptist. Although John did not work any miracles, he
as the forerunner had still been the preeminent human witness to our
Lord. All that John declared about Him was true, and it was no surprise
that "many believed in Him there."

Even now, many like the hostile and unbelieving Jews let their misconceptions about true religion and their love for sin blind their minds to
Christ's saving truth. But in spite of all obstacles, those whom the Holy
Spirit draws in repentance and faith will trust in the gospel and believe
who Jesus is (7:17). Such people will receive "the right to become children of God, even to those who believe in His name" (1:12).

ASK YOURSELF

Because of the resistance of so many to the gospel of Christ, it's easy to
lose confidence that He can work belief in the hearts of those around us.
What keeps you from giving up in times like these? What doubts and
fears need to be sacrificed in order to boldly declare the Word of God?

BELIEVERS AND DIVORCE

*"So they are no longer two, but one flesh. What therefore God
has joined together, let no man separate."* —MATT. 19:6

God once gave a stinging rebuke through the prophet Malachi to those Jews who "dealt treacherously" with their wives (Mal. 2:13). The Father established Himself as witness between husband and wife as they entered the marriage covenant; He is the One who ordains all marriages. Therefore "'I hate divorce,' says the Lord, the God of Israel, 'and him who covers his garment with wrong'" (v. 16).

God expects that believers, through the Spirit's indwelling power, will display the original beauty and mutuality of their marriage vows as well as the grace of forgiveness. Paul instructed the Ephesians,

> Wives, be subject to your own husbands, as to the Lord. For the husband is the head of the wife, as Christ also is the head of the church, He Himself being the Savior of the body. But as the church is subject to Christ, so also the wives ought to be to their husbands in everything. Husbands, love your wives, just as Christ also loved the church and gave Himself up for her. (Eph. 5:22–25)

Two crucial attitudes in a God-honoring marriage are self-denial and self-giving. If the husband and wife are walking in the Holy Spirit, they will manifest an unselfish humility and a forgiving, restoring love that puts the other first.

ASK YOURSELF

What are some of the purest, most powerful testaments to God's grace that can be seen in the lives of married couples? How is your perspective on marriage changed and enhanced by seeing it as a living demonstration of the love of God, a picture of His grand purposes on earth?

JESUS CHALLENGED ON DIVORCE

Some Pharisees came to Jesus, testing Him and asking, "Is it lawful
for a man to divorce his wife for any reason at all?" —MATT. 19:3

The Jews designed this adversarial question carefully, to place Jesus at odds with Moses, the great giver of God's law.

Because of erroneous interpretations of the Mosaic law to accommodate their lusts, the Pharisees were exponents of easy divorce. At the other extreme, some rabbis believed divorce was never permissible. This narrow view was unpopular and just as unscriptural as the Pharisaic view.

The Pharisees knew Christ didn't agree with their lenient position. He had said, "Everyone who divorces his wife, except for the reason of unchastity, makes her commit adultery; and whoever marries a divorced woman commits adultery" (Matt. 5:32). They now hoped He would repeat this teaching and thereby offend many other Jews who supported easy divorce, thus rallying public opposition to the Lord Jesus.

Ultimately, His enemies wanted to destroy Jesus, and they thought it might be easier in Perea, where the Lord now ministered. Likely the Pharisees hoped that Jesus' strong stand against easy divorce would lead to a condemnation of the adulterous tetrarch Herod Antipas, as John the Baptist had done. Maybe that would even cause Herod to execute Jesus, just as he had done with John (14:3–12). However, it was not His time and no man-centered scenario could change that.

ASK YOURSELF

What are some of the most common questions people ask today, not in trying to learn more about Jesus but in seeking to devalue Him? How would you answer a few of these if they were posed to you? What are the keys to turning pointless spiritual debate into productive discussion?

JESUS' ANSWER CONCERNING DIVORCE, PART 1

"'For this reason a man shall leave his father and mother and be joined to his wife, and the two shall become one flesh'? So they are no longer two, but one flesh. What therefore God has joined together, let no man separate."
—MATT. 19:5–6

Jesus quotes from Genesis to force the self-righteous Pharisees to confront Scripture, not just His viewpoint, regarding divorce. From two verses (1:27; 2:24) our Lord presents four reasons that divorce was never in God's plan. Here are the first two reasons.

First, the original text of Genesis 1:27 has "male" and "female" in the emphatic position, meaning "the one male and the one female." There was only one man and one woman in the beginning, not groups of males and females picking and choosing mates as they wished. Therefore divorce and remarriage was never intended to be an option.

Second, because Adam and Eve had no parents to leave, the leaving of father and mother is a principle applied to all future marriages. The word rendered "be joined" denotes the strong bonding of objects (Job 19:20; cf. Ruth 1:14; 2 Sam. 20:2). Sometimes it also defines holding to God in love and obedience (Deut. 10:20; Josh. 22:5).

Marriage as the Lord always intended it thus entails the total commitment of husbands and wives to each other and to Him as the Author of their permanent union and witness to their lifelong covenant.

ASK YOURSELF

No one should be surprised to recognize that God's stance on marriage is one of unbreakable strength and commitment. But inherent in such a noble undertaking is the reality of hardship and challenge. How much of a role does unrealistic expectation play in the marriage problems we face?

Jesus' Answer concerning Divorce, Part 2

"'For this reason a man shall leave his father and mother and be joined to his wife, and the two shall become one flesh'? So they are no longer two, but one flesh. What therefore God has joined together, let no man separate."
—MATT. 19:5–6

Jesus provides a third reason for divorce never being in God's plan—in marriage, "the two . . . become one flesh" (see 1 Cor. 7:4). In the marriage relationship, therefore, the husband and wife are indivisible and inseparable, until death. In God's eyes they become the complete possession of one another.

The act of adultery, harmful as it is to marriage, does not in itself dissolve the relationship. God declared that by divorcing his wife a man "dealt treacherously" with her "though she is your companion and your wife by covenant" (Mal. 2:14–16). For God, every wife is a "wife by covenant," not simply by sexual activity or human whim.

Fourth, Jesus says divorce is not in God's plan because every marriage is made in heaven. Beginning with Adam and Eve, "God has joined together" every husband and wife. No matter how humanity has disregarded God's part in it, marriage as a general social relationship originated with Him for the procreation, pleasure, and preservation of mankind. Whether undertaken sincerely or insincerely, with much or little commitment, our Lord's design for marriage is not divorce but permanence until one spouse or both should die.

ASK YOURSELF

Back away for a moment from any marriage difficulties you may be experiencing, long enough to remember that your marriage is the result of God's doing, not just your own. What can be gained by tuning your heart and mind to see how invested He is in seeing this through to success?

JESUS' ANSWER CONCERNING DIVORCE, PART 3

"'For this reason a man shall leave his father and mother and be joined to his wife, and the two shall become one flesh'? So they are no longer two, but one flesh. What therefore God has joined together, let no man separate."
—MATT. 19:5–6

When our Lord declared, "What therefore God has joined together, let no man separate," His point was and is that marriage is always from God, whereas divorce is always from sinful people. No man or woman—whoever they are, wherever they are, or for whatever reason they may have—has the permission or the authority to break apart what God has put together. Even unbelievers who divorce break God's law, as surely as believers who terminate their marriage. Ultimately, God ordains every marriage but never ordains any divorce.

At best, God only *permits* divorce and remarriage. He certainly never commands that outcome for marriage and never commends it, contrary to what many rabbis in Jesus' day taught. God permits divorce only because of sexual immorality (adultery) or desertion (1 Cor. 7:15), with these permissions being gracious concessions to human sinfulness (Matt. 19:8–9). Otherwise God would never lead a couple out of their marriage, and to say that He does or would is to make Him a liar.

ASK YOURSELF

Even if you've endured a divorce, you would not deny—in fact, you'd likely be the first to admit—the painful, deadening results of a marital collapse. What does it tell us about our hearts when Satan can mask these things as relief and freedom, and we're gullible enough to believe him?

THE PHARISEES' FAULTY DIVORCE ARGUMENT

They said to Him, "Why then did Moses command to give her a certificate of divorce and send her away?" —MATT. 19:7

Here the Pharisees undoubtedly sought to rebut Jesus' answer with their own appeal to Scripture. But they were not really interested in God's standard for marriage but in defending their own self-centered criteria. Rather than positively considering Jesus' words and seeking to amend their ways, the Jewish leaders were intent on discrediting and destroying the Lord. They epitomized unregenerate men who sought moral and spiritual loopholes to accommodate their sin.

To justify their lenient divorce practices, Christ's opponents appealed to Moses, trying to pit him against the Son of God. Because it is the only passage in the Mosaic law that mentions grounds for divorce, the Pharisees had to be appealing to Deuteronomy 24:1–4. But these verses definitely do not command divorce (cf. 22:19, 29; Lev. 21:7, 14).

If the Jews had carefully read their passage, they would have realized it does not teach about divorce at all but about a command concerning a specific case of remarriage. Moses simply refers to an unspecified case of indecency and mentions the granting of a divorce certificate, without commenting on the propriety of the procedure. Thus, any scriptural permission for divorce is implied rather than explicitly taught. It should not be difficult for us to surmise why the Old Testament does not specifically permit divorce. If the Jews so abused an implied permission, how much more would they have abused an explicit permission?

ASK YOURSELF

What causes us to revert to a legalistic way of dealing with the Lord, wanting to skirt the edges and still maintain our delusion of obedience? How is Christ able to free us from that?

JESUS' AFFIRMATION OF THE RIGHT VIEW ON DIVORCE, PART 1

He said to them, "Because of your hardness of heart Moses permitted you to divorce your wives; but from the beginning it has not been this way. And I say to you, whoever divorces his wife, except for immorality, and marries another woman commits adultery." —MATT. 19:8–9

We can't say there are never reasons for divorce. If God finally left idolatrous Israel after many years of forbearance (cf. Jer. 31:31–33), a person can leave his adulterous spouse after a long period of tolerance. Scripture suggests that because Joseph was a "righteous man" he believed he had to terminate the binding engagement with Mary, because she could have been pregnant by another man (see Matt. 1:18–19).

In today's passage, "hardness of heart" indicates a condition of prolonged adultery and unrepentance by the sinning spouse, making a normal marriage impossible. For such occurrences, God reluctantly through Moses "permitted . . . divorce." But divorce was never in God's original, ideal design for humanity—and it never will be.

The message here about "immorality" (adultery) and divorce is the same basic one in the Sermon on the Mount: "Everyone who divorces his wife, except for the reason of unchastity, makes her commit adultery; and whoever marries a divorced woman commits adultery" (Matt. 5:32). The point Jesus made with the exponents of easy divorce and remarriage is that illegitimate divorce followed by remarriage makes adulterers of everyone involved, and therefore easy divorce is wrong.

ASK YOURSELF

What other biblical teachings and commands, based on their difficulty to keep and our acceptance of failure, do we tend to excuse as being largely inapplicable to ourselves and our culture? What are the greatest dangers of treating God's Word with that kind of selective belief?

Jesus' Affirmation of the Right View on Divorce, Part 2

"And I say to you, whoever divorces his wife, except for immorality, and marries another woman commits adultery." —MATT. 19:9

If God was gracious to the sinning spouse by tolerating divorce instead of requiring execution, it was only fair that He was also gracious to the innocent spouse by permitting remarriage (cf. Rom. 7:2–3). God originally allowed divorce so that the adulterer in the marriage might have opportunity to repent instead of being executed. And He allowed remarriage by the innocent spouse so he or she could enjoy again the blessings of marriage that the sinning party's unfaithfulness destroyed. Jesus' clause "except for immorality" clearly permits the innocent partner to remarry, and to do so without committing adultery.

Christ's teaching here was a devastating indictment of His enemies. In contrasting God's genuine righteousness with the Pharisees' phony version, our Lord had said that even looking at a woman lustfully was the same as adultery (Matt. 5:28). Now Jesus' teaching in this text announced that divorce for any reason but immorality also resulted in adultery when there was remarriage. Thus the implication of this statement, which the Pharisees couldn't ignore and neither should anyone today, is that any person who fails to follow biblical guidelines for rightly divorcing a spouse is guilty of proliferating adultery—certainly not a position a believer should want to take.

ASK YOURSELF

How far has phoniness crept into your usual activities and interactions with others? What keeps you from living in free, full fellowship with Christ, not seeking to assert your self-righteousness or hiding behind hypocrisy? How would things be different if you simply followed Him?

APPROPRIATING JESUS'
TEACHING ON MARRIAGE, PART 1

"Not all men can accept this statement, but only those to whom it has been given.
For there are eunuchs who were born that way from their mother's womb; and
there are eunuchs who were made eunuchs by men; and there are also eunuchs who
made themselves eunuchs for the sake of the kingdom of heaven. He who is able to
accept this, let him accept it." —MATT. 19:11–12

The committed marriage is the only happy and lasting one. When two believers love each other unselfishly and live in accordance with God's Word, submitted to one another, a bond emerges that can withstand every temptation the world can aim at them. People in such marriages forge a sharing friendship that knows no limitations, secrets, or conditions.

Not unlike the apostles, however, some twenty-first-century believers seem afraid that a lifelong, unconditional commitment to marriage would consign them to a life of boring, frustrating restrictions. Therefore many conclude it's "better not to marry." But the Lord created marital commitment to bring enduring happiness and satisfaction—in ways a single person or uncommitted spouse can never realize. Far from being a reason to avoid marriage, with all its challenges and responsibilities, biblical commitment is the quality that makes marriage most desirable and fulfilling in the long run.

Of course, Christians must choose their marriage partner carefully and prayerfully. They should become committed only to someone who shares their biblical faith. No love or fulfillment can surpass what a believing couple knows when they live together in obedience to God's Word.

ASK YOURSELF

Are there certain relationships you avoid simply because they require too much of an emotional investment? Do you find that you often exchange genuine relationship with others for selfish, artificial reasons?

Appropriating Jesus'
Teaching on Marriage, Part 2

"Not all men can accept this statement, but only those to whom it has been given.
For there are eunuchs who were born that way from their mother's womb; and
there are eunuchs who were made eunuchs by men; and there are also eunuchs who
made themselves eunuchs for the sake of the kingdom of heaven. He who is able to
accept this, let him accept it." —MATT. 19:11–12

Celibate singleness is like a spiritual gift (1 Cor. 7:7), and "only those to whom it has been given" can hope to appropriate it and be happy and effective in Christian service.

Concerning "eunuchs," our Lord is referring to the voluntary celibacy of those to whom God has granted this gift. In such cases, celibacy can indeed be used in pleasing service to God's kingdom (see 1 Cor. 7:32–34).

Jesus concluded His teaching here by urging His hearers who by divine gift are "able to accept" a life of celibate singleness to do so as God's will for them. But more broadly, our Lord seems to urge the apostles and all believers to appropriate all He has taught concerning marriage, divorce, remarriage, and singleness. We must lay aside any false concepts and human practices on these matters, which may be simply inherited traditions. In other words, the saint's duty is to obediently accept all categories of Christ's teachings as God's Word and live accordingly.

ASK YOURSELF

If you are married, how might God want to change your perceptions of single life and make you more of an encourager to those around you who live without a mate at home? If you are single, what could God accomplish in you right now that having a spouse would only inhibit?

JESUS LOVES CHILDREN, PART 1

"Let the children alone, and do not hinder them from coming to Me; for the kingdom of heaven belongs to such as these." —MATT. 19:14

When word spread that the Messiah was in the vicinity, parents were drawn to the One whose reputation for loving children had become known across the region (cf. John 4:50).

The apostles, however, resented the parents' bringing the children and intruding into Jesus' time and other ministry. The tense of the Greek verb for "rebuked" (Matt. 19:13) suggests that as more and more brought their children to Jesus, His men continued to repulse them. Obviously the apostles, who had been witnesses to Jesus' ministry for two years, still did not fully share His mind and sentiments.

Not long before this, specifically for the apostles' benefit as they were arguing about who was the greatest, Christ said of the child in His arms, "Whoever then humbles himself as this child, he is the greatest in the kingdom of heaven" (Matt. 18:4). The Twelve should also have known that the Talmud taught parents to bring their children to respected rabbis for prayer and blessing. Accordingly, the Jewish parents in Perea, where Jesus now ministered (19:1), brought their children to Him to be blessed. If Jesus were indeed the Christ, these parents recognized a great opportunity for God's own Anointed One, the Deliverer of Israel, to bless their children.

ASK YOURSELF

Beyond the obvious, sugarcoated reactions to Jesus' tenderness toward children, what are some of the more far-reaching implications? How do His words and demeanor speak to the attitudes His followers should still exhibit today toward the young and their needs?

JESUS LOVES CHILDREN, PART 2

"Let the children alone, and do not hinder them from coming to Me; for the kingdom of heaven belongs to such as these." —MATT. 19:14

Jesus was not naively sentimental about children. He knew they were born with sinful natures and they didn't have to be taught to do wrong—their young hearts are naturally bent toward evil. Nevertheless our Lord loved children with a special compassion and, because of their innate openness and trustfulness, He said they are exemplary of the attitude needed for kingdom citizenship (Matt. 18:3–5).

From Mark 10:14 we learn that Jesus was actually angry with the apostles for trying to prevent the children from coming to Him. Undoubtedly there were several reasons He was indignant. First, He had a special love for all children because of the corrupt world they were born into and the evils they would face as they grew up. Second, Jesus also loved parents and understood the special anxieties they have on their children's behalf. Loving children was thus a way to gain parents' hearts. Third, He was angry because no one, not even the smallest baby, is beyond God's love. Fourth, the Lord's anger targeted the apostles' persistent lack of spiritual understanding. Finally, it was rank presumption for His men to hinder parents and children from approaching Him. In general, Jesus was upset with the disciples because the kingdom of heaven encompasses and characterizes such people as the young children.

ASK YOURSELF

What has life done to your "openness and trustfulness" toward God and His ways of dealing with you? What are some of the worst results of losing a childlike sincerity and simplicity toward Him? How could you begin to regain the sense of wonderment that a living faith requires?

CHILDREN AND THE KINGDOM, PART 1

"Let the children alone, and do not hinder them from coming to Me; for the kingdom of heaven belongs to such as these." —MATT. 19:14

The upshot of this text is that for those "such as these" who, because of a young age or mental deficiency, cannot apply saving faith before they die, God brings them into His kingdom by the sovereign work of His grace. Thus infants who die go into the presence of the Lord because He extends His special protection to them.

Regarding the infant son he lost, David said, "I will go to him, but he will not return to me" (2 Sam. 12:23). Although that may simply indicate they would both eventually be in the realm of the dead, the use of personal pronouns and David's confidence in the life to come (Ps. 16:8–11) imply something more. He was sure he belonged to God and would one day enter His presence, and that when he did, he would meet his son who had preceded him there.

God applies Christ's atoning death to children who die before they are able to embrace it by faith in the usual way. Therefore, in a postmodern culture that hinders the gospel in so many ways, it's an awesome responsibility for believing parents to teach their young ones the gospel and point them to saving faith in Christ as soon as the children can believe.

ASK YOURSELF

Do you know someone whose family has endured the loss of an infant or young child? How could you be looking for an opportunity to encourage their hearts and offer them your Christlike, sympathetic comfort?

CHILDREN AND THE KINGDOM, PART 2

"Let the children alone, and do not hinder them from coming to Me; for the kingdom of heaven belongs to such as these." —MATT. 19:14

The account in Mark 10:16 of this incident uses an intensive form of the Greek verb translated "blessing," which indicates a loving fervency by Jesus as He blessed the children. Scripture does not specify the nature of His blessing, but we can infer a divine promise of care for each child.

Soon after, as He had earlier, Jesus concluded, "Whoever does not receive the kingdom of God like a child will not enter it at all" (Luke 18:17). True members of the kingdom are only people who come to Christ in openness, dependency, and lack of hypocrisy, with childlike attitudes.

Over the years, a very effective means of winning converts in northern India has been a children's home. The home takes in orphaned and abandoned children and feeds, clothes, and shelters them. They attend public schools but also study God's Word in depth. Although adult Hindus and Muslims are very resistant to the gospel, the children from the home have been receptive and many have embraced Jesus as Lord and Savior. As children in both age and attitude, they have been genuinely open and responsive to Christ's claims in the gospel.

ASK YOURSELF

If you still have children at home, what deliberate efforts are you making to instill God's Word into their hearts? If you do not have children or your children are grown, how open should you be to asking God for opportunities to minister His grace to other children in Jesus' name?

FIVE KEY WORDS, PART 1

"Let the children alone, and do not hinder them from coming to Me; for the kingdom of heaven belongs to such as these." —MATT. 19:14

This passage suggests five key words helpful in leading children to Christ. Let's look at the first two words today. First of all, we must *remember* God has created every child and thus already owns every boy and girl (see Ps. 139:13–14). All "children are a gift of the Lord" (127:3*a*) and God wants parents to return each to Him for His use (cf. Prov. 22:6).

Our second key word is *teach*. Christian parents have the high calling of teaching their children "in the discipline and instruction of the Lord" (Gal. 6:4). Timothy's mother and grandmother taught him the Word, which molded him to serve the Lord with the apostle Paul (2 Tim. 3:15; cf. 1:5).

God set forth the pattern for righteous instruction early in Israel's history by commanding His people to believe and worship rightly, accepting the truth sincerely and uncompromisingly (Deut. 6:4–6). In addition, God commanded them to teach these things to their children: "You shall teach them diligently to your sons and shall talk of them when you sit in your house and when you walk by the way and when you lie down and when you rise up" (v. 7).

Parents should also provide visual reminders by posters and plaques. Truths depicted give reinforcement to God's wonderful Word (cf. vv. 8–9).

ASK YOURSELF

In trying to grow deeper in our theology and thinking, we can sometimes forget the more basic, foundational elements of belief. What are a few of these bedrock statements and how could you do a better job of having them ready to share with others?

FIVE KEY WORDS, PART 2

"Let the children alone, and do not hinder them from coming to Me; for the kingdom of heaven belongs to such as these." —MATT. 19:14

Our passage brings to mind three more terms that can aid parents in teaching children. Children need godly parents and teachers who *model* godly patterns to follow. Eli the priest showed what can happen when a parent is a negative example (1 Sam. 2:12–25). Similarly, David was a poor model, and Absalom sought to overthrow him (2 Sam. 14:21–19:7).

One Christian writer has observed,

It is the authenticity of parental commitment to truth apart from the lives of children that brings the freedom to share and to pass on that truth to them. In other words, a mature motive for passing on truth is that as a parent I hold that truth to have value for my life, independent of my children and their response to it.

Obviously, little needs to be said about our fourth key word, *love*. Parents who weep lovingly with their children, who both hurt and share joy with them, who make sacrifices of affection for them—such people will effectively influence their children for the Lord.

Finally, after parents have sought diligently to rear their children to obey the Lord, they must *trust* Him to make those efforts fruitful. Only the Holy Spirit can grant spiritual life and empower spiritual faithfulness.

ASK YOURSELF

Does spiritual truth sometimes feel disconnected from real life—a bit awkward and irrelevant to talk about? What has been descriptive of those times when you've experienced just the opposite—when you've seen truth transferring clearly to your ordinary choices and actions?

THE YOUNG RULER: WHAT HE SOUGHT, PART 1

*And someone came to Him and said, "Teacher, what good thing shall
I do that I may obtain eternal life?"* —MATT. 19:16

The "someone" here is likely a young synagogue ruler (Luke 18:18)
who came to Jesus seeking eternal life. The man was a religious leader—
devout, honest, wealthy, prominent, and influential—who seemed to
have everything. Thus it was surprising that he would admit to not having eternal life.

Although it clearly denotes an everlasting reality, eternal life does
not mean merely an unending existence. Even the pagans knew that such
an existence would not always be desirable. For example, when Zeus offered Aurora anything she wanted for her human lover Tithonus, she requested that he never die. But because she didn't ask that he stay forever
young, he was cursed to perpetual degeneration.

However, if it's correct that physical life involves active response to
our environment, then eternal life requires active response to the eternal,
namely, the heavenly realm. Eternal life is thus primarily a quality of existence, the ability given by the Spirit to be alive to God and His plan—
something the unsaved, being spiritually alive only to their sins, do not
know. For believers, it fills their hearts with the hope of life after death
and with the present reality of enjoying life with their indwelling Lord
and Savior, Jesus Christ.

ASK YOURSELF

What are the qualities of eternal, abundant life that are available to us
right now, freely enjoyed by all who truly apply what they believe?
What are your main obstacles to experiencing these spiritual realities,
and how desperate are you to live in the victory they provide?

THE YOUNG RULER: WHAT HE SOUGHT, PART 2

*And someone came to Him and said, "Teacher, what good thing shall
I do that I may obtain eternal life?"* —MATT. 19:16

The young man could not have grasped the complete implications of
what he requested, but he realized that an important dimension to his
present life was missing. Despite his prestigious status in the religious
community, he knew he lacked the God-given peace, assurance, hope,
and joy of which the Old Testament speaks. Simply by inquiring of Jesus
about eternal life, he placed himself beyond the cynical hypocrisy of the
scribes and Pharisees. The ruler realized he didn't possess the redeemed
life only God can grant, which satisfies us in the present and gives an un-
shakeable hope for our future life. And he was humbly and sincerely determined to obtain an answer to his question, regardless of what the
witnesses standing by might have thought of him.

For the man, he was deeply aware of his need and desperate to have it
fulfilled. Many people know and admit they don't have eternal life, yet at
the same time they seem to sense no need for it. Their lives have no divine
dimension and no hope for the life to come, but those crucial deficiencies
seem not to matter at all. The young ruler, however, felt his need so
strongly that he "ran up to [Jesus] and knelt before Him" (Mark 10:17).

ASK YOURSELF

How hungry would you say people are today for a secure belief in their
eternal future? Are you secure in yours? What are some of the best
questions to ask of others in getting them thinking about the importance
of receiving eternal life from the only One able and worthy to give it?

THE YOUNG RULER: WHOM HE SOUGHT

And someone came to Him and said, "Teacher, what good thing shall I do that I may obtain eternal life?" —MATT. 19:16

Even though the young ruler was undoubtedly in the middle of many parents who had brought their little children to Jesus for a blessing, he did not hesitate to ask a blessing for himself. Essentially he told Jesus, "I need Your blessing and favor just as much as these children." And instead of going into our Lord's arms, this man kneeled before Him, prostrating himself in a position of humility, yet also with utmost earnestness.

The young man sought the right thing—eternal life—and he came to the only One who could grant it. John writes, "God has given us eternal life, and this life is in His Son. . . . the true God and eternal life" (1 John 5:11, 20).

That the young ruler addressed Christ as "Teacher" indicates he considered Him to be a respected Old Testament authority and instructor of God's truth. But there is still no evidence he believed Jesus to be the promised Messiah and Son of God; yet the man no doubt viewed Him as one with a spiritual stature above that of the ordinary rabbi. Therefore, even though he did not believe Jesus to be the Messiah, the young man did see Jesus' extraordinary teaching and miracles as qualifying Him to know the way of eternal life; he had come to the right person (cf. Acts 4:12).

ASK YOURSELF

Who among your friends and family is one of your favorite people to be around, yet is resistant to surrendering his or her life to Christ's lordship and eternal care? What have you learned from navigating this relationship that contains such an obvious, important gap in agreement?

THE YOUNG RULER: HOW HE SOUGHT HIS GOAL

And someone came to Him and said, "Teacher, what good thing shall I do that I may obtain eternal life?" —MATT. 19:16

Many commentators have criticized the ruler's question, "What good thing shall I do that I may obtain eternal life?" as being too works oriented. No doubt the Pharisaic philosophy that doing religious things was the way to gain divine favor had influenced him, but his question by itself was a legitimate one. According to the Lord Jesus, there actually is something we must do in order to come savingly to God. When the people asked Him, "What shall we do, so that we may work the works of God?" Jesus told them, "This is the work of God, that you believe in Him whom He has sent" (John 6:28–29).

The point of the man's question was to find out how to "obtain eternal life," which is the most important question any person can ever ask. The whole purpose of evangelism and the very meaning of salvation is to bring eternal life to those who, because of sin, face eternal death (Rom. 6:23). For the young man on this occasion, we must be clear; the issue was not some advanced level of discipleship subsequent to salvation but rather his basic salvation. He already realized his need for salvation; now everything hinged on what Jesus would say and how the man would respond.

ASK YOURSELF

Has someone stumped you lately with a spiritual question? How do you respond when you don't know exactly how to answer? What would help you become more confident in engaging others in spiritual conversation and less likely to dodge matters that feel too probing and direct?

JESUS' RESPONSE, PART 1

And He said to him, "Why are you asking Me about what is good? There is only One who is good; but if you wish to enter into life, keep the commandments."
—MATT. 19:17

The Lord's response was even more amazing than the young ruler's request. Instead of superficially accepting his words and instructing him to "pray and receive Christ," Jesus tested his true motivation. Instead of jumping ahead with glee and hastily leading him to a "decision for Christ," the Savior asked him something that was very disconcerting.

Jesus' terse and seemingly evasive question, "Why are you asking Me about what is good?" shows that He can read the human heart. Our Lord's next comment, "There is only One who is good," perhaps sought to elicit exactly who the man thought Jesus was. Did he realize that the One he was talking to was Himself the "One who is good," namely, God, the Father's Son? Since the young ruler had no answer for this, it's very likely he viewed Jesus as merely a gifted human teacher. The man had truly come to the right person for the answer to his inquiry and the fulfillment of his need for salvation, but he did not yet know who Christ really was.

The Lord Jesus did not press the man for an immediate "acceptance" of the redemptive message because he lacked an essential understanding—the sense of his own sinfulness. Pointing this out to him was the most immediate and next crucial task for Jesus.

ASK YOURSELF

What do you fail to accomplish when you view most every conversation with unbelievers as an "altar call"? Why is listening to someone and really getting to know them so valuable for both of you?

Jesus' Response, Part 2

*And he said to him, "Why are you asking Me about what is good? There is only
One who is good; but if you wish to enter into life, keep the commandments."*
—Matt. 19:17

Leviticus 18:5 clearly refers to the importance of keeping the commandments: "So you shall keep My statutes and My judgments, by which a man may live if he does them." In referring to the law, Jesus in effect told the young man, "You know what to do. You're a devoted Jew who knows what God's law requires. Go do it."

But more crucial yet, the ruler's heart needed to trust Messiah; he was not ready to believe, however. He was probably filled with anxiety and frustration. He longed for peace and assurance—the inner blessings of Scripture associated with spiritual life. In other words, the man wanted God's blessings, but he did not care about knowing God.

Many today also look just for fulfillment of their felt needs, but that is insufficient to bring them genuine salvation. Knowing this reality, Jesus didn't offer any kind of instant relief for the young ruler's felt needs. Instead, He told him he was an offense to the Father. Balanced, biblical evangelism will lead a sinner to measure himself against the perfect law of God so he can realize his deficiency. Salvation is for those who hate their sins and want to abandon them.

ASK YOURSELF

In your zeal to help others, have you sometimes compromised biblical truth to make them feel better about themselves? What have you experienced from dealing squarely with people's true needs and spiritual standing? How have they usually responded—if not immediately, over time?

JESUS' RESPONSE, PART 3

*Then he said to Him, "Which ones?" And Jesus said, "You shall not
commit murder; You shall not commit adultery; You shall not steal;
You shall not bear false witness; Honor your father and mother;
and you shall love your neighbor as yourself."* —MATT. 19:18–19

The young man's brief reply of "Which ones?" must have contained a
tone of perplexity and sounded like a rhetorical question regarding the
commandments. No doubt he had memorized them all, read them many
times, and carefully "kept" every one. Which ones could Jesus mean?

Our Lord answered the ruler by citing five of the Ten Commandments and adding the second greatest commandment (see Ex. 20:12–16;
Lev. 19:18; Matt. 22:39). Christ did not even mention the first four commandments or the first and greatest commandment, all of which center
on people's attitude toward God (Ex. 20:3–11; Deut. 6:5; cf. Matt.
22:38)—these are even more impossible for anyone to keep.

The young ruler would have been very familiar with the Scripture
Jesus quoted, but he again missed His point. He failed to grasp that the
commandments in themselves could not give the spiritual life to which
they point. If a man or woman could somehow perfectly keep all the
commandments for a lifetime, that person would indeed have eternal life.
But as Jesus strived to show the young man, no one apart from divine,
saving grace can obey even one of the commandments perfectly.

ASK YOURSELF

If the commandments of Scripture are not intended to earn right standing
with God, then what good do they accomplish? What tends to happen to
you when you disregard them? How is your relationship with Christ
cemented by obeying Him, by following closely after Him as Lord?

THE YOUNG RULER'S RESPONSE, PART 1

But when the young man heard this statement, he went away grieving;
for he was one who owned much property. —MATT. 19:22

Like most of the religious leaders of Jesus' day, the young ruler's deceptive mind convinced him that he had kept all of God's law (Mark 10:20).
He considered himself nearly perfect in God's eyes simply because he
had never committed physical murder or adultery, was not a thief or liar,
and did not blaspheme God or worship idols.

The man's question, "What am I still lacking?" (Matt. 19:20), implied that he thought observance beyond the law was necessary for salvation. Because his outward behavior was moral and religious, he did not
suspect that his inner life could be corrupt (cf. Matt. 23:27). Thus far he
had not confessed lust as a form of adultery, hatred as a form of murder,
or swearing by any heavenly or earthly thing as a form of taking God's
name in vain (see Matt. 5:22, 28, 34–35). And the young man seemed totally ignorant that "whoever keeps the whole law and yet stumbles in one
point, he has become guilty of all" (James 2:10).

The eager young ruler failed to see that the commandments are not
standards of performance but pictures of divine righteousness. God gave
them to show people how they themselves can't possibly obey His standards. Obedience is imperfect because the human heart is imperfect.

ASK YOURSELF

Being unable to follow God's law perfectly, and not needing to in order
to receive God's grace and favor through faith in His Son, how do you
keep yourself from falling into laziness toward God's Word? What
remains your motivation for loving and serving Him with all your heart?

THE YOUNG RULER'S RESPONSE, PART 2

But when the young man heard this statement, he went away grieving;
for he was one who owned much property. —MATT. 19:22

A major strategy of the Devil is to deceive sinners about their sin, thus exploiting their pride and natural inclination toward self-deception. The young ruler had too much spiritual pride to admit that he was by nature sinful and that his entire life fell short of God's standard for holiness (Rom. 3:23). Instead, his yearning for eternal life revolved around only his personal, felt needs.

Real salvation, on the other hand, is for people who have abandoned their own efforts for spiritual or religious betterment, realizing that in their own strength they are incapable of coming to God. Redemption is for those who repent of sin and cast themselves on God's mercy, recognizing that anything good they receive or accomplish occurs only by God's sovereign, gracious provision in Christ.

The young ruler most needed to understand and believe that "the Law was given through Moses; grace and truth were realized through Jesus Christ" (John 1:17; cf. Gal. 3:24). But all he wanted from the Lord was to know about some additional commandment, a novel and legalistic formula for living, another rite or ceremony he could complete and make himself acceptable to God—any or all of which would be insufficient for genuine salvation.

ASK YOURSELF

How does legalism show itself most readily in your life? What are some of the ceremonial, surface matters you perform that make you feel better about yourself, even though your heart is rarely invested in them? How often do you refer to these when comparing yourself to others?

THE YOUNG RULER'S RESPONSE, PART 3

But when the young man heard this statement, he went away grieving;
for he was one who owned much property. —MATT. 19:22

The young man's response prompted Jesus to turn his focus toward God. He sought to demonstrate to the rich ruler that his real problem was not a feeling of incompleteness, as present as that may have been, but his sinful separation from God and his total inability to conquer it. He desperately needed to see that "God is a righteous judge, and a God who has indignation every day" with those who reject Him (Ps. 7:11; cf. Rom. 5:10; Eph. 2:3). Christ wanted the man to know that the Father will not save any who endeavor to come to Him still harboring sin.

Most important, Jesus did not make the mistakes that well-meaning evangelists so often make today—not confronting people with their utter sinfulness and spiritual helplessness, not urging them to confess and repent of those sins. Our Lord knew that God's grace can't be faithfully preached to unbelievers like the rich young ruler until His law is preached and mankind's corrupt nature is exposed. It is impossible for a person to fully realize his need for mercy until he clearly ascertains the magnitude of his guilt. As the Puritan Samuel Bolton wisely noted, "When you see that men have been wounded by the law, then it is time to pour in the gospel oil."

ASK YOURSELF

How much of your dismay over sin is wrapped up more in your loss of peace and settledness—your personal sense of regret—rather than your grief at offending the grace of God? How can you daily reinforce your heart to desire nothing greater than to bless and glorify the Lord?

THE YOUNG RULER'S RESPONSE, PART 4

But when the young man heard this statement, he went away grieving; for he was one who owned much property. —MATT. 19:22

In response to Jesus' concern about the law, the young ruler was essentially self-satisfied, surely not convicted or wounded by its message. The man earnestly sought eternal life, but only on his terms and by his own power. He would not or could not confess his sin and repent of it, both of which are utterly essential to salvation. John the Baptist began his ministry preaching repentance (Matt. 3:2), as did Jesus Himself (4:17). The apostles Peter and Paul both recognized how crucial repentance is (Acts 2:38; 26:20). In fact Peter saw repentance as a synonym for salvation when his second letter declared, "The Lord . . . is patient toward you, not wishing for any to perish but for all to come to repentance" (2 Peter 3:9).

Real confession and repentance of sin both are works of the Holy Spirit, just as are other elements of salvation (see John 6:44; 16:8–9). But both of these necessities require action by the sinner's will, the same as receiving Christ as Lord and Savior does. It is not that the young man or any other seeker must fully grasp all aspects of salvation all at once, but true belief demonstrates a willingness to do whatever God requires, something sadly that the young ruler did not demonstrate.

ASK YOURSELF

Are you being resistant right now to anything the Spirit is bringing to your attention, whether in prayer, in the Word, or in the teaching you've been hearing? What is keeping you from conforming yourself to His will? What might be waiting on the other side of your obedience?

JESUS' COMMAND TO THE YOUNG RULER, PART 1

Jesus said to him, "If you wish to be complete, go and sell your possessions and give to the poor, and you will have treasure in heaven; and come, follow Me."
—MATT. 19:21

Here our Lord sought again to make the self-satisfied ruler confront his true spiritual condition. In the context, Jesus uses "complete" as a synonym for salvation. He essentially told the young man, "If you truly desire eternal life, you will obey My command and prove your sincerity by selling everything and giving what you receive to the poor." The ruler's willingness to obey would not earn him salvation but would prove that he desired salvation above everything else (see Matt. 13:44–46).

The real issue was, "Will you follow My instructions, no matter what? Who will rule your life, you or Me?" There is hardly a better way to find out if a person is ready to accept Christ's sovereignty than to ask him or her to surrender their wealth. It soon became clear that material things were the man's priority, and he therefore did not realize the Father's salvation.

Our Lord's command to sell all and give to the poor was capable of obedience in the man's own power. But he refused to obey, not because he *could* not but because he *would* not. This attitude proved conclusively he really did not desire God's will that he be spiritually complete, or saved.

ASK YOURSELF

In what way does desire for money—or the fear of losing it—affect your freedom and immediacy in responding to the Lord? What would be different about your walk with Him if financial pressure were less of an issue, if you were following His command not to worry about such things?

JESUS' COMMAND TO THE YOUNG RULER, PART 2

Jesus said to him, "If you wish to be complete, go and sell your possessions and give to the poor, and you will have treasure in heaven; and come, follow Me."
—MATT. 19:21

Because of his dismay at the prospect of giving up all his possessions, the young man perhaps didn't even hear Christ tell him, "Come, follow Me." The divine call to discipleship always falls on deaf ears when there is no willingness to sacrifice all and follow the Lord (cf. Matt. 8:19–22).

Contrary to his own assessment, the rich ruler did not comply with any of God's law, especially not in the category of materialism. He thought he owned his property, but he was actually its slave, insistent on placing it above Christ's call to salvation.

The man "went away grieving" because he came seeking eternal life but realized he was leaving without it. Every person finds a certain sin or group of sins especially hard to turn from. For the young ruler it was his love of material things and the prestige that accompanies having them. Merely relinquishing his possessions would not have saved him, but it would have revealed a heart listening to the Holy Spirit and ready for salvation.

Many materially destitute people can be as far from the kingdom as the rich young ruler was. They too have to be willing to sacrifice whatever they do own (Luke 14:33), even if it is only their sinful pride.

ASK YOURSELF

Why is sacrifice such a key element of our sanctification? What have you learned from relinquishing rights, desires, and other demands in order to make your heart more fully His?

DIFFICULTIES FOR THE RICH, PART 1

*And Jesus said to His disciples, "Truly I say to you, it is hard for a rich man to enter the kingdom of heaven." —*MATT. 19:23

Generally speaking, it's been difficult for the wealthy to enter the kingdom of God. First of all, they tend to derive a false sense of security from their wealth. Because an abundance of money and possessions can provide for all sorts of physical needs and wants, the affluent usually rely on money to purchase whatever they desire, thus finding little reason to trust God. Therefore there are "not many wise . . . mighty, . . . noble; but God has chosen the foolish, . . . weak, . . . base, . . . despised" (1 Cor. 1:26–28). The poor were also the special targets of Christ's teaching (Luke 4:18).

People who have large earthly resources often think they do not need heavenly resources. Thus Paul commanded Timothy to "instruct those who are rich in this present world not to be conceited or to fix their hope on the uncertainty of riches, but on God, who richly supplies us with all things to enjoy" (1 Tim. 6:17). The apostle goes on: "Instruct them to do good, to be rich in good works, to be generous and ready to share, storing up for themselves the treasure of a good foundation for the future, so that they may take hold of that which is life indeed" (vv. 18–19). The Lord wants the rich as well as the poor to be useful servants of His kingdom.

ASK YOURSELF

The spiritual obstacles of the wealthy are the most obvious to ascertain. But have you before—or are you now—experiencing shortage in your finances? What are some of the challenges to Christian faith, lifestyle, and servanthood that are unique to those who must make do with less?

DIFFICULTIES FOR THE RICH, PART 2

And Jesus said to His disciples, "Truly I say to you, it is hard for a rich man to enter the kingdom of heaven." —MATT. 19:23

Their large financial accounts and many possessions tend to anchor the wealthy close to this world. Our hearts are where our treasures are (Matt. 6:21), and the rich often find it difficult to treasure the things of God. Jesus' parable of the soils describes their reception of the gospel this way:

> And others are the ones on whom seed was sown among the thorns; these are the ones who have heard the word, but the worries of the world, and the deceitfulness of riches, and the desires for other things enter in and choke the word, and it becomes unfruitful. (Mark 4:18–19)

In Luke 12, the proud and successful farmer of Jesus' parable is oblivious to his soul's welfare: "Soul, you have many goods laid up for many years to come; take your ease, eat, drink and be merry" (v. 19). But because of his greed and sinful self-reliance, "God said to him, 'You fool! This very night your soul is required of you; and now who will own what you have prepared?' So is the man who stores up treasure for himself, and is not rich toward God" (vv. 20–21).

Even believers can get sidetracked and trapped by their possessions. We dare not give the Lord only what remains after we have taken all we want and fulfilled all our earthly plans.

ASK YOURSELF

How do some of the same deceptions inherent in financial wealth show up in other areas? What have you done to try limiting your temptation to rely on earthly things?

IMPOSSIBILITIES FOR EVERYONE, PART 1

"With people this is impossible, but with God all things are possible."
—MATT. 19:26*b*

Here Christ makes it clear that the impossibility to attain salvation by human strength or means extends to everyone, not just the rich. In Mark's parallel account, our Lord declares, "Children, how hard it is to enter the kingdom of God!" (Mark 10:24). The young ruler's barrier to the kingdom was not simply his wealth but rather his trust in it and in his personal confidence that he could fulfill God's standards. But Jesus emphasizes that the reason it is so difficult to be saved by our own efforts and on our own terms is because it's absolutely impossible.

Each of the Ten Commandments and the two great commandments (Ex. 20:3–17; Matt. 22:36–40) was intended to demonstrate the impossibility of sinners' meeting God's perfect requirements in their own power. Good deeds or moralistic efforts have never produced salvation.

The apostle Paul later expressed the same truth:

Now we know that whatever the Law says, it speaks to those who are under the Law, so that every mouth may be closed and all the world may become accountable to God; because by the works of the Law no flesh will be justified in His sight; for through the Law comes the knowledge of sin. (Rom. 3:19–20)

ASK YOURSELF

With the unavoidabilty of this truth—that no amount of human effort is enough to earn salvation—why do the majority of people still cling to the hope of it? What are some of the ways you hear this expressed? What would you say to someone who was depending on it?

IMPOSSIBILITIES FOR EVERYONE, PART 2

"With people this is impossible, but with God all things are possible."
—MATT. 19:26b

Every person since Adam and Eve is by nature "accustomed to doing evil" (Jer. 13:23). It would be more possible for someone to change his skin color or the leopard to change its spots (v. 23) than for anyone to attain salvation by human wisdom or strength.

Jesus here is not singling out the wealthy as being basically further from salvation than others. He is simply noting on the one hand that wealth is usually a formidable roadblock; furthermore, money provides no advantage whatsoever, even though the rich of Jesus' day thought they could buy more sacrifices, give more alms, and make more offerings than the poor.

Wealth tends to make those who have it more self-centered. They often devote much time and effort to protecting, enlarging, and enjoying all they have, at the expense of the needs and interests of the less affluent. Although there are certainly exceptions, many of the wealthy resemble the self-indulgent rich man who was oblivious to the destitute Lazarus, the one who was essentially a beggar outside the rich man's gate (see Luke 16:20–31).

So if the impossibilities of attaining salvation apart from God, though a bit different for rich and poor, result in the same hopelessness, we can ask, with the apostles, "Then who can be saved?"

ASK YOURSELF

What are some of the greatest reminders in your life that God's grace is your only hope? Why is this sometimes so hard for us to accept and rejoice in? How has God grown your ability to be thankful for needing Him, not burdened by the thought of having to impress Him?

POSSIBILITIES WITH GOD

And looking at them Jesus said to them, "With people this is
*impossible, but with God all things are possible." —*MATT. 19:26

By one simple statement, "With people this is impossible", our Lord once and for all destroyed any hope people might have in their own righteousness and good deeds to earn salvation. Whatever their status of earthly success and wealth, all people stand condemned before a righteous God, and because of human depravity (spiritual powerlessness), they can do nothing to merit His forgiveness.

But with God it is possible for Him to save helpless sinners. He can do what men and women cannot. The young ruler departed from Jesus without eternal life because he had sought it on the basis of his own merit. But as we have stressed, salvation is entirely a gracious and sovereign work of God.

The work of believing witnesses is simply to proclaim the gospel clearly and lovingly and allow the Holy Spirit to apply that truth to an unbeliever's heart, bringing him or her to repentance and faith. Those actions by the unbeliever require human willpower, but they are works sovereignly performed by God's Spirit. Jesus Himself clearly set forth the true possibilities of God in salvation when He taught the crowds, "No one can come to Me unless the Father who sent Me draws him; and I will raise him up on the last day" (John 6:44; cf. v. 37).

ASK YOURSELF

What are some of the other impossibilities you face in life—matters that could be accomplished only by the God with whom "all things are possible"? What keeps your trust in Him from being blind faith? What have you had to live without while trying to make things happen yourself?

PETER'S LEGITIMATE QUESTION

Then Peter said to Him, "Behold, we have left everything and
followed You; what then will there be for us?" —MATT. 19:27

We can expand Peter's question as follows: "Lord, we came on Your
terms, didn't we? Does that qualify us for eternal life? We left everything, including family and friends, to be Your disciples. We've repented
of sin, surrendered to Your lordship, and taken up our crosses for Your
sake. Will we now receive a place in Your kingdom?"

The apostles, except for Judas Iscariot, had truly yielded themselves
to Jesus. For the time being they clung to some misconceptions about
Messiah's kingdom, perhaps expecting Him to establish it during their
lifetimes. This made it difficult at first for them to accept the concept of
Christ's suffering and death. However, they still followed and obeyed
Him. As Peter had asserted, "You have words of eternal life. We have believed and have come to know that You are the Holy One of God" (John
6:68–69).

Peter and his colleagues were sure Jesus had some divine reward in
store for them, although it was undoubtedly not a refined and mature understanding of such matters. We could criticize Peter for his expectation
of blessing and reward, but Jesus did not. Instead He acknowledged that
they were His genuine and sincere disciples, calling them "you who have
followed Me" (Matt. 19:28).

ASK YOURSELF

What does Jesus' promise of eternal reward reveal about His love for us
and His understanding of us? Why would He not consider it more than
sufficient simply to confirm that He has forgiven our sins, without having
to spell out what it would mean for us? Are we wrong to need that?

JESUS' PROMISE, PART 1

"Truly I say to you, that you who have followed Me, in the regeneration when the Son of Man will sit on His glorious throne, you also shall sit upon twelve thrones." —MATT. 19:28

Today's text is a unique promise from Jesus about the believer's role in His millennial kingdom. He uses "regeneration" to signify the rebirth of the earth under His sovereign reign after He returns. This event will be a global parallel to the individual rebirth of believers. Although it will not yet be completely new (Rev. 21:1), earth will still be far superior to the present fallen and unredeemed planet (cf. Isa. 65:17; 66:22; Rev. 20:1–6). Peter called it "the period of restoration of all things about which God spoke by the mouth of His holy prophets from ancient time" (Acts 3:21).

The redeemed will join Christ at His throne (Rev. 3:21) and exercise authority over the population of the earth (2:26), and at the same time the apostles will rule restored Israel. On the millennial earth, righteousness will prosper, God will exalt Jerusalem, health and healing will prevail, abundant food will grow as never before, the lion will be at peace with the lamb, deserts will bloom, and people will have longevity. The Lord will limit the curse of sin that came with the fall. This limitation will anticipate the eradication of sin in the eternal state—the glory of heaven that follows the millennium (see Rev. 22:3).

ASK YOURSELF

In light of the turmoil, fear, and worry that dominates our average news cycle, how marvelous it is to think about a coming time when all will be peace and freedom! How can the reality of this promised hope impact your thinking and perspective on daily life right now?

JESUS' PROMISE, PART 2

"Truly I say to you, that you who have followed Me, in the regeneration when the Son of Man will sit on His glorious throne, you also shall sit upon twelve thrones." —MATT. 19:28

In His renewed earthly kingdom, the Messiah, the Lord's Anointed, will receive all the nations as His inheritance and have the ends of the earth as His possessions, as Scripture had long before predicted (cf. Ps. 2:2, 8–9). At this time "the Son of Man will sit on His glorious throne," as King of kings and Lord of lords (cf. Rev. 19:16). This refers to Daniel 7:13–14 in which God the Father, "the Ancient of Days," presents the kingdom to the Son of Man.

At this time believers from all the ages will also reign with Christ. God will also restore the nation of Israel, and the apostles will share Christ's rule over her, as they sit on twelve thrones and judge the twelve tribes. Writing about both the earthly and heavenly phases of the kingdom (cf. Rev. 20:4; 21:27), Daniel declares, "Then the sovereignty, the dominion and the greatness of all the kingdoms under the whole heaven will be given to the people of the saints of the Highest One; His kingdom will be an everlasting kingdom, and all the dominions will serve and obey Him" (Dan. 7:27).

ASK YOURSELF

The Christ who rules with power in the prophetic writings of Scripture is the same One who rules on the throne of your heart, if you've repented of your sin and received His forgiveness. How are you seeing His power applied to your life today? Are you taking full advantage of it?

JESUS' PROMISE, PART 3

"And everyone who has left houses or brothers or sisters or father or mother or children or farms for My name's sake, will receive many times as much, and will inherit eternal life. But many who are first will be last; and the last, first."
—MATT. 19:29–30

People who renounce their material assets and become poor for Jesus Christ are going to share with the disciples in His triumph and kingdom rule. Mark's gospel tells us that anyone who relinquishes "houses or brothers or sisters or father or mother or children or farms" for Jesus' sake and the gospel's "will receive a hundred times as much now in the present age . . . and in the age to come, eternal life" (Mark 10:30).

When someone trusts in Christ, that person often has to renounce certain other relationships, even with those who would otherwise be very close. Frequently a man's or woman's conversion turns family and close friends against them—in some cases to the point of being disinherited or killed. But the person who gives up all to follow Jesus will come to know a multitude of new parents and siblings with whom he or she will forever be united in God's spiritual family. Throughout the world, Christians find those who share their sorrows, encourage their spirits, and help meet their needs, material and spiritual.

Jesus promises believers abundant blessings now, in the millennial kingdom, and throughout all eternity.

ASK YOURSELF

Have you been forced either to sever or suspend certain relationships because of your allegiance to Christ and His kingdom? What have been some of the other costs involved in proclaiming Christian faith? How does His promise of exponential blessing encourage your heart?

BLIND MEN'S PERSISTENCE, PART 1

They cried out all the more, "Lord, Son of David, have mercy on us!"
—MATT. 20:31*b*

The two blind men in today's text were absolutely desperate, knowing that the final possible hope of their gaining sight would soon depart. The word translated "cried out" is a term that denoted any sort of screaming or anguished shout, such as the rantings of insane people and women's cries at childbirth. This usage here underscores the men's desperation. They no doubt were unaware of Jesus' impending crucifixion, but they seemed to realize they would never encounter Him again. Thus they shouted at the top of their voices, not caring what impression it left on others as long as Jesus heard them.

Because the blind men addressed Jesus as "Lord" does not necessarily mean they recognized Him to be Messiah. However, their request for mercy and their calling Him by the messianic title "Son of David" demonstrates their recognition of who Jesus was. Most Jews knew "the Scripture said that the Christ comes from the descendants of David" (John 7:42; cf. Matt. 21:9; Luke 1:32).

The astounding thing was not the two men's physical blindness, common in that day, but their spiritual sight, uncommon in any day. They could see nothing physically, but they saw very much spiritually.

ASK YOURSELF

How restricted or inhibited are you in seeking, worshiping, and aligning yourself with Christ? Are there certain lengths you hope you never have to go in declaring publicly your desperate need for Him? What can you learn from those who approach Him without fear of reputation?

BLIND MEN'S PERSISTENCE, PART 2

They cried out all the more, "Lord, Son of David, have mercy on us!"
—MATT. 20:31*b*

In asking Jesus for healing, the blind men admitted their unworthiness and cast themselves completely on His mercy. Their actions were loud and intrusive in order to be noticed, but their hearts were in the right place. They realized they deserved nothing from Jesus and that only His grace could remove their blindness.

When we approach God with all the faith we have, even though it's incomplete and weak, He will meet us at that point and draw us on to salvation. As He proclaimed through the prophet Jeremiah, "You will seek Me and find Me when you search for Me with all your heart" (Jer. 29:13). Scripture historian Alfred Edersheim has commented of these men: "the faith of the blind rose to the full height of divine possibility."

But the crowds following Jesus resented the men's interruption and "sternly told them to be quiet." The world, and even many believers, can so often be harsh and indifferent toward others' needs. The people here thought only of their own selfish interests, and by comparison the men were merely a nuisance.

However, commentator F. F. Bruce has noted that the men "refused to be bludgeoned into silence by the indifferent crowd." Instead, with genuine believing persistence, "they cried out all the more, 'Lord, Son of David, have mercy on us!'"

ASK YOURSELF

What are some of the cries for help you've heard in the last few days? What needs have been expressed by your family, your friends, your coworkers, or perhaps a random stranger who caught your eye? How do you keep from seeing these as intrusions, but rather as opportunities?

BLIND MEN'S SUPERNATURAL PRIVILEGE, PART 1

Moved with compassion, Jesus touched their eyes; and immediately they regained their sight and followed Him. —MATT. 20:34

After years of blindness, the blind men's gripping desire was to see. Our Lord felt much compassion toward them, and so He "touched their eyes; and immediately they regained their sight." As the Creator of the universe, Christ reached out to the pleading men, suspended His own natural laws, and with infinite, divine compassion bestowed His perfect mercy on some very definite human needs for healing.

The fact that Matthew says "they regained their sight" (cf. Mark 10:51) tells us that the men had formerly possessed normal eyesight. No doubt they were more acutely aware of what they had been missing than would have been other blind people who had never seen anything.

The Lord Jesus performed His healing miracles in many different ways. Sometimes He asked the afflicted person to do something for himself. Sometimes He merely uttered a word, and at other times the Savior applied some action, such as placing His fingers in deaf ears or making salve from mud and anointing blind eyes. In this instance He "touched their eyes." Jesus' miracles were always complete, and normally, as here, they were instantaneous and definitely supernatural or divine in origin, showing once again He was the Son of God.

ASK YOURSELF

What forms of blindness perhaps still exist in your life, your attitudes, or your limitations of faith? To what would you ask the Lord to open your eyes so you can see more clearly? Is there any reason you would be less vocal and persistent than these men to see your sight restored?

BLIND MEN'S SUPERNATURAL PRIVILEGE, PART 2

Moved with compassion, Jesus touched their eyes; and immediately
they regained their sight and followed Him. —MATT. 20:34

We can infer from our passage that the blind men sought deliverance from both physical and spiritual blindness. Sad to say, but the vast majority of people whom Jesus encountered during His earthly ministry were spiritually blind. He "was the true Light which, coming into the world, enlightens every man. He was in the world, and the world was made through Him, and the world did not know Him. He came to His own, and those who were His own did not receive Him" (John 1:9–11; cf. 8:12). People were spiritually blind then, and are spiritually blind today; they simply do not want to see God's truth. Christ explained this to the Jewish leader Nicodemus:

This is the judgment, that the Light has come into the world, and men loved the darkness rather than the Light, for their deeds were evil. For everyone who does evil hates the Light, and does not come to the Light for fear that his deeds will be exposed. (3:19–20; cf. Matt. 6:22–23)

To people's innate blindness, Satan adds additional blinders (2 Cor. 4:4), and to sinners who persistently refuse to believe, God may choose to reinforce that hardness (Isa. 6:9–10). But, as with the blind men, it doesn't have to be that way, thanks to divine mercy.

ASK YOURSELF

How often have you stood on the other side of Christ's eye-opening work in your life, looking back to see how deceived you had been by Satan's lies? What have you learned from situations like these, not only about the liberating power of God but about the capabilities of your foe?

BLIND MEN'S SUPERNATURAL PRIVILEGE, PART 3

*Moved with compassion, Jesus touched their eyes; and immediately
they regained their sight and followed Him.* —MATT. 20:34

Of unbelieving first-century Jews, Paul wrote, "Their minds were
hardened; for until this very day at the reading of the old covenant the
same veil remains unlifted, because it is removed in Christ" (2 Cor. 3:14;
cf. Rom. 11:25). But the leading Jewish religious leaders, in the persons
of the hypocritical and censorious scribes and Pharisees, epitomized
spiritual blindness and unbelief. Jesus called them "blind guides of the
blind" (Matt. 15:14; cf. 23:16, 24).

In contrast, the two men gave genuine evidence of a desire to be rid
of spiritual as well as physical blindness. In fact, after the Lord restored
their eyesight, the text says they "followed Him." Likely most of the
crowd following Jesus outside Jericho were not disciples; but on the
other hand Bartimaeus and presumably his friend here were "glorifying
God" (Luke 18:43). That's reason enough to believe Jesus healed them
spiritually as well as physically.

In addition, Jesus instructed them, "Go; your faith has made you
well" (Mark 10:52). "Made . . . well" derives from the Greek *sozo*, a common term for physical restoration (cf. 13:20; Luke 23:35) *and* spiritual
salvation. The saving deliverance from sin through faith in Christ is the
final meaning Jesus' words conveyed to the formerly blind men.

ASK YOURSELF

How many of your own appeals to God are merely for the elimination of
physical need, wanting to be delivered primarily to relieve your pain and
distress? What would happen if God dealt mercifully with your spiritual
situation but left you in the same physical shape as before?

BLIND MEN'S SUPERNATURAL PRIVILEGE, PART 4

*Moved with compassion, Jesus touched their eyes; and immediately
they regained their sight and followed Him.* —MATT. 20:34

Jesus did not make faith a requirement to receive His physical healings.
For one thing, He healed many at the request of someone else (see Matt.
8:5–13). The healed infants and those raised from the dead, of course,
could not exercise any kind of faith. But the New Testament does not report a single instance of a person receiving salvation without faith. Only
by God's sovereign grace, working through trusting faith, does He save
anyone (Eph. 2:8).

Thus it seems inherent in the Lord's pronouncement "Your faith has
made you well" (Mark 10:52) that He was assuring the men's salvation.
Christ made precisely the same statement to the individual leper who
glorified God for his healing and returned to thank the Savior (see Luke
17:12–19). Jesus healed the other nine men of leprosy, but only the one
man was "made . . . well" because of his faith, which strongly suggests a
spiritual healing as well as a physical cleansing.

The account of the two blind men reveals three elements of Jesus'
healing ministry. First, this powerful and dramatic demonstration of
God's compassion proves Jesus' messiahship. Second, the story previews
the millennium and its ideal, disease-free environment. Finally, the incident symbolizes God's healing of spiritual blindness. What Jesus did for
blind eyes He likewise desires to accomplish for blind souls.

ASK YOURSELF

How would you rate the strength of your faith right now? Are you walking
in the freedom of expectation and spiritual confidence? Or do you rather
feel as if your trust in Him is lagging, either fatigued from long weeks of
waiting, or merely apathetic—too busy to give Him much thought?

MARTHA'S HEARTFELT SERVICE

So they made Him a supper there, and Martha was serving; but
Lazarus was one of those reclining at the table with Him. —JOHN 12:2

Luke's narrative of Jesus' visit to Mary and Martha several months earlier than this event gives some background concerning Martha's attachment to serving. On that occasion, because her concern for serving should not have been the priority, our Lord had to rebuke her: "Martha, Martha, you are worried and bothered about so many things; but only one thing is necessary, for Mary has chosen the good part" (Luke 10:41–42; cf. vv. 38–40).

Even after that loving reprimand, Martha was again involved in serving an important meal. She primarily directed her service toward Christ. This was commendable for two reasons: loving gratitude to the Lord motivated her, and a desire to generously honor Him guided her actions. Jesus had no reason to admonish Martha this time.

And like Martha, all believers should be involved in selfless service (Rom. 12:11; cf. Col. 3:24). Our Lord declared, "The greatest among you shall be your servant" (Matt. 23:11) and said of Himself, "I am among you as the one who serves" (Luke 22:27; cf. Matt. 20:28). Christ promises those who serve Him: "If anyone serves Me, he must follow Me; and where I am, there My servant will be also; if anyone serves Me, the Father will honor him" (John 12:26).

ASK YOURSELF

How deeply do you struggle with a resistance to expend yourself and make sacrifices for others? In thinking of those who have most clearly modeled a servant's heart to you, what are the things you highly admire about them? How have they benefited from being the first to give?

MARY'S HUMBLE SACRIFICE

*Mary then took a pound of very costly perfume of pure nard, and
anointed the feet of Jesus and wiped His feet with her hair; and
the house was filled with the fragrance of the perfume.* —JOHN 12:3

In an amazing and spontaneous outpouring of love for her Lord, Mary
here anointed Jesus' feet with very expensive perfume. "Nard" was a fragrant oil extracted from a plant native to northern India. Mary used a
high-quality, pure nard, which made it even more costly.

She broke the expensive alabaster vial (Mark 14:3), thus relinquishing everything—contents and container, which likely constituted most of
her net worth. Like David (2 Sam. 24:24), she refused to offer the Lord
that which cost nothing; hers was an act of unrestrained, lavish love.

In an act that shocked eyewitnesses even more than the pouring out
of costly perfume, Mary "wiped His feet with her hair." The Jews saw
footwashing of others as a degrading but necessary task, to be done by
only the lowest slaves (cf. John 1:27). But the onlookers considered it
even more shocking that Mary let down her hair. That was considered indecent, even immoral behavior for respectable Jewish women. But Mary
was focused only on honoring Christ and pouring out her love for Him,
with no concern for any perceived shame that would come to her. This
total abandonment to the Lord was the measure of her love for Him.

ASK YOURSELF

What do you hold back from offering to the Lord? What among your
possessions, talents, and resources do you rarely if ever consider as a
potential gift to Him? How could you transfer it from trivial use into a
thankful expression of honor and glory to the One who made you?

JUDAS'S HYPOCRISY, PART 1

But Judas Iscariot, one of His disciples, who was intending to betray Him, said, "Why was this perfume not sold for three hundred denarii and given to poor people?" Now he said this, not because he was concerned about the poor, but because he was a thief. —JOHN 12:4–6a

Judas's false statement of philanthropic concern actually revealed his long-standing avarice and selfishness, which ultimately led to his betrayal of Jesus. In becoming one of the disciples, he ambitiously hoped for a high position in a political kingdom Jesus would soon usher in. But when the crowds sought to make Him head of such a kingdom, Jesus did not cooperate (John 6:14–15) and even foretold His death to the Twelve, effectively dashing Judas's grandiose ambitions.

The disillusioned Judas therefore apparently sought to get as much "compensation" as possible for his wasted three years with Jesus. Seeing potentially a year's wages ("three hundred denarii") slip away infuriated Judas and he rebuked Mary. Commentator Colin Kruse writes, "Judas' disapproval of Mary's action related not to loss of opportunity to do more for the poor but to his own loss of opportunity to steal from the common purse." The hypocritical and self-righteous false disciple's remarks so convinced others of his "righteous indignation" that many joined in his protest (see Matt. 26:8–9; Mark 14:4–5). No doubt even some genuine disciples were carried away, at least temporarily, by his words.

ASK YOURSELF

What are some statements you often hear that sound right in theory but fail to stand up to biblical scrutiny? Why is logic not always enough in judging whether an argument is sound or complete? How much of our selfish desire is often wrapped up in our perceptions and outlooks?

JUDAS'S HYPOCRISY, PART 2

*"Let her alone, so that she may keep it for the day of My burial. For you always have the poor with you, but you do not always have Me." —*JOHN 12:7–8

Could Judas have had noble motives in what he said—speaking as a misguided patriot seeking to get Jesus to bring in His kingdom as soon as possible? Not according to the New Testament (cf. John 6:70–71; 13:2, 27). Judas lived daily with God's Son for three years, yet in the end rejected and betrayed Him, succumbed to severe guilt (but no real repentance), committed suicide, and went "to his own place," that is, hell.

The Lord Jesus defended Mary right away and rebuked Judas, telling him, "Let her alone, so that she may keep it for the day of My burial." The best way to understand this puzzling statement is to supply an ellipsis of missing words: "Let her alone; *she did not sell the perfume as you wish she had*, so that she could keep it for the day of my burial." (We know Jesus could not mean Mary should keep the perfume until His burial, since she had just poured it out.) Mary's spontaneous action of love and devotion to Christ was far superior to Judas's hypocritical statements. And it carried a much deeper significance than appears at first reading, as Jesus explained, "When she poured this perfume on My body, she did it to prepare Me for burial" (Matt. 26:12; cf. Mark 14:8).

ASK YOURSELF

What are some of our actions, ceremonies, and expressions of worship that seem on the surface not to accomplish much, when in reality they perform a much higher service than mere productivity can measure?

JUDAS'S HYPOCRISY, PART 3

"For you always have the poor with you, but you do not always have Me."
—JOHN 12:8

Our Lord did not want to minimize giving to the poor but wanted to challenge the apostles to keep their priorities straight. They would not have much longer to perform good deeds to Him because He would not always be physically with them. Jesus was again looking ahead to His death, now less than a week away.

Unmasked as a hypocrite regarding his concern for the poor, Judas now faced the ultimate sort of pivotal decision. He could bow before Jesus in penitent repentance, asking forgiveness of his sin. Or he could harden his heart, refuse to repent, and betray Christ at Satan's direction. Sadly, Judas chose the latter, sinful course and was solely responsible for its consequences, although his actions fulfilled the purpose of God in the death of His Son (cf. John 13:18–19). That he was not just an ordinary follower of Jesus, but part of the Lord's inner circle, makes Judas's betrayal of Him all the more heinous. His hypocrisy led to history's most despicable act and merited these chilling words from the Master: "Woe to that man by whom the Son of Man is betrayed! It would have been good for that man if he had not been born" (Matt. 26:24), an admonition no one should ever want to hear.

ASK YOURSELF

Is there any of Judas's heart and reaction in you? When the weight of biblical authority speaks against a cherished sin or attitude of yours, how do you typically respond? What are the usual motives and red flags that routinely resist repentance when it is most clearly called for?

The People's Superficiality

And they came, not for Jesus' sake only, but that they might also
see Lazarus, whom He raised from the dead. —JOHN 12:9b

The term "Jews" here doesn't refer to the religious leaders but to a group of ordinary laypeople (cf. John 11:55–56). After the Sabbath, the crowd of Jewish people who were in Jerusalem for Passover discovered that our Lord was in Bethany. News of His raising Lazarus from the dead had spread, and the crowd was curious to see both the miracle worker and the one He had brought back to life.

These people were not hostile to Jesus, like Judas and the religious leaders, but they were not faithfully committed to Him either, as were Mary and Martha. Instead they were thrill seekers, looking for the latest sensation, superficially interested in the Lord, but spiritually indifferent and ultimately antagonistic toward Him. Similar to the congregation in Laodicea, they were "lukewarm, and neither hot nor cold" (Rev. 3:16). They would be enthusiastic toward Him at the triumphal entry: "Hosanna! Blessed is He who comes in the name of the Lord, even the King of Israel" (John 12:13). Just days later many of the same people would shout, "Away with Him, away with Him, crucify Him!" (19:15). Such inconsistency would not produce faith, in spite of overwhelming evidence for the Messiah, but would lead some to even mock Jesus as He hung on the cross (Matt. 27:39–40).

ASK YOURSELF

What are some of the most distressing evidences of fickleness and disloyalty in your heart? What must be the reason for our perspective to swing so far so quickly? What is missing inside when we are infatuated with scoop and gossip, when we are swayed from side to side by public opinion?

The Leaders' Hostile Scheming

But the chief priests planned to put Lazarus to death also; because on account of him many of the Jews were going away and were believing in Jesus.
—John 12:10–11

The resurrected Lazarus, as living proof of Christ's supernatural power, presented a real threat to the Sadducees because his miraculous rising from the grave, at the Lord's command, was causing many Jews to believe in Jesus (see John 11:48). Lazarus was an undeniable testimony to Jesus and a great embarrassment to the Sadducees, who denied any resurrection from the dead (Matt. 22:23).

Unable to counter the incontrovertible evidence the living Lazarus presented against their erroneous doctrine, the Sadducees sought to destroy the evidence by killing him. The Jewish leaders' deceptive web was growing, as Leon Morris notes: "It is interesting to reflect that Caiaphas had said, 'it is expedient for you that one man die for the people' (11:50). But one was not enough. Now it had to be two. Thus does evil grow."

There is no neutrality concerning the Lord: "He who is not with Me is against Me," Jesus said (Luke 11:23a). Whether with Him, like Mary and Martha, ambivalent toward Him, like the crowd, or against Him, like Judas and the Jewish leaders, everyone takes a stand eventually. And that stand determines each person's eternal destiny, because "there is salvation in no one else; for there is no other name under heaven that has been given among men by which we must be saved" (Acts 4:12).

ASK YOURSELF

Why does any church's attempt at making Jesus a trendy, culturally accommodating figure guarantee that many of the people it reaches will not be long-term followers?
Why must faith in Jesus force the taking of sides?

The Triumphal Entry: the Multitude

The large crowd who had come to the feast, when they heard that Jesus was coming to Jerusalem, took the branches of the palm trees and went out to meet Him.
—John 12:12–13a

In this familiar story the excited multitude waved palm branches, a symbol of victory and celebration. In their emotional fervor the people also offered up their hosannas, which is an acclamation that means "Help, I pray" (v. 13b). In addition, the crowd affirmed its hope in Messiah by proclaiming, "Blessed is He who comes in the name of the Lord" (see Ps. 118:26). The people underscored their belief by further hailing Jesus as "King of Israel" (cf. John 1:49; 19:15).

Previously, Jesus had refused to be acclaimed as the king and military conqueror the people wanted (cf. 6:14–15). This time He raised their hopes by accepting their praises. But this time Christ accepted their salutes only on His terms. As the one who came to save (Matt. 1:21), who came in the name of the Lord (John 5:43), and the true King of Israel (1:49), He was certainly entitled to the multitude's praise. But when the religious leaders saw what was happening and how children were praising Him, "they became indignant and said to Him, 'Do You hear what these children are saying?'" (Matt. 21:15). To that criticism Jesus affirmed to the leaders His right to receive praise: "Yes, have you never read, 'Out of the mouth of infants and nursing babies You have prepared praise for Yourself'?" (v. 16).

ASK YOURSELF

Does it surprise you to realize that people are naturally inclined to "worship," to want to be part of something bigger than themselves? Knowing this, how does it affect the way you share Christ with others?

THE TRIUMPHAL ENTRY: AS PREDICTED

Jesus, finding a young donkey, sat on it; as it is written, "Fear not, daughter of Zion; behold, your king is coming, seated on a donkey's colt." —JOHN 12:14–15

When Jesus came to Jerusalem, He . . .

sent two disciples, saying to them, "Go into the village opposite you, and immediately you will find a donkey tied there and a colt with her; untie them and bring them to Me. If anyone says anything to you, you shall say, 'The Lord has need of them,' and immediately he will send them." (Matt. 21:1–3)

The disciples obeyed and came back with a colt and its mother. Not sure which animal Jesus planned to ride, they placed coats on both (see 21:6–7). The Lord decided to ride the colt, and as the procession went forward, "most of the crowd spread their coats in the road, and others were cutting branches from the trees and spreading them in the road" (v. 8). Spreading garments in Jesus' path signified respect for Him as Israel's King.

Christ's actions were a purposeful, conscious fulfillment of Zechariah 9:9—"Fear not, daughter of Zion; behold, your king is coming, seated on a donkey's colt." If He had been the kind of conquering warrior the people wanted, He would have more appropriately ridden a warhorse. But He chose to ride a donkey's colt and thus entered Jerusalem as the humble Prince of Peace. Only when He returns in judgment will the Lord Jesus ride the conqueror's white stallion (see Rev. 19:11).

ASK YOURSELF

In what way is Christ's humility the ultimate expression of power? Why do all exhibitions of pride, even if more subtle than showy, leave people hungry for even more attention and acceptance?

THE TRIUMPHAL ENTRY: THE APOSTLES' REACTION

These things His disciples did not understand at the first; but when Jesus
was glorified, then they remembered that these things were written of
Him, and that they had done these things to Him. —JOHN 12:16

The disciples initially couldn't grasp that Jesus' earthly mission was not as conqueror but as Savior. Shortly before His ascension, they still asked, "Lord, is it at this time You are restoring the kingdom to Israel?" (Acts 1:6). It was not until the coming of the Holy Spirit, after "Jesus was glorified," that the apostles remembered and understood the significance of these events. As Jesus promised them, "The Helper, the Holy Spirit, whom the Father will send in My name, He will teach you all things, and bring to your remembrance all that I said to you" (John 14:26; cf. 16:13).

Our Lord was and is a unique King. Instead of the majestic pageantry normally connected with earthly monarchs, during His earthly ministry Jesus was meek and lowly (Matt. 11:29); instead of defeating His foes by force, He conquered them by His atoning death (Heb. 2:14). But although He was originally despised and rejected by many (Isa. 53:3), Christ will one day return as the all-victorious King and Lord (Rev. 19:11–16), who will destroy His enemies with a fierce and final judgment (Ps. 2:9; Rev. 19:15). He perfectly fulfilled all biblical prophecies concerning His first coming, and He will likewise return in precisely the manner foretold by Scripture.

ASK YOURSELF

Are you going through a situation right now that is confusing to you? How do you think God wants you to respond to circumstances that are not currently making sense?

JESUS' DIVINE MISSION AND THE TEMPLE

And Jesus entered the temple and drove out all those who
were buying and selling in the temple. —MATT. 21:12a

During His earthly ministry, Jesus certainly saw much social injustice, economic inequity, deprivation and poverty, and many oppressive acts by Rome. However, He came to conquer the far more severe predicament of sin. Men and women can't solve their problems with each other until their sinful rebellion toward and separation from God is resolved through faith and obedience.

It was in His Father's temple and at the hands of His chosen people that Christ endured the most offense, denial, and unbelief. So it was in God's house that cleansing had to begin. Worship is always the divine focal point, and so society's most pervasive evil has been its abandonment of God. Today, as in ancient Israel, God's people must be revived and renewed before they can be instruments of change on the culture around them.

Even though our Lord cleansed the temple just three years earlier (John 2:14–16), it was likely here more profane and corrupted than ever. Why then would Jesus bother again to try cleaning up the temple? Although a second cleansing would simply be temporary and would in the long run not transform the religious leaders' hearts, Christ was compelled to testify of the Father's holiness and perfect judgment concerning sacrilege, carnal tradition, and unbelief. In so doing, our Lord showed He was on a divine mission for His Father.

ASK YOURSELF

Are you aware of a wrong or injustice that, rather than needing a nice, tolerant treatment and response, perhaps invites your indignant anger? How do you know when something demands this?

JESUS SHOWS DIVINE AUTHORITY, PART 1

And Jesus entered the temple and drove out all those who
*were buying and selling in the temple. —*MATT. 21:12*a*

J esus on this occasion confronted the religious leaders and temple
guards and merchants with complete, sovereign authority. Men in those
positions had absolutely no power over the Messiah. Many of them
would have key roles in Jesus' trial and death, but none could exert that
influence without the Father's permission. As He told the Pharisees
earlier:

> For this reason the Father loves Me, because I lay down My life so
> that I may take it again. No one has taken it away from Me, but I lay
> it down on My own initiative, I have authority to lay it down, and I
> have authority to take it up again. (John 10:17–18; cf. 19:11)

Soon Jesus would allow the Jews to do with Him as they pleased; but
now they were unable to prevent Him from making this dramatic demonstration of divine authority. Christ unilaterally expelled both merchants
and customers from the temple and put the commercial tables out of operation. In the presence of thousands of eyewitnesses, He made a sham-
bles of the sacrilegious bazaar and proclaimed the sin and shame of those
who had profited from it. The merchants, "money changers," and priests
could not lift even a voice against what the Son of Man did, any more
than the lions could harm the prophet Daniel (Dan. 6:22).

ASK YOURSELF

How badly, in light of some current situation in your life, do you need the
biblical reminder that Christ is the final authority on all things? What
would this change about the way you approach and think through its
various elements? How could you encourage another to remember this?

JESUS SHOWS DIVINE AUTHORITY, PART 2

And Jesus entered the temple and drove out all those who were buying and selling in the temple. —MATT. 21:12a

Eyewitnesses to Jesus' display of divine authority did not resist His actions for several reasons. The Jewish leaders feared the populace, many of whom had just hailed Jesus as Messiah (Luke 19:48). The merchants also feared the people, whom they had defrauded for many years. But those reasons don't fully explain what happened to the commercializers who were desecrating the temple. Jesus was in such powerful control that He would not even "permit anyone to carry merchandise through the temple" (Mark 11:16). It seems He made everyone immediately drop what they were carrying and leave empty-handed. Christ's commanding presence was so powerful that it caused fear and submission in everyone there, no matter what their overall opinion of Him and His ministry.

Jesus' earthly ministry was generally one of *quiet* submission to the Father's will, but on this and several other occasions, He forcefully showed divine hatred against what profanes God's name and tarnishes His holiness. Here His powerful display of authority symbolically cleansed the temple, albeit briefly, of overt moral defilement.

Luther's famous opposition to indulgences, the would-be financial purchase of God's grace, helped spark the Reformation. Similarly, today's Christians should oppose the many contemporary defilements of the church, including the merchandising of the gospel. Judgment still must "begin with the household of God" (1 Peter 4:17).

ASK YOURSELF

Anger in the church is often vented toward petty grievances and preferences that are not worth expending the energy over. Why do we waste our influence over things that don't really matter? When have you seen someone's passionate call for righteousness shake up a congregation?

JESUS' COMMITMENT TO SCRIPTURE

*And He said to them, "It is written, 'My house shall be called a house
of prayer'; but you are making it a robbers' den." —MATT. 21:13*

Jesus' cleansing of the temple was consistent with the Word of God,
which He quoted here (Isa. 56:7). The temple was to be a place of worship and quiet meditation (cf. 1 Kings 8:28–30), not a mercantile exchange where hucksters and charlatans conducted their greedy
enterprises under the guise of serving the Lord.

It was to the tabernacle, the temple's predecessor as the central place
of worship, that Hannah went when she was grieving over her childless-
ness. There God granted her request for a son—Samuel, who became
one of God's choice servants (1 Sam. 1:9–20). David affirmed, "One
thing I have asked from the Lord, that I shall seek: that I may dwell in the
house of the Lord all the days of my life, to behold the beauty of the
Lord and to meditate in His temple" (Ps. 27:4).

In claiming that the Jewish leaders had turned the temple into "a
robbers' den," Jesus cited this expression from Jeremiah 7:11 as His authority. Instead of being a safe place where believers could come and
worship, the temple had become a place where extortion was protected.
The sanctuary of God had become a sanctuary for robbers, a reality
Jesus knew Scripture condemned.

ASK YOURSELF

How have the church building and the people of God been a
refuge for you in times past? What could you and your church
do to make yourselves an even greater oasis for those needing
spiritual food and drink? How have you perhaps failed to
be as open as you should to human need?

CHRIST'S COMPASSION AND POWER, PART 1

And the blind and the lame came to Him in the temple, and He healed them.
—MATT. 21:14

Following Jesus' dramatic display of righteous indignation against the temple money changers, a number of blind and lame souls rightly sensed that the Lord's fury was not at all directed at them. Just as the unrepentant can expect God's wrath, those who humbly and faithfully seek Him can expect His compassion.

Most of the beggars in Jesus' day were diseased and crippled and regularly gathered at the temple. They hoped to receive at least a little money and maybe the miracle of healing if Jesus came by. Their fellow citizens mostly despised and ignored them, primarily because people considered the handicapped and poor to be suffering as a direct result of their sins or their parents' sins (cf. John 9:2). The selfish and arrogant Jewish leaders had little compassion for them at all.

Had it not been for the thousands of suffering people in Palestine, with disease and demon possession, we would not know of Jesus' great compassion and power of healing. Compared to heaven's infinite duration, our earthly afflictions are so temporary. Nevertheless they are real and sometimes extremely trying, and our Lord never minimizes them. Thus He healed a wide variety of ailments, did not turn away or chide those who sincerely came to Him, and thereby manifested His divine power and authority.

ASK YOURSELF

The level of suffering in any of our communities is too great for us even to imagine, much less to hope that we can alleviate or offer comfort to more than a small portion of the hurting. What should be our ministry response to needs so numerous? What would Christ have us do?

CHRIST'S COMPASSION AND POWER, PART 2

And the blind and the lame came to Him in the temple, and He healed them.
—MATT. 21:14

Christ's compassion demonstrates not only supreme power but also the gracious, divine love that contrasts so vividly to fallen human nature. The Lord told John the Baptist's disciples, "Go and report to John what you hear and see: the blind receive sight and the lame walk, the lepers are cleansed and the deaf hear, the dead are raised up, and the poor have the gospel preached to them. And blessed is he who does not take offense at Me" (Matt. 11:4–6).

Christians know Jesus sovereignly controls the destinies of every person who has ever lived; He has the right to send unbelievers to hell forever. But like the suffering and needy who came to Him, believers confidently turn to the Lord, realizing He will not turn them away. They know He always treats them well, even if it's through discipline (Heb. 12:6).

A mighty expression of divine power accompanied Christ's demonstration of the Father's compassion. Implicitly, right after the blind and lame came for relief, "He healed them." Only the healing power that derives from God could restore eyesight or give it for the first time. And only divine power could repair or replace diseased or defective limbs or supply those that were missing. And only He can provide true spiritual salvation and healing.

ASK YOURSELF

What are the two or three greatest needs in your life right now? How is God responding to them, bringing you both healing and comfort? Or how is He helping you persevere as you keep your trust in Him, even in the absence of immediate relief? What has His love proven to you?

ACCEPTANCE AND REJECTION OF JESUS, PART 1

They became indignant and said to Him, "Do You hear what these children are saying?" And Jesus said to them, "Yes; have you never read, 'Out of the mouth of infants and nursing babies You have prepared praise for Yourself'?"
—MATT. 21:15c–16

Like the Pharisees, "the chief priests and the scribes" felt piously superior to the average people, especially toward the poor or those with physical ailments. They felt that the afflicted deserved their fate. No amount of exposure to sufferings could elicit compassion from those unbelievers.

When the temple elite asked Jesus, "Do You hear what these children are saying?" they essentially said, "Don't You know these children are blasphemously calling You the Messiah?" Actually the Jews could not tolerate the Lord's compassionate godliness, because it was such a harsh denunciation of their calloused ungodliness.

Jesus was fully aware of His opponents' words and knew their meaning. Nevertheless, as He had done before, He quoted the Old Testament (here Ps. 8:2) against those supposed experts in the law. The two Hebrew words in Psalm 8:2 for "infants" and "nursing babies" refer to children under three years of age, the age of weaning. However, the children who hailed Jesus here were past the age of weaning. Jesus' point is that if even tiny children would praise Him, how much more could older children be expected to do so? Jesus Christ *will* be praised, and if people won't do so, He told the Pharisees, "the stones will cry out" (Luke 19:40b).

ASK YOURSELF

Does anything keep words of praise from filling your heart, even in the busy paces of the day? How have you been kept at peace by worshiping Him as you go along, maintaining a continual attitude of thanks?

ACCEPTANCE AND REJECTION OF JESUS, PART 2

They became indignant and said to Him, "Do You hear what these children are saying?" And Jesus said to them, "Yes; have you never read, 'Out of the mouth of infants and nursing babies You have prepared praise for Yourself'?"
—MATT. 21:15c–16

God knew that His Son would be "despised and forsaken of men" (Isa. 53:3). Yet at any time Jesus could have defeated His foes: "Or do you think that I cannot appeal to My Father, and He will at once put at My disposal more than twelve legions of angels?" (Matt. 26:53).

Christ soon left the Jewish leaders because they would not believe in Him. Instead they challenged Him again the next day:

> "By what authority are You doing these things, and who gave You this authority?" Jesus said to them, "I will also ask you one thing, which if you tell Me, I will also tell you by what authority I do these things. The baptism of John was from what source, from heaven or from men?" And they began reasoning among themselves, saying, "If we say, 'From heaven,' He will say to us, 'Then why did you not believe him?' But if we say, 'From men,' we fear the people; for they all regard John as a prophet." And answering Jesus, they said, "We do not know." He also said to them, "Neither will I tell you by what authority I do these things." (Matt. 21:23–27)

Instead of attacking secular Rome, Jesus confronted pseudoreligious Judaism. Instead of promoting revolution, He preached righteousness.

ASK YOURSELF

As people who follow Christ, why can we never expect to be free from persecution if we take our faith seriously? How can you learn to live without everyone's acceptance?

THE FIG TREE'S SIGNIFICANCE

Now in the morning, when He was returning to the city,
He became hungry. Seeing a lone fig tree by the road, He came to it
and found nothing on it except leaves only. —MATT. 21:18–19a

Fig trees as tall as twenty feet are common in the Middle East and are much prized as shade trees. Thus a favorite place for people to gather in biblical times was under a fig tree (Zech. 3:10; cf. Deut. 8:8). When Jesus called Nathanael to discipleship, he was under a fig tree, probably in his own yard (John 1:48). But if the presence of a healthy fig tree symbolized blessing and prosperity for the Jews, its absence or defect would symbolize judgment and deprivation.

Normally a fig tree produced fruit prior to leaves. Thus Jesus was disappointed when He found this tree with only leaves on it. Fig trees bore fruit twice annually, the first time in early summer. In April, the likely time of this event, a fig tree at Jerusalem's altitude would not usually have either fruit or leaves, because "it was not the season for figs" (Mark 11:13). However, if this particular tree produced leaves early, it should have also produced early fruit.

Jesus used many natural objects to illustrate His teachings. Here He used a barren fig tree to portray a spiritually barren Jewish nation.

ASK YOURSELF

Are there ways in which you give the impression and profession of being a Christian, yet fail to produce anything that brings help and nourishment to those around you? What are the kinds of fruit we should expect to see growing in our lives? When we don't, what does that mean?

THE PARABLE OF THE FIG TREE, PART 1

"No longer shall there ever be any fruit from you."
And at once the fig tree withered. —MATT. 21:19*b*

Jesus' somber statement here placed the fig tree under a divine curse (cf. Mark 11:21) and rendered it perpetually unproductive. Although the tree may have died "at once," the withering was not necessarily apparent until the next day. Then the Lord and the apostles came by the tree again and saw it "withered from the roots up" (Mark 11:20).

Jesus saw the fig tree as representing spiritually dead Israel, with its leaves symbolizing the nation's external religiosity, and its absence of fruit her spiritual barrenness. As Paul later described the Jews, they had "a zeal for God, but not in accordance with knowledge" (Rom. 10:2; cf. 2 Tim. 3:5).

The fruit they bear always demonstrates people's right relationship to God. Our Lord earlier taught that "a good tree cannot produce bad fruit, nor can a bad tree produce good fruit" (Matt. 7:18). In His parable of the soils, the good soil represents the one in whom the Word takes root and flourishes: "the man who hears the word and understands it; who indeed bears fruit and brings forth, some a hundredfold, some sixty, and some thirty" (v. 23). Fruitfulness is always evidence of salvation and godliness (cf. John 15:5), whereas barrenness, as portrayed by the fig tree in today's text, is always evidence of lostness and ungodliness.

ASK YOURSELF

What are Jesus' motivations in calling for fruitfulness from our lives? How does the production of visible fruit confirm the reality of our salvation, our life-giving relationship with Christ? What would be the point of Christian living that had nothing for others to see and share in?

The Parable of the Fig Tree, Part 2

"No longer shall there ever be any fruit from you."
And at once the fig tree withered. —Matt. 21:19*b*

This episode was not Jesus' first instance of using the barren fig tree illustration. In an earlier parable, He taught the following:

> A man had a fig tree which had been planted in his vineyard . . . And he said to the vineyard-keeper, "Behold, for three years I have come looking for fruit on this fig tree without finding any. Cut it down! Why does it even use up the ground?" And he answered and said to him, "Let it alone, sir, for this year too, until I dig around it and put in fertilizer; and if it bears fruit next year, fine; but if not, cut it down." (Luke 13:6*a*, 7–9)

The owner's willingness to wait for the fig tree to produce fruit describes God's patience with the Jews before bringing judgment on them. Jesus makes no explicit comparison of those three years to the three years of His earthly ministry, but it was at the end of His ministry that the Jews finally rejected Him and had Him executed.

God's judgment on Israel, as illustrated by the cursed fig tree, was finally fulfilled around A.D. 70 when God allowed the Romans to sack Jerusalem and raze the temple. That's because Israel had not borne any spiritual fruit, and has not to this day.

ASK YOURSELF

For those who see only the harsh, condemning judgment of God, what are some of your most compelling testimonies to His patience and long-suffering? How has He continued to work with you despite your failings and inconsistency? How does His patience show itself in the world at large?

THE PARABLE OF THE FIG TREE, PART 3

"No longer shall there ever be any fruit from you."
And at once the fig tree withered. —MATT. 21:19b

God once reminded Israel that, like a vinedresser, He had nurtured and cared for her. But the vineyard produced only worthless fruit, and the man vowed to remove its protective boundaries and let it be ravaged. "For the vineyard of the Lord of hosts is the house of Israel and the men of Judah His delightful plant. Thus He looked for justice, but behold, bloodshed; for righteousness, but behold, a cry of distress" (Isa. 5:7; see vv. 1–6). Then the prophet records a long series of woes (curses), outlining the calamities God's people would suffer because of their spiritual unfaithfulness (vv. 8–30). The empty fig tree in a sense encapsulates all such barrenness.

In the twentieth century, secular Jews returned to Palestine and established the state of Israel in 1948. But the Jews are not yet regathered redemptively, because Christ will accomplish that when He returns to establish His earthly kingdom. In the meantime, Israelis live in constant turmoil and danger, far from the peaceable kingdom Christ will bring.

Israel won't be destroyed, because God protects her. But she isn't being blessed because she won't have Jesus as her Messiah (cf. John 1:11). No one comes to the Father who does not come through the Son (14:6). And because Israel won't embrace the Son now, she has no claim on the Father.

ASK YOURSELF

Learn of those who even now are ministering to the Jews (and Arabs as well) in Jesus' name, and ask God to show you how you can be involved in serving His ancient people.

Lesson of the Fig Tree, Part 1

"And all things you ask in prayer, believing, you will receive."
—Matt. 21:22

When the apostles saw the fig tree had withered (cf. Mark 11:20), Jesus moved from a visual parable to another truth. The parable said that religious profession without spiritual reality is accursed before God. Now the Lord took the opportunity to instruct about the power of faith joined to the purpose of God, which can do far more than wither a fig tree.

When referring to mountains (Matt. 21:21), Christ was obviously speaking metaphorically. Neither He nor the disciples ever used miraculous powers to perform spectacular but useless supernatural feats. But He had performed numerous healing miracles, many of which the unbelieving Jews had witnessed. But they wanted a sign on a grandiose scale (cf. Matt. 12:38), and a literal casting of a "mountain . . . into the sea" would have been just the kind of miracle the Jewish leaders sought to see.

However, the applicable principle Jesus wanted to teach us is essentially this: "Believers have unimaginable power available to them, and if they sincerely believe and don't doubt, they will witness God's tremendous powers at work." In the upper room, Christ said, "Whatever you ask in My name, that will I do, so that the Father may be glorified in the Son. If you ask Me anything in My name, I will do it" (John 14:13–14). The key to answered prayer is to ask in Jesus' name, according to His will.

ASK YOURSELF

In trying to remain guarded and logical about life, have you failed to develop a faith that believes God for the impossible? How can you balance a bold, expectant spirit with a humble, healthy perspective on God's sovereignty? What might God be urging you to believe Him for today?

LESSON OF THE FIG TREE, PART 2

"And all things you ask in prayer, believing, you will receive."
—MATT. 21:22

Mountain-moving faith is unselfish, undoubting, and unqualified confidence in God. It trusts in His revelation. When a Christian asks for something that's consistent with Scripture, and he or she trusts in His power to supply it, that request will be honored, because it honors Christ and the Father. God honors genuine obedience to His commands and provides what is sought when any request comes in faith and according to His will.

When the apostles wondered why they couldn't cast out a demon from a young boy, "He said to them, 'Because of the littleness of your faith; for truly I say to you, if you have faith the size of a mustard seed, you will say to this mountain, "Move from here to there," and it will move; and nothing will be impossible to you'" (Matt. 17:20). Our Lord was not commending small faith; it was actually such faith that prevented the apostles from expelling the demon. Jesus rebuked them for having a small faith that stayed small. However, He exhorted them to have a faith like the mustard seed, which begins small, continues to grow, and reaches greatness.

Sincere and genuine prayerfulness to God activates mountain-moving faith. Furthermore, persistent prayer is the type that also produces faith that can move mountains, because it is truly believing prayer (cf. Luke 11:5–8; 18:1–8).

ASK YOURSELF

Do you frequently lose patience with God, exasperated by His perceived slowness at hearing and answering your prayer? Why does He often require us to wait longer than we'd like before seeing Him take action on our or another's behalf? Who models well this kind of persistence to you?

LESSON OF THE FIG TREE, PART 3

"And all things you ask in prayer, believing, you will receive."
—MATT. 21:22

Persistent, believing prayer is not inconsistent with God's sovereign will, because in His sovereign plan He commands persistent prayer and promises to honor it. Thus the Christian who wants what God wants can ask and expect His answer.

Of course, God's will for us does not always involve things we might naturally prefer. His will for believers sometimes entails the need to sacrifice, suffer, or even die for Him. For the followers of Christ who truly seek God's will, it is never primarily about succeeding or failing, prospering or being poor, living or dying, but about being faithful (1 Cor. 4:2). That's why Paul says, "If we live, we live for the Lord, or if we die, we die for the Lord; therefore whether we live or die, we are the Lord's" (Rom. 14:8).

Much of today's church is powerless because so many believers are powerless. And they are so weakened because they aren't persistent in praying for God's will and believing that He will reveal it. The Father wants His children to tirelessly persist and be relentless in following these words of Jesus: "Ask, and it will be given to you; seek, and you will find; knock, and it will be opened to you. For everyone who asks receives, and he who seeks finds, and to him who knocks it will be opened" (Matt. 7:7–8).

ASK YOURSELF

What are some of the greatest lessons you have learned in prayer throughout your lifetime? How has your latest, most urgent season of need prepared you for the one you're dealing with today?

GENTILES INTERESTED IN JESUS, PART 1

"Sir, we wish to see Jesus." —JOHN 12:21*b*

In their wish to have an audience with Jesus, certain Gentiles—who had abandoned their pagan religions and come to worship the true God—stood in sharp contrast to the hostile and superficially fickle Jews. Ironically, just days before Jesus' own people would cry for His crucifixion, certain Gentiles sought to know more about Him. God eventually set the Jewish nation aside and extended the gospel to the Gentiles (cf. John 10:16; 11:52) and commissioned those who believed to witness on His behalf.

The Old Testament foresaw Israel's rejection, but Paul understood that God will ultimately restore her (Rom. 9:25–27; cf. 11:25). God has temporarily set aside Israel in favor of the church, which consists of believing Gentiles and a believing remnant of Jews (cf. 11:5, 17). Thus God's setting aside Israel doesn't prevent individual Jews from salvation (10:1). Nor is it a final abandonment of Israel:

> And so all Israel will be saved; just as it is written, "The deliverer will come from Zion, He will remove ungodliness from Jacob." "This is My covenant with them, when I take away their sins." From the standpoint of the gospel they are enemies for your sake, but from the standpoint of God's choice they are beloved for the sake of the fathers; for the gifts and the calling of God are irrevocable. (Rom. 11:26–29)

In a significant way, the apostle John illustrates in today's text the interplay between Gentiles and Jews regarding the gospel's expansion.

ASK YOURSELF

Is there someone in your life that you've largely given up on? How do God's promises to Israel encourage you to keep believing for those who continue to reject His grace and mercy?

GENTILES INTERESTED IN JESUS, PART 2

"Sir, we wish to see Jesus." —JOHN 12:21*b*

These Gentiles perhaps approached Philip because Jesus was then beyond the Court of the Gentiles and in that part of the temple they could not enter. Thus they could have seen Philip in the Court of the Gentiles, recognized him as an apostle, and approached him. That Philip "was from Bethsaida of Galilee" (v. 21*a*) could also be why the men spoke to him. They may also have been from that region, which was near the Gentile area called the Decapolis (cf. Mark 5:20; 7:31).

It seems as though Philip was uncertain how to handle these Greeks; therefore he told Andrew about their request to see Jesus. Philip may have hesitated to go immediately and directly to Jesus because he recalled the Savior's admonition, "Do not go in the way of the Gentiles, and do not enter any city of the Samaritans" (Matt. 10:5; cf. 15:24). Also, with the Jews spying on our Lord's every move, Philip perhaps considered it dangerous for them to see Jesus talking with Gentiles. Because they were both from Bethsaida, it was natural for Philip and Andrew to tell Jesus of the Gentiles' interest in Him.

Why is this incident even included in John's gospel? Likely because the Greeks represent a Gentile interest in Christ and the gospel—the coming of the church, composed of Jews and Gentiles who would proclaim the Lord's message to the world.

ASK YOURSELF

Do you ever feel so bound by decorum and tradition that you resist immersing yourself into the great river of God's kingdom and His plans for this age? How have you seen churches lose their relevancy by making caution a primary motivator—and being habitually slow to act?

JESUS' INVITATION TO ALL, PART 1

"If anyone serves Me, he must follow Me; and where I am, there My servant will be also; if anyone serves Me, the Father will honor him." —JOHN 12:26

The Son of Man would be glorified (v. 23), not by conquering the Romans and setting up His kingdom right away, but by dying and seeing His disciples obediently willing to serve Him and also die if necessary. This realization perhaps disillusioned many followers, including the apostles. Nevertheless, Jesus emphasized His teaching by using an agricultural illustration His audience would have understood. His point, "unless a grain of wheat falls into the earth and dies, it remains alone; but if it dies, it bears much fruit" (v. 24), was simply that He would be glorified, but only through death and resurrection. Christ's glorious kingdom, with all its wonderful, scripturally promised features, could not come to be without first the cross and its various somber and agonizing features.

Anyone who thinks the cross was merely the by-product of Israel's rejection of Christ is foolish, just as He declared it to the Emmaus disciples, "O foolish men and slow of heart to believe in all that the prophets have spoken! Was it not necessary for the Christ to suffer these things and to enter into His glory?" (Luke 24:25–26).

ASK YOURSELF

How often do you meditate on the reality of Jesus' suffering—the painful dishonor He chose to endure because of His love for you and His faithful obedience to the Father's will? When do these thoughts and reflections prove the most helpful and worshipful?

JESUS' INVITATION TO ALL, PART 2

"If anyone serves Me, he must follow Me; and where I am, there My servant will be also; if anyone serves Me, the Father will honor him." —JOHN 12:26

Our Lord knew that after Calvary the gospel would go far beyond Israel to all the nations of the world. Therefore He responded to the Gentiles' inquiry by pointing to His upcoming death. Christ knew that the only way they could truly see Him and enjoy genuine spiritual fellowship with Him was through His atonement. Even as the wheat grain produces a full harvest after it goes into the soil and dies, so Jesus' death bears much fruit by providing salvation for people of every ethnic group (cf. Rev. 5:9). These Greeks would be representative of the many in that group.

The Lord then applied that truth with an invitation that shows the heart attitude required of anyone who would be saved. Any person who loves his temporal life (cf. 1 John 2:15–17) more than the things of God's kingdom ultimately loses that life. By contrast, the one "who hates his life in this world" by making Christ rather than himself the top priority will preserve his life for all eternity. And here this means preferring the Lord Jesus over your family, wealth, plans, and desires—even your own life (Luke 14:27). This kind of appeal is a continual, unmistakable demand Jesus makes throughout the Gospels (cf. Matt. 13:44–46).

ASK YOURSELF

What is clouding your singleness of focus on Christ today, luring you away from heartfelt allegiance to Him, trying to deceive you into thinking that other pursuits are more valuable than loving and serving God? What do these other ways always end up costing and always fail to deliver?

JESUS' INVITATION TO ALL, PART 3

"If anyone serves Me, he must follow Me; and where I am, there My servant will be also; if anyone serves Me, the Father will honor him." —JOHN 12:26

The Lord Jesus often warned all who would follow Him to think about the heavy cost this could involve: "If anyone wishes to come after Me, he must deny himself, and take up his cross daily and follow Me" (Luke 9:23; cf. v. 24; 14:26–33). Right after saying this, He counseled, "Whoever is ashamed of Me and My words, the Son of Man will be ashamed of him when He comes in His glory, and the glory of the Father and of the holy angels" (9:26). Willingness to give up everything to follow the Lord is what distinguishes genuine disciples from false professors.

To those who truly follow Him, Jesus makes two wonderful promises. First, His servants will be right where He is, which guarantees they will spend eternity in heaven (cf. 2 Tim. 2:10). "If I go and prepare a place for you," Jesus said, "I will come again and receive you to Myself, that where I am, there you may be also" (John 14:3; cf. 17:24). Second, God will honor all those who faithfully serve His Son. All human honors fade into insignificance compared to this eternal honor. The world may hate believers (John 15:18–19), but God's promise, "Those who honor Me I will honor" (1 Sam. 2:30), is still true.

ASK YOURSELF

How do you experience the honor of God being returned to you? In what ways does your sincere, steady desire to apply His Word and submit to His lordship come back to you in blessing, in confidence, and in the assurance of salvation?

JESUS' INVITATION TO ALL, PART 4

"If anyone serves Me, he must follow Me; and where I am, there My servant will be also; if anyone serves Me, the Father will honor him." —JOHN 12:26

Jesus' perfect atonement for the sins of all who believe eliminated every artificial barrier that had previously separated Jews from Gentiles (see Eph. 2:14–16). As a result, "the Gentiles are fellow heirs and fellow members of the body, and fellow partakers of the promise in Christ Jesus through the gospel" (3:6), and "there is no distinction between Greek and Jew, circumcised and uncircumcised, barbarian, Scythian, slave and freeman, but Christ is all, and in all" (Col. 3:11; cf. Gal. 3:28).

In accordance with God's sovereign plan, good resulted out of the tragedy of Israel's rejection of Jesus: "By [the Jews'] transgression," the apostle Paul explains, "salvation has come to the Gentiles" (Rom. 11:11). Furthermore, Paul outlines additional good results of Gentile salvation:

> Now if [the Jews'] transgression is riches for the world and their failure is riches for the Gentiles, how much more will their fulfillment be! But I am speaking to you who are Gentiles. Inasmuch then as I am an apostle of Gentiles, I magnify my ministry, if somehow I might move to jealousy my fellow countrymen and save some of them. For if their rejection is the reconciliation of the world, what will their acceptance be but life from the dead? (Rom. 11:12–15; cf. Zech. 12:10; 13:1)

ASK YOURSELF

What are some of the real-life implications of being one with all believers in Christ, with "no distinction" made for class, gender, or nationality? Why is this not always practiced? Can there be room for disagreement on nonessentials—a lack of total conformity—without shattering unity?

THE THEME OF THE CROSS, PART 1

"For this purpose I came to this hour. Father, glorify Your name."
—JOHN 12:27b–28a

It's clear that here Jesus is speaking of His impending death. From beginning to end, the Bible underscores the indispensable significance of His sacrifice as an offering for the sins of all who would believe. It was a substitutionary sacrifice that satisfied the wrath of God for His own (see Isa. 53:4–6; 1 Peter 2:24).

First of all, Christ's death fulfilled prophecy. According to Daniel, "the Messiah will be cut off " (see Dan. 9:25–26). Through Zechariah God said,

> I will pour out on the house of David and on the inhabitants of Jerusalem, the Spirit of grace and of supplication, so that they will look on Me whom they have pierced; and they will mourn for Him, as one mourns for an only son, and they will weep bitterly over Him like the bitter weeping over a firstborn. (Zech. 12:10; cf. 13:1)

Isaiah 52:13–53:12 contains the most detailed prophecy of Christ's death, as it predicts He would be "pierced through for our transgressions" and "crushed for our iniquities" (53:5). Many other Old Testament texts give specific, prophetic details concerning Messiah's death—each one fulfilled in Christ's death (see Pss. 22:6–8, 14–18; 31:5; 34:20; Isa. 50:6; Zech. 11:12–13). Furthermore, the substitutionary death of our Lord was the fulfillment of all the Old Testament sacrifices (e.g., Lev. 1:3–17; 4:1–5; 5:14–6:7), as the New Testament letter to the Hebrews confirms (especially 9:11–10:18).

ASK YOURSELF

How do the many Old Testament prophecies concerning Christ's death inspire you with God's remarkable plan for your salvation? What confidence do they give you today that He is working for your good?

THE THEME OF THE CROSS, PART 2

"For this purpose I came to this hour. Father, glorify Your name."
—JOHN 12:27b–28a

His atoning death on the cross, with all its agony and pain, was the ultimate goal of the incarnation and Jesus' earthly ministry. Far and away this work of redemption is the most important New Testament theme. Christ made this plain, "For even the Son of Man did not come to be served, but to serve, and to give His life a ransom for many" (Mark 10:45). The writer of Hebrews elaborates on the same truth:

> Therefore, since the children share in flesh and blood, He Himself likewise also partook of the same, that through death He might render powerless him who had the power of death, that is, the devil, and might free those who through fear of death were subject to slavery all their lives. (Heb. 2:14–15; cf. 1 John 3:5, 8)

Summarizing the importance of the Lord's death, theologian Henry Thiessen observes,

> Christ did not come primarily to set us an example, or to teach us doctrine, but to die for us. His death was not an afterthought or an accident, but the accomplishment of a definite purpose in connection with the incarnation. The incarnation is not an end in itself; it is but a means to an end, and that end is the redemption of the lost through the Lord's death on the Cross.

ASK YOURSELF

In contemplating Jesus' suffering on your behalf, how deeply does it make you hate the sin that has penetrated your life? How warmly does it surround you with the faithful, unending love of God? How strongly does it motivate you to express your gratitude through trust and obedience?

THE THEME OF THE CROSS, PART 3

"For this purpose I came to this hour. Father, glorify Your name."
—JOHN 12:27b–28a

The cross was the constant theme of our Lord's own teaching ministry. Right after Peter's confession of Christ (Matt. 16:16), "Jesus began to show His disciples that He must go to Jerusalem, and suffer many things from the elders and chief priests and scribes, and be killed, and be raised up on the third day" (v. 21). He instructed Nicodemus, "As Moses lifted up the serpent in the wilderness, even so must the Son of Man be lifted up" (John 3:14; cf. 8:28; Luke 24:25–26).

The cross of Christ was also the main theme of apostolic preaching and teaching. On Pentecost, Peter preached this to the crowds: "[Jesus], delivered over by the predetermined plan and foreknowledge of God, you nailed to a cross by the hands of godless men and put Him to death. But God raised Him up again, putting an end to the agony of death" (Acts 2:23–24; cf. 3:13–15; 7:52; 13:27–29). Paul reminded the Corinthians, "For I delivered to you as of first importance what I also received, that Christ died for our sins according to the Scriptures" (1 Cor. 15:3).

Paul also summarized the theology of Christ's death: "For if while we were enemies we were reconciled to God through the death of His Son" (Rom. 5:10a)—a glorious reality for all believers.

ASK YOURSELF

What are some of the other great themes of God's Word that speak of the vastness of His sovereign plan and His covenant love for His people? How could you apply these more directly to your specific situations in life, growing your ability to trust in His care and His purposes for you?

THE THEME OF THE CROSS, PART 4

"For this purpose I came to this hour. Father, glorify Your name."
—JOHN 12:27b–28a

Today we conclude our look at the scriptural theme of the cross by noting that it is a subject of supreme interest in heaven. At Jesus' transfiguration, Moses and Elijah "appearing in glory, were speaking of His departure which He was about to accomplish at Jerusalem" (Luke 9:31). It was heavenly messengers at the empty tomb following Christ's death and resurrection who announced the news to the women (Luke 24:6–7). And further, the "sufferings of Christ" are something "into which angels long to look" (1 Peter 1:11–12).

Such heavenly interest will always be present:

> Then I [John] looked, and I heard the voice of many angels around the throne and the living creatures and the elders; and the number of them was myriads of myriads, and thousands of thousands, saying with a loud voice, "Worthy is the Lamb that was slain to receive power and riches and wisdom and might and honor and glory and blessing." (Rev. 5:11–12; see also vv. 9–10)

Finally, the cross anchors the ordinances of baptism (Rom. 6:1–4) and Communion (1 Cor. 11:26), which is a blessing to every true saint.

ASK YOURSELF

Make this a season of specific, intensive worship and thanksgiving for the love of God, displayed in all its severity and sincerity on the cross of Christ. How could you more deliberately keep these familiar thoughts from becoming standard and stale—filled with wonder instead?

JESUS' ANGUISH OVER THE CROSS

"Now My soul has become troubled; and what shall I say,
'Father, save Me from this hour'?" —JOHN 12:27a

In His humanity, Jesus felt all the pain of bearing sin's curse (Gal. 3:13). Thus, "He offered up both prayers and supplications with loud crying and tears to the One able to save Him from death, and was heard because of His piety" (Heb. 5:7). Here, as in Gethsemane, Christ agonized over the horrific death that awaited Him.

Nevertheless the Lord did not deviate from the Father's eternal plan of redemption (1 John 2:2; 4:10). In fact, He voluntarily gave up His life:

> For this reason the Father loves Me, because I lay down My life so that I may take it again. No one has taken it away from Me, but I lay it down on My own initiative. I have authority to lay it down, and I have authority to take it up again. (John 10:17–18)

To underscore this resolve (cf. 12:28), Jesus prayed, "Father, glorify Your name," basically the same prayer He would soon offer in Gethsemane: "Not My will, but Yours be done" (Luke 22:42).

God does receive glory when His attributes are displayed (cf. Ex. 33:18–19), and nowhere do we see His love for sinners (Rom. 5:8), His holy wrath against sin (5:9), His perfect justice (3:26), His redeeming grace (Heb. 2:9), or His wisdom (1 Cor. 1:22–24) more clearly than at the cross.

ASK YOURSELF

Are you dreading a certain upcoming event or challenge that is sure to ask more of you than you want to give? What could God be wanting to accomplish through it? How does Jesus' struggle and confidence encourage you in your own battle?

The Father's Voice, Part 1

*Jesus answered and said, "This voice has not come
for My sake, but for your sakes." —*John 12:30

God's voice here (v. 28) attested His approval of His Son (cf. Matt.
3:17; 17:5). This authentication reassured the apostles that Christ's death
would in no way signify the Father's disapproval of the Son. On the contrary, even as God had already glorified His name through Jesus' life, He
would soon glorify it again through Jesus' death. Our Lord's death and
resurrection would eventuate in His return to full glory in the Father's
presence. This culmination is what Christ prayed for in His High Priestly
prayer:

> Father, the hour has come; glorify Your Son, that the Son may glo-
> rify You, even as You gave Him authority over all flesh, that to all
> whom You have given Him, He may give eternal life. This is eternal
> life, that they may know You, the only true God, and Jesus Christ
> whom You have sent. I glorified You on the earth, having accom-
> plished the work which You have given Me to do. Now, Father, glo-
> rify Me together with Yourself, with the glory which I had with You
> before the world was. (John 17:1–5)

God's audible voice proving He had heard and answered Christ's
prayer was unmistakable. But the bewildered audience, similar to those
with Paul on the Damascus road (Acts 9:7), was unable to appreciate the
words.

ASK YOURSELF

How hard is it to embrace the fact that because of Christ's sacrifice and
your faith in Him, you are accepted and highly valued by your Father?
What keeps you from enjoying this fullness of relationship?

THE FATHER'S VOICE, PART 2

*Jesus answered and said, "This voice has not come
for My sake, but for your sakes."* —JOHN 12:30

The people's inability to interpret the words God uttered reveals the spiritual callousness so typical of the crowds (cf. Mark 4:15; John 8:43). The issue is not God's silence but that sinners are spiritually deaf because of God's sovereign judgment (cf. Isa. 6:9–10; Matt. 13:14–15). Unbelievers, being dead in sin (Eph. 2:1), members of Satan's domain (Col. 1:13), and blinded by him to gospel truth (2 Cor. 4:4), simply cannot grasp God's Word. As Paul asserts: "a natural man does not accept the things of the Spirit of God, for they are foolishness to him; and he cannot understand them, because they are spiritually appraised" (1 Cor. 2:14).

It's reasonable to understand that the divine voice did not come exclusively for Jesus' sake; He didn't need to hear such a voice to know the Father had answered His prayer. God spoke audible words from heaven primarily to strengthen the onlookers' faith. R. C. H. Lenski rightly observes,

> This miraculous reply was for the disciples, that they might hear directly and with their own ears both that the Father had, indeed, answered Jesus and what that answer was. It was another attestation of the Father, of the clearest and the strongest kind, that Jesus was his well-beloved Son.

Even though the eyewitnesses were uncertain of its precise meaning, God's audible utterance still told them of His affirmation of His Son, which we also can be sure of.

ASK YOURSELF

What are some of the affirmations of God's love and grace that others continue to turn a deaf ear to? How might you bring these to someone's attention, inviting them to look and see what God has done?

CHRIST ANTICIPATES VICTORY

*"Now judgment is upon this world; now the ruler of this world will be cast out.
And I, if I am lifted up from the earth, will draw all men to Myself."*
—JOHN 12:31–32

Here our Lord anticipates three significant triumphs of the cross. First, it would judge the satanic world system (cf. John 8:23, 44; 1 John 2:15–17). The world's apparent victory over Jesus at the cross was in reality the sealing of its unbelieving doom (cf. Acts 17:31). Those who reject the Lord condemn themselves to eternal hell (cf. John 3:18, 36).

Jesus' death also would judge the world's wicked ruler, Satan (Luke 4:5–6; 2 Cor. 4:4), by stripping away his authority and influence (cf. Rev. 12:10; 20:1–3, 10). "Through [His] death [Christ would] render powerless him who had the power of death, that is, the devil" (Heb. 2:14; cf. 1 Cor. 15:25–26).

The third triumph the cross would accomplish Jesus states in positive terms. When He is "lifted up from the earth" (which His hearers all understood as a reference to the crucifixion), Jesus would "draw all men to" Himself. The phrase "all men" refers to those (the "much fruit" of John 12:24) whom the Spirit would draw to salvation from all types and classes of people. It also underscores that all such are saved by believing in Christ's work on the cross. Only through His death is sin satisfactorily atoned for (Rom. 3:24–25; 1 Peter 1:18–19) and divine forgiveness granted (Matt. 26:28; Col. 1:13–14).

ASK YOURSELF

What evidence does Satan give that he is a defeated foe? What could help you more forcibly apply God's promised victory on a daily basis, assuring yourself more certainly that the Devil's time is limited?

THE CROWD'S ABANDONMENT OF JESUS

The crowd then answered Him, "We have heard out of the Law that
the Christ is to remain forever; and how can You say, 'The Son of Man
must be lifted up'? Who is this Son of Man?" —JOHN 12:34

The crowd here asked Jesus some doubting and critical questions about His messianic identity. Their disrespectful query, "Who is this Son of Man?" (in other words, "What kind of Messiah are You talking about?"), simply demonstrated blatant unbelief. The people couldn't reconcile a prediction of Jesus' death (John 12:23–26) with their conviction that Messiah would be a triumphant conqueror (Isa. 9:7; Ezek. 37:25; Dan. 7:13).

But Jesus did not allow these questions or any temptations to turn Him away from His mission or to keep Him from the agony of the cross. He fulfilled His mission in five main ways. First, His death was a sacrificial payment to God for sinners' lawlessness (Heb. 7:27; 9:26). Second, Jesus' death was an act of submission to the Father (Phil. 2:8; Heb. 5:8). Third, His death offered a substitution for sinners to God (Isa. 53:4–6). Fourth, for all who believe, our Lord's death satisfied God's wrath against sin (Rom. 3:25; 1 John 2:2), which removed all their condemnation (Rom. 8:1). Fifth, Christ's death redeemed believers to God (Rom. 5:10–11; 1 Peter 1:18–19) as His children (Gal. 3:26; 4:5–6; Heb. 2:10).

Because of Christ's perfect atonement, believers will enjoy glorious eternal life.

ASK YOURSELF

How have you endured the pain of being misunderstood by others? How do these experiences typically lead you to react? How do you compensate for the rejection? How does it help you to know that Jesus has a firsthand understanding of being harshly treated, ignored, and laughed at?

Jesus' Final Call to Belief, Part 1

"While you have the Light, believe in the Light,
so that you may become sons of Light." —John 12:36a

Despite the Jews' rejection of Him, Jesus in His persistent love for them invited them once more to acknowledge Him as Lord and Savior. The invitation included both a cry for Israel's salvation and a warning (v. 35; cf. Luke 13:34–35). This was a reference to Himself as the Light of the world (cf. John 8:12). Paul called Christ "the Light of the knowledge of the glory of God" shining in the darkness (2 Cor. 4:6). Soon Jesus would leave the people to whom He came and they would again be in total darkness (cf. 2 Cor. 3:14–16).

He had already told some unbelieving Jews, "For a little while longer I am with you, then I go to Him who sent Me" (John 7:33). He would tell the apostles in the upper room, "Little children, I am with you a little while longer. You will seek Me; and as I said to the Jews, now I also say to you, 'Where I am going, you cannot come'" (13:33; cf. 16:16). Christ knew that only a short time remained for people to hear and respond to Him. The "day of salvation" (2 Cor. 6:2) was fading away and the darkness of eternal separation from Him quickly approached.

Those who fail to appropriate the Light will lose it.

ASK YOURSELF

With so much else to worry about, with His awful suffering weighing heavily on His mind, the fact that Jesus continued reaching out to others makes a powerful statement. How could you display this same others-oriented heart and approach in the midst of your most pressing situations?

JESUS' FINAL CALL TO BELIEF, PART 2

*"While you have the Light, believe in the Light,
so that you may become sons of Light."* —JOHN 12:36a

Before the invention of electric lights, people traveled only in the clarity and safety of daylight. Jesus compares those who don't heed His warning to ancient travelers caught out after nightfall. The only way for those listeners to avoid being lost in spiritual darkness was to believe in the Light (Christ) while they still had Him. Those who do trust in Him will surely "become sons of Light" (cf. 1 John 1:5–7) and radiate the glorious light of Christ into a dark and generally lost world (Matt. 5:14–16).

When sinners stubbornly and consistently reject God, He may remove His grace and judge them. God had extraordinary patience with the Old Testament Jews: "You bore with them for many years, and admonished them by Your Spirit through Your prophets" (Neh. 9:30a). However, when "they would not give ear . . . [God] gave them into the hand of the peoples of the lands" (9:30b; cf. Judg. 10:13). God further lamented, "My people did not listen to My voice, and Israel did not obey Me. So I gave them over to the stubbornness of their heart, to walk in their own devices" (Ps. 81:11–12; cf. Isa. 63:10; Hos. 4:17).

People who reject Christ's light, never embracing Him in saving faith, inevitably face God's wrath in eternal punishment (see Heb. 10:26–27).

ASK YOURSELF

Are there any matters of spiritual or relational significance that you have been putting off and avoiding? While inaction is sometimes the right course when you're not sure what to do, is your delay more the result of fear and selfishness, perhaps a reluctance to forgive or confront?

Cause for Israel's Unbelief: Divine

He has blinded their eyes and He hardened their heart, so that they would not see
with their eyes and perceive with their heart, and be converted. —John 12:40

Israel's unbelief and rejection of Jesus was within God's perfect plan. Predicting their unbelief, the prophet Isaiah asked, "Lord, who has believed our report?" (Isa. 53:1). The answer, of course, is very few (cf. Luke 13:23–24), which was so even though God revealed His arm to the Jews through Christ's miracles. Essentially the Father blinded their eyes and hardened their hearts so they would not see, understand, and be saved (cf. Isa. 6:10; Rom. 9:18). Israel's general rejection of Messiah was not simply foreseen, it was by God's sovereign design—an act of judgment by Him.

In His infinite wisdom, God did bring good out of the Jews' rejection. It was "by [Israel's] transgression [that] salvation has come to the Gentiles" (Rom. 11:11). His plans will never be thwarted by the evil things sinners do (cf. Gen. 50:20; Ps. 76:10).

The Jews' rejection of Jesus did not occur overnight but was the culmination of centuries of rebellion, squandered privileges, and leaving divine truth. Tragically, when God's truth came to them in the person of the Lord Jesus, many just could not believe. They thought their perception was clear, but actually they were spiritually blind (cf. Matt. 23:16–17, 19, 24, 26).

ASK YOURSELF

How do you handle biblical truths that are hard to grasp and difficult to communicate? How can you discern when grappling over a confusing truth has yielded all the understanding you need for now, that you can lay it down with awe and acceptance of who God is and how He acts?

CAUSE FOR ISRAEL'S UNBELIEF: HUMAN

But though He had performed so many signs before them,
yet they were not believing in Him. —JOHN 12:37

God's judicial hardening of many of the Jews did not nullify the human fault of those who would not believe in Jesus. Commentator Leon Morris observes, "When John quotes 'he hath blinded their eyes . . .' he does not mean that the blinding takes place without the will, or against the will of these people. . . . These men chose evil. It was their own deliberate choice, their own fault. Make no mistake about that." Donald Carson provides more insight: "God's judicial hardening is not presented as the capricious manipulation of an arbitrary potentate cursing morally neutral or even morally pure beings, but as a holy condemnation of a guilty people."

Sadly, sinners who insist on hardening their hearts toward God may find that He will harden them. For example, Pharaoh hardened his heart ten times and God hardened it ten times (see Ex. 4, 7, 8, 9, 10, 11, 13, 14). Isaiah exhorted his listeners, "Seek the Lord while He may be found; call upon Him while He is near" (Isa. 55:6), before He withdraws and ultimately hardens the heart. The two causes of unbelief, one divine and the other human, in combination illustrate the perfect interface between divine sovereignty and human responsibility.

The Lord Jesus promises true believers, "If anyone serves Me, he must follow Me; and where I am, there My servant will be also; if anyone serves Me, the Father will honor him" (John 12:26).

ASK YOURSELF

How do you handle personal responsibility and accountability in your home, family, workplace, and personal life? Why are we so quick to pass blame? How could you improve in this area and thus encourage others?

FATEFUL CONSEQUENCES OF
BELIEF AND UNBELIEF, PART 1

"He who rejects Me and does not receive My sayings, has one who judges him;
the word I spoke is what will judge him at the last day." —JOHN 12:48

These words constitute a summary of Jesus' public ministry to Israel and underscore its importance and the fateful error of refusing to believe in Him. Jesus' opening words on faith emphasize the impossibility of believing in the Father apart from the Son (cf. 5:24; 8:19) and reveal that those who believe in Jesus enjoy a personal knowledge of both Father and Son (14:9, 23).

Christ's words "If anyone hears My sayings and does not keep them" shift the focus from the blessings of belief to the dire results of unbelief. Failure to obey the Savior identifies unbelievers (3:36); therefore Paul calls them "sons of disobedience" (Eph. 2:2). During His earthly ministry, Jesus' objective was to save such people, not judge them (Luke 19:10; John 3:17). Yet He will one day judge unrepentant sinners (Rev. 20:11–15). People who reject the gospel actually condemn themselves (Matt. 7:24–27) and will receive a divine and just judgment. Scripture warns: "See to it that you do not refuse Him who is speaking. For if those did not escape when they refused him who warned them on earth, much less will we escape who turn away from Him who warns from heaven" (Heb. 12:25).

ASK YOURSELF

Seeing the primary role Christ's saving mission played in His heart and teachings, why are we guilty of treating it without importance in our conversations with others? How is the church showing signs of losing confidence in Jesus' ability to save and in the sufficiency of His gospel?

FATEFUL CONSEQUENCES OF BELIEF AND UNBELIEF, PART 2

"The things I speak, I speak just as the Father has told Me." —JOHN 12:50*b*

Our Lord's words determine eternal destinies, not only because He is the Son of Man but also because He speaks for the Father (cf. John 4:34; 5:30). Thus, nobody can spurn His statements without consequences. Jesus did not speak strictly from His own agenda, but He proclaimed His Father's redemptive plan (cf. 6:63, 68). He taught only from the Father's words, which are unchangeable and absolute (Matt. 5:18).

As God's chosen people, the Jews had received many blessings (Rom. 9:4–5), the greatest of which was that the Messiah was one of their own. However, when He came to them they refused to accept His call to believe in Him and ignored His warnings of the serious consequences of such unbelief. Our Lord declared Israel's judgment with these sobering words: "Behold, your house is left to you desolate; and I say to you, you will not see Me until the time comes when you say, 'Blessed is he who comes in the name of the Lord!'" (Luke 13:35). A few decades later the Romans would destroy Jerusalem and the temple, and the Jews would be scattered and under God's discipline even until now. But because of His great love for His chosen people, God will one day redeem a remnant, "and so all Israel will be saved" (Rom. 11:26).

ASK YOURSELF

What are some of the common doubts about God's existence and His saving power that permeate today's discussions? Do these doubts seem to be getting deeper and more entrenched in our society? What is usually required for spiritual openness to show itself in a person's heart?

JESUS' AUTHORITY CHALLENGED, PART 1

*"By what authority are You doing these things,
and who gave You this authority?"* —MATT. 21:23*b*

Here Jesus was likely reiterating some of the truths He had taught many times before—no doubt matters related to "the gospel of the kingdom" (Matt. 9:35). Whatever the topic, "all the people were hanging on to every word He said" (Luke 19:48).

The "these things" the Jews referred to means all Christ had been doing and teaching, but especially the cleansing of the temple the day before. They had been powerless to prevent it, and were certainly devastated and embarrassed by it, and now they were demanding an explanation.

Jesus possessed no rabbinic ordination and thus no official recognition by the religious establishment. Its leaders had long wondered why He not only taught and preached but healed the sick, cast out demons, and raised the dead. Now they demanded to know why He forced the merchants and money changers out of the temple.

Even though the religious authorities doubted the source and legitimacy of the Lord's power, they did not contest that He had authority from someone, somewhere. Jesus' miracles were so obvious and well-attested that the authorities never doubted that He did them. But the leaders were not ready to assign the proper supernatural origin to all Jesus was doing and saying. They would not agree with the common people who "were awestruck, and glorified God, who had given such authority to men" (Matt. 9:8). The Jews preferred to believe His power came from Satan, not God.

ASK YOURSELF

Do others sometimes feel that you don't deserve the notice you attract? Why is authority so quickly and easily challenged in the human heart, and why are lies often preferable to believe rather than the truth?

JESUS' AUTHORITY CHALLENGED, PART 2

"By what authority are You doing these things,
and who gave You this authority?" —MATT. 21:23b

The Jewish leaders also conceded that Jesus taught authoritatively. As the crowds recognized, He instructed with a clarity, definitiveness, and certainty that the scribes' teachings lacked (Mark 1:22). For those teachers, when Scripture conflicted with human tradition, tradition prevailed (Matt. 16:6). For them, there were many sources of wisdom and authority, but none that was exclusively commanding, not even Scripture.

Our Lord's ministry definitely demonstrated authoritativeness by granting those who believed in Him the right to become children of God (cf. John 1:12). God "gave Him authority to execute judgment" (5:27) and "authority over all flesh" to grant eternal life to those the Father has given Him (17:2). Even over His own life, Jesus had "authority to lay it down," and concerning His resurrection, "authority to take [His life] up again" (10:18).

Christ had both great power and the right to exercise it, because both His power and authority derived from His heavenly Father. "For just as the Father raises the dead and gives them life, even so the Son also gives life to whom He wishes. . . . just as the Father has life in Himself, even so He gave to the Son also to have life in Himself" (John 5:21, 26). "For I have come down from heaven, not to do My own will, but the will of Him who sent Me" (6:38; cf. 7:16; 8:18).

ASK YOURSELF

What traditions do you see in today's church life and religious practice that trump the teachings of Scripture in people's minds? Why do we gravitate toward form and comfort even when challenged or invited to enter the adventure of spiritual freedom with Christ?

JESUS' COUNTERQUESTION, PART 1

Jesus said to them, "I will also ask you one thing, which if you tell Me,
I will also tell you by what authority I do these things. The baptism of
John was from what source, from heaven or from men?" —MATT. 21:24–25a

As they talked among themselves, the Jews recognized they would be in trouble no matter what answer they gave (vv. 25b–26). If they acknowledged that John the Baptist's ministry was from heaven, the Lord would ask them, "Then why did you not believe him?" They had not merely spurned John himself but also his clear testimony of Jesus, whom the forerunner identified as "the Lamb of God who takes away the sin of the world" and the very "Son of God" (John 1:29, 34). To accept John logically meant the Jews should also accept Jesus as Messiah—but they refused to do that.

The scribes and Pharisees were trained to rationalize away any teachings inconsistent with their doctrine, as the following illustrates:

> "God does not hear sinners; but if anyone is God-fearing and does His will, He hears him. Since the beginning of time it has never been heard that anyone opened the eyes of a person born blind. If this man [Jesus] were not from God, He could do nothing." They answered him, "You were born entirely in sins, and are you teaching us?" So they put him out. (John 9:31–34)

Stubborn unbelief is always biased against spiritual truth.

ASK YOURSELF

Jesus was not cowed by manipulative attempts to discredit His character or to cheapen the authority He was claiming. Do you struggle to maintain this level of calm confidence when challenged to defend your beliefs or explain your actions? What could help you with that?

JESUS' COUNTERQUESTION, PART 2

*Jesus said to them, "I will also ask you one thing, which if you tell Me,
I will also tell you by what authority I do these things. The baptism of
John was from what source, from heaven or from men?"* —MATT. 21:24–25a

The religionists of Jesus' day persistently rejected the light He offered
them, and therefore He withdrew it. For such arrogant, self-satisfied people who saw no need for the gospel, Christ would bring them no further
teaching. Instead, He would declare to them only further warning and
condemnation (see Matt. 23).

When He was before Caiaphas the high priest, "Jesus kept silent,"
refusing to give further testimony of Himself (Matt. 26:63). When Pilate
asked Him to answer the Jews' many charges against Him, the Lord "did
not answer him with regard to even a single charge" (27:14).

When men and women continually reject God's truth and grace, He
may withdraw from them: "My Spirit shall not strive with man forever"
(Gen. 6:3). But Jesus revealed that He took no pleasure in the Jews' unbelief:

> Jerusalem, Jerusalem, who kills the prophets and stones those who
> are sent to her! How often I wanted to gather your children together,
> the way a hen gathers her chicks under her wings, and you were un-
> willing. Behold, your house is being left to you desolate! For I say to
> you, from now on you will not see Me until you say, "Blessed is He
> who comes in the name of the Lord!" (Matt. 23:37–39)

ASK YOURSELF

How do you know when silence is the best response to a person's
attitudes or questions? How can your prayers for a belligerent person
stay strong even though talking with him seems a waste of time?

CONTRASTING RESPONSES TO THE GOSPEL

"'Son, go work today in the vineyard.'" And he answered, "'I will not'"; but afterward he regretted it and went. The man came to the second and said the same thing; and he answered, "'I will, sir'"; but he did not go. Which of the two did the will of his father?" They said, "The first." —MATT. 21:28b–31a

Our Lord characterizes in this brief parable two contrasting responses to the gospel. The first son initially refused to go, saying "I will not." However, "afterward he regretted it and went." The father also asked the second son "the same thing," and at first that son said he would go, but ultimately he didn't. Jesus implies that the second son lied to his father to falsely indicate that he would obey.

When Christ asked, "Which of the two did the will of his father?" the Jews replied with the obvious answer, "The first."

The point of this parable is clearly that actions are more important than mere words. Of course, the preferable scenario is for us to agree to do God's will and then do it. However, it is far better, if we at first refuse to do the Lord's will, that we repent and obey the divine command, rather than giving a hypocritical yes to His directives but failing to obediently follow through with actions. Here the obedience to God's will relates to embracing the gospel, receiving Jesus as the Messiah and as Savior and Lord.

ASK YOURSELF

Does Jesus' parable speak to an issue in your life right now—a point of rebellion or avoidance that has put you at odds with God's will? What would obedience bring to your heart even if it comes at a great cost?

How a Gospel Parable Applied, Part 1

Jesus said to them, "Truly I say to you that the tax collectors and prostitutes will get into the kingdom of God before you." —MATT. 21:31*b*

In the preceding parable, the Jews did not correspond to "the first" son, who obeyed his father, but to the latter who did not. On a later occasion, Jesus would say of the Jews, "They say things and do not do them" (Matt. 23:3). They claimed to obey God, but their behavior revealed they really had no place for Him or His Son in their hearts.

The men who heard Jesus' words were the religious elite. They claimed to live in obedience to God's law and had the false notion that their elevated positions and many religious works rendered them favored persons in His sight. Yet Jesus told those arrogant leaders that "tax collectors and prostitutes," who first chose to sinfully disregard God but later repented, would "get into the kingdom of God before" they would. Jesus used the expression "before you" not to indicate that the leaders would eventually enter heaven (no unbelievers ever do) but simply to illustrate the divine reversal of human standards for salvation. The so-called sinners of that day were closer to heaven than the religionists because they were more ready to admit their need for God's grace.

Mere pompous claims of religion don't qualify anyone for the kingdom, and even gross sins, when repented of, will not exclude someone.

ASK YOURSELF

How does Jesus' open invitation to the lowest classes of society square with the ministry model of the church today? When faced with the risks of reaching out to the most hardened of sinners, how interested are you in the matching opportunities to see God transform hurting lives?

HOW A GOSPEL PARABLE APPLIED, PART 2

Jesus said to them, "Truly I say to you that the tax collectors and prostitutes will get into the kingdom of God before you." —MATT. 21:31b

The Jewish leaders had an unbelieving skepticism of the Baptist from the beginning (see Matt. 21:32) and even sent some of their representatives to question him (John 1:19–25). As a result, when John

saw many of the Pharisees and Sadducees coming for baptism, he said to them, "You brood of vipers, who warned you to flee from the wrath to come? Therefore bear fruit in keeping with repentance; and do not suppose that you can say to yourselves, 'We have Abraham for our father'; for I say to you that from these stones God is able to raise up children to Abraham." (Matt. 3:7–9)

In contrast, "the tax collectors and prostitutes did believe" (21:32) John, meaning they believed the gospel, even in its incomplete form as taught by the Baptist. Manifesting a repentant sincerity in being baptized for cleansing from sin, the tax collectors asked John, "Teacher, what shall we do?" (Luke 3:12). Although Scripture contains no specific examples, Jesus points out that some whom John baptized were repentant prostitutes who, like the tax men, confessed their sins and received forgiveness (see Matt. 3:5–6).

Again, what contrasting responses we see to the gospel—unbelief by those who were outwardly righteous, and belief by the outwardly immoral and dishonest.

ASK YOURSELF

Why are those who don't find themselves in a state of perceived need or desperation less likely to trust Christ with abandon? Would you confess in yourself any pattern of disbelief?

JESUS ILLUSTRATES THE
REASON FOR JUDGMENT, PART 1

*"But when the vine-growers saw the son, they said among themselves,
'This is the heir; come, let us kill him and seize his inheritance.' They took
him, and threw him out of the vineyard and killed him."* —MATT. 21:38–39

The scene described in this parable was familiar to the people in Palestine's agrarian society, so Jesus' audience could easily identify with the grape vineyard, a mainstay of the economy.

Under the Holy Spirit's guidance, Matthew here condenses several episodes into one (21:33–39). Mark's account tells us the first three slaves came to the vineyard separately, one by one (12:2–5). The evil caretakers probably scourged the first slave, leaving him wounded and bloody, then killed a second slave outright and stoned a third man, which very likely killed him. Subsequently, the vineyard owner sent an even larger group of slaves to gather his produce, but the growers responded in the same way, "beating some and killing others" (Mark 12:5).

The owner had given the caretakers an excellent opportunity to cultivate the vineyard and earn a good living, all under the owner's complete trust. But the tenants, who represented the Christ-rejecting Jews, were not content with those benefits. They were greedy for the entire harvest and were brutally remorseless in pursuing that end. This second in a trilogy of judgment parables vividly illustrates the sin of the unbelieving Jewish leaders in their willful rejection of God and His Son.

ASK YOURSELF

What would you consider your baseline of blessing that you don't allow God's supply to drop beneath before you turn on Him?

JESUS ILLUSTRATES THE
REASON FOR JUDGMENT, PART 2

"But when the vine-growers saw the son, they said among themselves, 'This is the heir; come, let us kill him and seize his inheritance.' They took him, and threw him out of the vineyard and killed him." —MATT. 21:38–39

The murder of the son was cruelly premeditated ("This is the heir; come, let us kill him and seize his inheritance"). Those entrusted with the vineyard did not mistake him for some other servant; they knew exactly who he was. Because he was the owner's son, they were eager to kill him and grab his inheritance.

This parable generates much sympathy for the betrayed, grieving owner, as well as indignant anger toward the cold, calculating, and brutal tenants. In fact, the details of the story are so astounding, unrealistic, and extraordinary that Scripture critics claim Jesus overstated the account or that the Gospel writers exaggerated the original version. But such extremes were necessary for our Lord to make His point. He wanted members of His audience and any who read this today to ponder the owner's uncommon patience and the growers' unprecedented wickedness as they consider their own positions before God and their ultimate, eternal destinies.

ASK YOURSELF

If not rejecting them and treating them with contempt, how have you at least ignored some of the Scripture's calls for you to produce works "in keeping with repentance" (Matt. 3:8), to be held accountable for what God has invested in you? What fruit could you bring to Him today?

JUDGMENT EXPLAINED AND CONCLUDED, PART 1

*"Did you never read in the Scriptures, 'The stone which the
builders rejected, this became the chief corner stone; this came about
from the Lord, and it is marvelous in our eyes'?"* —MATT. 21:42

For years Israel had been the stone that the world's empire builders had
rejected as unimportant and despised. But in God's sovereign plan He
chose Israel to be "the chief corner stone" in His redemptive plan, the
people through whom the Savior would come.

However, the cornerstone symbol has a greater significance than
that:

> Let it be known to all of you and to all the people of Israel, that by
> the name of Jesus Christ the Nazarene, whom you crucified, whom
> God raised from the dead . . . He is the stone which was rejected by
> you, the builders, but which became the chief corner stone. And
> there is salvation in no one else; for there is no other name under
> heaven that has been given among men by which we must be saved.
> (Acts 4:10–12)

The greater stone than Israel is the Lord Jesus Christ, and the
builders who rejected Him were the religious leaders who represented all
Israel, and more broadly, the entire unbelieving world.

Jesus linked the messianic psalm—He quoted 118:22—to bolster His
point. The rejected stone is the crucified Christ, and the restored "chief
corner stone" is the resurrected Christ. It is He who will one day judge
all unbelievers for their rejection of Him.

ASK YOURSELF

What are some of the "cornerstones" people try to build their
lives upon? How have you seen these unstable supports give way,
not only for others but for you? How can you tell each morning
if you're leaning all your weight on Him?

JUDGMENT EXPLAINED AND CONCLUDED, PART 2

"Did you never read in the Scriptures, 'The stone which the builders rejected, this became the chief corner stone; this came about from the Lord, and it is marvelous in our eyes'?" —MATT. 21:42

Israel mishandled her stewardship of the Promised Land and robbed God of the honor due His name. According to tradition, Isaiah was sawed in two. His people threw Jeremiah into a slime pit and probably later stoned him to death. The Jews also rejected many of the other prophets (cf. 1 Kings 22:24). They actually murdered Zechariah in the temple (2 Chron. 24:20–22). Such hateful behavior led them to kill the Son of God.

Presenting this parable was one of Jesus' clearest claims to deity. The story even alludes to His being crucified outside the city (cf. Heb. 13:12), analogous to the vineyard owner's son being killed after he was cast outside the vineyard. His audience knew He had to be God's Son, but they refused to honor and accept Him as such, so their attitudes and actions were inexcusable. The Jews wanted Christ dead, not because He was evil and ungodly but because He threatened their sinful control of the temple and the entire Jewish religious system.

Throughout redemptive history, right down to the present, many have refused to embrace Jesus Christ as Lord and Savior not because of lack of evidence but simply because they have *not wanted* to believe the evidence—and for this they are justly judged.

ASK YOURSELF

Most people today have a similar motive. They do not consider Jesus evil; they just do not want Him to have authority in their lives. Is there any part of you that doesn't want Christ's complete claim?

Judgment Explained and Concluded, Part 3

"Did you never read in the Scriptures, 'The stone which the builders rejected, this became the chief corner stone; this came about from the Lord, and it is marvelous in our eyes'?" —Matt. 21:42

I n his first epistle, Peter, quoting the Old Testament, reiterates the truth about Jesus as the cornerstone:

> "Behold, I lay in Zion a choice stone, a precious corner stone, and he who believes in Him will not be disappointed." This precious value, then, is for you who believe; but for those who disbelieve, "The stone which the builders rejected, this became the very corner stone," and, "A stone of stumbling and a rock of offense"; for they stumble because they are disobedient to the word, and to this doom they were also appointed. (1 Peter 2:6–8; cf. Eph. 2:19–20)

After David heard the prophet Nathan's parable about the rich man who took a poor man's lamb to feed a traveler,

> David's anger burned greatly against the man, and he said to Nathan, "As the Lord lives, surely the man who has done this deserves to die. He must make restitution for the lamb fourfold, because he did this thing and had no compassion." Nathan then said to David, "You are the man!" (2 Sam. 12:5–7)

Effectively, Jesus told the Jewish leaders, "You are the men! You deserve condemnation and death for killing the owner's servants and then his son. The owner is God, the vineyard His kingdom, the servants His prophets, and the son is Me. Such harsh, unbelieving actions as you've perpetrated demand My judgment."

ASK YOURSELF

Have you been avoiding an area of guilt that is staring you in the face? Confess every sin, and receive Christ's peace and forgiveness.

JUDGMENT APPLIED, PART 1

"And he who falls on this stone will be broken to pieces; but on whomever it falls, it will scatter him like dust." —MATT. 21:44

From the outset of his kingdom preaching, John the Baptist demanded that the Jewish leaders who wanted to be baptized "bear fruit in keeping with repentance" first (Matt. 3:8). Such fruit is the demonstrated righteousness deriving from a life that has turned from sin (see Col. 1:10). The unbelieving Jews, however, refused to repent and therefore could not produce kingdom fruit. They were willfully barren spiritually, and for that reason were divinely cursed, like the fig tree with leaves but no figs (Matt. 21:18–19).

By God's grace Israel will one day return to Him and bear fruit: "God has not rejected His people whom He foreknew. . . ." And when "the fullness of the Gentiles has come in . . . all Israel will be saved; just as it is written, 'The Deliverer will come from Zion, He will remove ungodliness from Jacob'" (Rom. 11:2, 25–26).

In the meantime God has selected another people, redeemed Gentiles, to be His witnesses. Paul, quoting the prophet Hosea, asserts, "'I will call those who were not My People, "My people," and her who was not beloved "beloved." 'And it shall be that in the place where it was said to them, "You are you are not My people," there they shall be called sons of the living God.'" (Rom. 9:25–26; cf. Hos. 1:10; 2:23). That group, constituting the Lord's church, is free from the judgment that befell unbelieving Israel.

ASK YOURSELF

Do you ever find yourself overlooking the deep privilege of being drawn by God's grace into fellowship with Him? What are the best ways to keep your appreciation of His mercy fresh in your heart?

JUDGMENT APPLIED, PART 2

*"And he who falls on this stone will be broken to pieces; but on
whomever it falls, it will scatter him like dust."* —MATT. 21:44

Peter, quoting in part from Isaiah, writes this about the people who are
the church: "you are a chosen race, a royal priesthood, a holy nation, a
people for God's own possession, so that you may proclaim the excellen-
cies of Him who has called you out of darkness into His marvelous light"
(1 Peter 2:9; cf. Isa. 43:20; 61:6; 66:21). Only believers are Spirit-
equipped to produce kingdom fruit: "I am the vine, you are the branches;
he who abides in Me and I in him, he bears much fruit, for apart from Me
you can do nothing" (John 15:5).

The Jewish leaders who, as it were, fell on Christ and killed Him
would themselves "be broken to pieces." And "on whomever it [Jesus the
stone] falls, it will scatter him like dust." Just as God has given all salvation to His Son (John 14:6), He has also "given all judgment to the Son"
(5:22).

So anyone, not just the Jewish leaders of Jesus' day, who "does not
love the Lord, he is to be accursed," the apostle Paul wrote in a solemn
closing to the Corinthians (1 Cor. 16:22). Enemies of the gospel, unless
they repent, are destined to be crushed into nothingness—"broken to
pieces" and scattered "like dust" (cf. Dan. 2:32–35).

ASK YOURSELF

The blessed alternative is to let ourselves (our pride, sin,
and self-will) be broken on the altar of submission to Christ,
so the ashes of our lives can be transformed for holy, eternal
purposes. How would you allow your hard places to be broken
open and replaced with Christ's character?

THE JEWS REACT TO THE PARABLE

When the chief priests and the Pharisees heard His parables, they understood that He was speaking about them. When they sought to seize Him, they feared the people, because they considered Him to be a prophet. —MATT. 21:45–46

The Jewish leaders' only concerns were for self-justification and retribution; therefore their reaction to the Lord's words was "to seize Him" and murder Him. What prevented those things from happening right away was that "they feared the people, because they [the people] considered Him to be a prophet." It was the classic case of being men-pleasers rather than God-pleasers. As a result, the leaders waited to arrest the Lord until they were sure they could turn the crowds against Him, which occurred shortly after this. Finally disillusioned with a Messiah and King unlike what they wanted or expected, the people gave the leaders no more reason to fear them. When Pilate, for instance, asked what should be done "with Jesus who is called Christ," the people's answer was "Crucify Him!" (Matt. 27:22).

The passage we've considered pictures God's gracious provision for men and women, His patience with their unbelief and rejection, and His love in sending them His one and only Son for their salvation. However, it also reveals His righteous judgment against sinners who exhaust His patience.

The passage also depicts Christ's deity as God's Son and His willing obedience to accomplish redemption, resurrection, and ascension—with eternal life for believers and judgment for rejecters.

ASK YOURSELF

Can you spot evidence of hypocrisy in your own heart, such as that which existed in the religious leadership of Jesus' day? What would be some of the freedoms to be experienced by rejecting your people-pleasing tendencies and becoming a whole person all day long, in any situation?

REJECTION OF THE ROYAL INVITATION, PART 1

"But they paid no attention and went their way, one to his own farm, another to his business, and the rest seized his slaves and mistreated them and killed them."
—MATT. 22:5–6

A wedding invitation from a king brought not only honor but obligation. To spurn that favor was a serious, inconceivable offense. Jesus' shocked listeners had to be thinking, *Who would behave as the people in the story? Their very unwillingness to attend the wedding is preposterous.*

Those hearing the parable had to be amazed also at the king's initial patient and humble response (vv. 3–4), especially in the face of open insult. But the king sent other servants, in effect, to remind those invited of all the preparations that had been made.

But those urged to come to the feast were so selfishly preoccupied with personal profit-making concerns that the king's patient and gracious calls for them to attend his son's wedding were totally ignored. These invitees deliberately forfeited the splendid aspects of the royal wedding for the sake of their mundane, selfish endeavors. The next invitees reacted even more wickedly with an act of unbelievably brutal arrogance. Offended at the king's persistence, they seized the king's messengers and killed them—an act of flagrant and unspeakable rebellion against their sovereign.

Because Christ said the parable was about the kingdom of heaven, its meaning needed no interpretation. It was obviously another warning and indictment to the Jews and, by extension, any who would proudly flout the Father's gracious offer of salvation.

ASK YOURSELF

How have you let trivial interests and activities distort your discernment of what is truly relevant and significant? What is the greatest danger of letting inconsequential matters become of such importance to us?

REJECTION OF THE ROYAL INVITATION, PART 2

"But they paid no attention and went their way, one to his own farm, another to his business, and the rest seized his slaves and mistreated them and killed them."
—MATT. 22:5–6

The ones God had sent to repeatedly call those already invited to the feast were John the Baptist, the Lord Jesus in His earthly ministry, the prophets, apostles, and other preachers and teachers. God's repeated message to Israel, His already-invited guests, was essentially what He'd said from heaven at Christ's baptism: "Here is My Son; come and give Him honor." But the establishment rejected John the Baptist and beheaded him, rejected Jesus and crucified Him, rejected the prophets and apostles and killed many of them.

The indifferent invitees in the parable are basically the secular-minded people of today, more interested in temporal pursuits than anything spiritual. They are materialists, desirous of accumulating "stuff," ambitious, wanting only to get ahead in life. They simply have no time for the kingdom of God.

Those aggressively hostile to the invitation represent false religions that are actively opposed to the gospel. Such false religions would include humanistic, postmodern philosophies, New Age mysticism, naturalistic scientism, outspoken atheism, as well as cults and sects of Christianity. Historically, the main persecutor of true, biblical religion has been false religion. It is therefore inevitable, as God's Word predicts (2 Thess. 2:3–4), that the final world system of Antichrist will be religious, not secular. But through it all, as Jesus' parable illustrates, God's patience, grace, and forbearance have been immense.

ASK YOURSELF

How could you exhibit such patience and grace toward those in your life who take great offense at Christian faith and your practice of it?

REJECTERS PUNISHED

"But the king was enraged, and he sent his armies and destroyed those murderers and set their city on fire. Then he said to his slaves, 'The wedding is ready, but those who were invited were not worthy.'" —MATT. 22:7–8

As in the parable of the vineyard, here God's patience proves to have its limit. In fact, the king (representing God) would have been justified in punishing the irresponsible invitees when they first ignored his call. After his several pleas and the people's persistent refusal to attend the wedding, the king became "enraged." This reminds us of what God said concerning the pre-Flood generation: "My Spirit shall not strive with man forever" (Gen. 6:3).

The royal wedding was ready, as the king explained, "but those who were invited were not worthy" to attend. Such unworthiness was not because the people weren't righteous enough. None of the urgings to come was based on the subjects' merit but entirely on the king's gracious favor (cf. Matt. 22:10).

Only saying yes to God's invitation and faithfully embracing His Son as Lord and Savior makes us worthy to receive eternal life—not any kind of human goodness, philanthropic deeds, or spiritual accomplishments. Because God's chosen people, Israel, rejected His Son, He has rejected them for a season. Because they would not accept their own Messiah, God would temporarily cast them off as His unique, chosen people.

ASK YOURSELF

Why do so many believe that their own best attempts at living a good life should be sufficient to earn them a place in heaven? How do you discuss this error in judgment with them, and why must you ultimately trust God, rather than your convincing arguments, to open their hearts to truth?

New Guests Invited

"Those slaves went out into the streets and gathered together all they found,
both evil and good; and the wedding hall was filled with dinner guests."
—Matt. 22:10

The king here commanded his servants to go everywhere, find everyone they could, and invite them to the wedding hall. Jesus would command the same kind of thing: "Go therefore and make disciples of all the nations" (Matt. 28:19). And Paul told the Romans, "salvation has come to the Gentiles" (Rom. 11:11; cf. 9:25–26; Hos. 1:10; 2:23).

The king's servants invited the morally evil and good alike, their being equally unworthy in themselves to come to the festivities. Our Father has always extended His saving call to both good and bad people—neither category is righteous apart from Him, thus both equally need salvation.

Paul makes it clear that people characterized by any of the infamous sins of 1 Corinthians 6:9–10 will have no part in God's kingdom. But He will savingly receive any person guilty of any or all of those evils—anyone who truly repents and trusts Christ's atonement. Thus the apostle could tell the Corinthian believers, "Such were some of you; but you were washed, but you were sanctified, but you were justified in the name of the Lord Jesus Christ and in the Spirit of our God" (v. 11). All who respond to God's call, who follow Christ as Lord, will be wedding guests for eternity.

ASK YOURSELF

What are some of the sins and failures you could recall today in thinking about all that God has delivered you from? What are some of the transgressions that you continue to divert toward when your spirit flags and your thinking is deceived? Make this a moment of repentance and worship.

THE INTRUDER EXPELLED, PART 1

"'Bind him hand and foot, and throw him into the outer darkness;
in that place there will be weeping and gnashing of teeth.'
For many are called, but few are chosen." —MATT. 22:13–14

At first reading, you have to wonder how this man or anyone invited to the dinner could have come properly attired (vv. 11–12). That the other banquet guests, however, except for this one man, apparently wore their wedding clothes indicates the king must have made provision for such dress. It would have been a mockery for such a gracious ruler to invite the wickedest of people to his feast and then exclude one merely for lack of proper attire.

The man was completely accountable for being inappropriately dressed, but the king still respectfully asked him what happened: "Friend, how did you come in here without wedding clothes?" (v. 12). The man was unable even to offer a feeble excuse; instead he was speechless. Thus it's obvious that he could have come in wedding clothes if he'd been willing.

Until the king confronted him, the man had presumed he could come to the feast on his own terms, in whatever clothes he desired. But that is arrogant and self-willed, inconsiderate of other guests, and insulting to the king himself. This case is much like those today who presume to find salvation on their terms, apart from obedience to the gospel.

ASK YOURSELF

What would be the result if even one shred of our salvation was dependent on our own effort? Why is it so important that the redemption of our souls is the complete work of God, without any assistance on our part, without a single expectation for us to meet Him halfway?

THE INTRUDER EXPELLED, PART 2

"'Bind him hand and foot, and throw him into the outer darkness;
in that place there will be weeping and gnashing of teeth.'
For many are called, but few are chosen." —MATT. 22:13–14

When the presumptuous man couldn't answer the king's question, the monarch had him bound and thrown into the outer darkness of endless suffering. There he would be permanently expelled from the king's presence and would experience overwhelming regret and remorse. (The binding of his hands and feet likely represents prevention of his resisting or of any attempt to return.) Although the man had a great opportunity, he thoroughly lacked the godly sorrow that leads to repentance and saving faith (2 Cor. 7:10).

Ever since Cain's early attempt to satisfy God by offering a self-appointed sacrifice (Gen. 4:3–5), people have striven for salvation on human terms. They might join a church and associate with believers, become diligent in church activities, donate to support the church, and claim devotion to the Lord. But in the last day their hypocrisy will be obvious and their doom certain. How we should all trust, serve, and obey Christ so that we don't have to say to Him, "Lord, Lord, did we not prophesy in Your name, and in Your name cast out demons, and in Your name perform many miracles?" or hear Christ say, "I never knew you; depart from Me, you who practice lawlessness" (Matt. 7:22–23).

ASK YOURSELF

Are there any terms in which you approach God on the basis of your own worthiness, pointing to your performance of certain religious duties, expecting His opinion of you to improve because of your devotion to His commands? Why do we resist being totally dependent on grace?

The Intruder Expelled, Part 3

"'Bind him hand and foot, and throw him into the outer darkness;
in that place there will be weeping and gnashing of teeth.'
For many are called, but few are chosen." —MATT. 22:13–14

For the Christian, the only acceptable spiritual wedding garment is God-imputed righteousness, without which no one can see Him. Unless our righteousness is greater than the phony self-righteousness of the Jewish leaders, we "will not enter the kingdom of heaven" (Matt. 5:20). The only garment God accepts is the biblical "sanctification without which no one will see the Lord" (Heb. 12:14).

Many of the Jews hearing Jesus' parable would have, or should have, remembered Isaiah's words, "I will rejoice greatly in the Lord, my soul will exult in my God; for He has clothed me with garments of salvation, He has wrapped me with a robe of righteousness" (Isa. 61:10). Believing Jews understood that, contrary to what the rabbis taught by their humanly devised, legalistic traditions, God demands inner righteousness of His followers—and He offers it to people as a gift.

Only the Lord knows for sure whether our righteousness is of our own making or His granting. Only He sees the internal righteousness imputed to our hearts, but everyone sees the external righteousness He imparts to our lives. Peter teaches that believers will manifest holy lives, noting that they "have in obedience to the truth purified [their] souls" (1 Peter 1:22).

ASK YOURSELF

What does it mean, in practical terms, for Christ's righteousness to take the place of our own? What are some of the real-life ways that we restrain our own self-will and allow the Spirit of Christ to work His righteousness through us? How do we let His character come through?

THE INTRUDER EXPELLED, PART 4

"'Bind him hand and foot, and throw him into the outer darkness;
in that place there will be weeping and gnashing of teeth.'
For many are called, but few are chosen." —MATT. 22:13–14

Our Lord no doubt would have been pleased if someone listening to this parable had interrupted to ask Him, "How can the correct wedding garment be my attire? How can I avoid being thrown into the outer darkness like this man?" Jesus would have answered, as He had many times and in various ways in the past, "Come to Me so that you may have life" (John 5:40; cf. Matt. 11:28–30). Furthermore, Paul implicitly points to this saving wedding garment of righteousness: "He made Him who knew no sin to be sin on our behalf, so that we might become the righteousness of God in Him" (2 Cor. 5:21).

Our Lord closes this parable with the sobering statement "For many are called, but few are chosen," which encapsulates the biblical balance between God's sovereignty and humanity's responsibility. God offers the gospel to every person because He is not willing that anyone be condemned to hell forever (see 1 Tim. 2:3–4; 2 Peter 3:9). But not everyone wants God, and many who say they do want Him want Him only on their terms. But the chosen enter God's kingdom because of their divinely aided acceptance of His grace. Those not among the chosen are ultimately excluded by their own willing rejection of that same sovereign grace.

ASK YOURSELF

How does the "many are called, but few are chosen" concept affect your evangelism? Do you sometimes let the sovereign reality of God's call inhibit your desire to be involved in sharing the gospel with others?

THE PHARISEES AND HERODIANS ATTACK JESUS

*"Tell us then, what do You think? Is it lawful to
give a poll-tax to Caesar, or not?"* —MATT. 22:17

Because the Pharisees were afraid to take direct action against Jesus,
they tried to trap Him into making a subversive statement against Rome
that would ensure His arrest and execution. They wanted to "deliver
Him to the rule and the authority of the governor" (Luke 20:20), who at
that time was Pontius Pilate. The pro-Roman Herodians were useful co-
conspirators who would make perfect witnesses against Jesus. The two
groups strongly disagreed about religion and politics, but the two didn't
mind making common cause against Christ.

Thus with everything aligned, the Pharisees' representatives, described as "spies who pretended to be righteous" (v. 20), told the Lord,
"Teacher, we know that You are truthful and teach the way of God in
truth, and defer to no one; for You are not partial to any" (Matt. 22:16).
The men outwardly praised Him for His personal and doctrinal integrity.
They conceded He would not be intimidated by opposition threats but
would stand His ground with courage and conviction.

The Pharisees' representatives could not have been more accurate, if
only they had actually believed what they said. Flattery often involves
lying, but it is most disingenuous and wicked when it uses the truth to
achieve its sinful purposes, as was the case here.

ASK YOURSELF

Do you ever stoop to insincerity in trying to advance your objectives or
in clearing the paths for your ambition? Why must we be on such careful
guard against trusting in our own wiles and persuasion? How deeply
does honesty really reign in your heart, able to lead in any situation?

Jesus' Answer regarding the Poll Tax, Part 1

*Then He said to them, "Then render to Caesar the things that are Caesar's; and to God the things that are God's." —*MATT. 22:21

Christ knew the flattering tongues of the pharisaic emissaries were poisonous, and thus He had the perfect response for them: "Why are you testing Me, you hypocrites?" (22:18). Although He had never met them before, He knew what these men were up to.

Disregarding the Lord's sharp words, the men quickly gave Him a denarius, hoping to pull Him into their snare. The denarius of that day equaled the daily wage of a soldier or common laborer in Palestine. The denarius and all Roman coins had an engraving of the emperor on one side and an identifying inscription on the other. This made the coins especially offensive to the Jews. First, the emperor's picture reminded them of Rome's oppression, and second, such rendering of images was against the Mosaic law (Ex. 20:4). Hence the Jews were extremely interested in what Jesus' response would be.

The men immediately answered "Caesar" to Jesus' question about the likeness and inscription on the coin (Matt. 22:20–21a). They hoped at last He was about to speak incriminating words against Rome that they could use against Him. But the Lord was going to surprise them with a most insightful and perceptive answer, the meaning of which we shall see tomorrow.

ASK YOURSELF

One of the clear teachings of Scripture is that we are not to "test" the Lord (Deut. 6:16; Matt. 4:7). How have you been guilty of going against this warning by making God stand trial for perceived injustices in your life? But does this mean it is ever wrong to question Him?

Jesus' Answer regarding the Poll Tax, Part 2

Then He said to them, "Then render to Caesar the things that are Caesar's; and to God the things that are God's." —MATT. 22:21

Here Jesus affirms the God-ordained obligation of Christian citizens to pay taxes to whatever government rules them. Paying taxes is particularly binding on Christians because they are specially obligated to God's Word. Notice that Christ gives us no waivers or special exemptions, even under harsh rulers such as the ones who soon would nail Him to a cross.

Living under the same Roman Empire, Paul writes this:

> Every person is to be in subjection to the governing authorities. For there is no authority except from God, and those which exist are established by God. . . . Therefore it is necessary to be in subjection . . . For because of this you also pay taxes, for rulers are servants of God, devoting themselves to this very thing. Render to all what is due them: tax to whom tax is due; custom to whom custom; fear to whom fear; honor to whom honor. (Rom. 13:1, 5–7; cf. 1 Tim. 2:1–3)

Peter teaches the same: "Submit yourselves for the Lord's sake to every human institution, whether to a king as the one in authority, or to governors as sent by him for the punishment of evildoers and the praise of those who do right. For such is the will of God that by doing right you may silence the ignorance of foolish men" (1 Peter 2:13–15).

ASK YOURSELF

How do these teachings affect your behavior and attitudes as a citizen of your nation? Should a Christian feel certain restraints and boundaries in criticizing his or her government and leadership figures? How does this apply when the ruling bodies seem to be acting in error?

Jesus' Answer regarding the Poll Tax, Part 3

Then He said to them, "Then render to Caesar the things that are Caesar's; and to God the things that are God's." —Matt. 22:21

God's sovereign decree has placed rulers over us at all levels—national, regional, state, and local—who stand in His place to preserve society. To avoid taxes, therefore, is to disobey God and His Word.

If in an era of pagan despotism and persecution, as during Jesus' and Paul's time, believers had to pay their taxes, how much more should contemporary saints who live in free and democratic cultures? To argue that sending tax money to secular governments is wrong is spurious and contradicts what Jesus teaches here on the subject. Unquestionably, Scripture commands that we must pay our taxes because they are part of "the things that are Caesar's." All things are God's, but He has ordained that a certain amount of the resources entrusted to men and women must go to human governments as taxes.

In addition to submitting to authorities in taxes and other matters, we are to pray for them: "First of all, then, I urge that entreaties and prayers, petitions and thanksgivings, be made on behalf of all men, for kings and all who are in authority, so that we may lead a tranquil and quiet life in all godliness and dignity" (1 Tim. 2:1–2).

ASK YOURSELF

Why is it important that the Bible not only be confined to strict religious instruction but also apply to each of our interactions with others, covering all of life? In what ways has the Scripture impacted your role as a member of your family, as a worker, as a part of society?

JESUS' ANSWER REGARDING THE POLL TAX, PART 4

Then He said to them, "Then render to Caesar the things that are Caesar's; and to God the things that are God's." —MATT. 22:21

To wrap up our consideration of what Jesus taught about the believer's responsibility toward taxes, we could imagine Him saying, "Yes, it is entirely appropriate to pay taxes because they are the government's, belonging to the things of that domain."

As representatives of human government, presidents, prime ministers, and other officials have the right to assess taxes; but as representatives of human religion, as the Caesars frequently were, they have no right to command worship. The government's realm is social, economic, and military, and to the extent that it steps outside that realm, its authority ceases and people's obligation to it ceases. When the Sanhedrin (the Jewish ruling council of Jesus' day), which had political and religious authority in Jerusalem, gave the apostles "strict orders not to continue teaching in this [Jesus'] name," Peter answered for all of them, declaring, "We must obey God rather than men" (Acts 5:28–29).

Totalitarian countries, such as mainland China and some Islamic nations, persecute Christians for not giving total allegiance to the state. Although most believers in every country are good citizens who pay their taxes, they refuse to surrender their souls to the government. Such complete allegiance must be reserved for the Lord.

ASK YOURSELF

Are there any statutes or prohibitions established by your government that go beyond what a Christian is entitled to obey? If not, are there any leanings that could reach that level if they continue on their present course? How will you know when certain things have gone too far?

JESUS EXPOSES IGNORANCE OF GOD'S POWER

*But Jesus answered and said to them, "You are mistaken, not understanding the Scriptures nor the power of God. For in the resurrection they neither marry nor are given in marriage, but are like angels in heaven." —*MATT. 22:29–30

Christ here explains that marriage and its related activities do not occur in heaven, because there is no birth and death there as on earth. Also, there will not be any exclusive relationships in heaven because everyone will be perfectly related to everyone else. Exposing the Sadducees' erroneous views of the resurrection, Jesus adds that people will be "like angels," equally spiritual, deathless, glorified, and eternal. In Luke's account, he notes that our Lord said resurrected believers "are sons of God, being sons of the resurrection" (20:36).

Years later, the Christians in Corinth were also confused about this subject. Using understandable terms, Paul explained the resurrection body:

> So also is the resurrection of the dead. It is sown a perishable body, it is raised an imperishable body; it is sown in dishonor, it is raised in glory; it is sown in weakness, it is raised in power; it is sown a natural body, it is raised a spiritual body. If there is a natural body, there is also spiritual body. (1 Cor. 15:42–44)

The foolish idea that God is restricted to raising bodies in the same form as when they died undermines His power. It is also no reason to deny the resurrection.

ASK YOURSELF

Even with the mysteries surrounding exactly how our resurrected bodies will appear and what life will be like in eternity, how do the revelations God has given in His Word excite you about your future?

JESUS EXPOSES IGNORANCE OF GOD'S WORD

*"Have you not read what was spoken to you by God: 'I am the God of Abraham, and the God of Isaac, and the God of Jacob'? He is not the God of the dead but of the living." —*MATT. 22:31*b*–32

Jesus based His irrefutable argument on the emphatic present tense use of "I am" in the Pentateuch (Ex. 3:6; cf. Gen. 28:13). The Lord was still the God of the three patriarchs long after their deaths—even more so now because their souls have fellowship in His eternal presence.

Christ used the present tense because the Father "is not the God of the dead but of the living." And if He is now the God of the three patriarchs, then they obviously live in heaven. They would still be alive so God could fulfill His promises to them that He didn't while they were on earth.

And indeed if they had been thinking of that country from which they went out, they would have had opportunity to return. But as it is, they desire a better country, that is, a heavenly one. Therefore God is not ashamed to be called their God; for He has prepared a city for them. (Heb. 11:15–16; see also vv. 13–14)

Jesus proved the resurrection from the Pentateuch, a source the Sadducees accepted, and thus "silenced the Sadducees" (Matt. 22:34).

ASK YOURSELF

The fact that God's relationship with His people did not begin a few days ago but extends centuries past—even into eternity past—should anchor our trust in His faithful, covenant love. How are you experiencing this? How often do you reflect on the rich depth of your faith heritage?

A LAWYER'S QUESTION

"Teacher, which is the great commandment in the Law?" —MATT. 22:36

By inference we can say the lawyer here asked Jesus what was the greatest commandment of Moses. The religious leaders respected the entire Old Testament as authoritative, and considered Moses to be the foremost human figure and teacher in Scripture. Our Lord noted that the scribes and Pharisees had placed themselves on Moses' seat (Matt. 23:2) because it represented ultimate religious authority. And because Jesus' teaching of Scripture was so different from theirs, the Pharisees were sure He had a message He considered to be greater than Mosaic law. They hoped Jesus would disclose evidence to that effect, because to supersede or contradict Moses was to supersede God and reveal oneself as an apostate. Thus they could turn the people against Him. The single question here assumed that Jesus' naming one "great commandment" rather than many, as they did, would allow them to condemn Him as sufficiently nonorthodox.

However, from the start of His earthly ministry, Christ had assured His Jewish listeners that He had not come "to abolish the Law or the Prophets . . . but to fulfill" (5:17). Though He was the Messiah and Son of God, Jesus made clear He was not teaching anything to nullify the law. He further emphasized that "until heaven and earth pass away, not the smallest letter or stroke shall pass from the Law until all is accomplished" (v. 18).

ASK YOURSELF

What are some of the "great" commandments of Scripture that have meant the most to you in recent days? How is God working with you to wrestle obedience from your resistant heart? How does compliance with His Word bring you confidence that He is your Lord and Savior?

THE GREAT COMMANDMENT, PART 1

"'You shall love the Lord your God with all your heart, and with all your soul,
and with all your mind.' This is the great and foremost commandment."
—MATT. 22:37–38

To the ancient Jews, "heart" denoted the essence of someone's personal being (Prov. 4:23). "Soul" closely approximates emotion, and Jesus used the word in the garden of Gethsemane (Matt. 26:38). "Mind" equates to what is usually rendered "might" in Deuteronomy 6:5, from which Jesus quoted. The Hebrew word has the broad connotation of moving ahead with energy and strength. "Mind" carries both the meaning of willful intellectual endeavor and determined strength.

Genuine love for God always involves intelligence, sensitivity, and willing action and service wherever possible and appropriate. God seeks neither empty words nor hollow ritual but the entire person and all that he or she possesses. Just as He loves us with His whole being, we are to return that love with our whole being. His love for humanity was so great "that He gave His only begotten Son" to save sinners (John 3:16). Godly love does not love because of what it can obtain but simply because love is right and good. Therefore, the distinguishing mark of saving faith in the Lord is real love for Him (John 14:23–24; 1 John 4:12–13). So-called faith in Christ not characterized by consuming love for Him is not saving faith at all but rather the bare intellectual kind that even the demons have (cf. James 2:19).

ASK YOURSELF

What is God's Word calling forth from you today? What areas of submission to Him demand more than halfhearted, automatic responses of faith, but rather deep and costly sacrifices? What would keep you from giving Him your all today, from following Him at any expense?

THE GREAT COMMANDMENT, PART 2

"'You shall love the Lord your God with all your heart, and with all your soul, and with all your mind.' This is the great and foremost commandment."
—MATT. 22:37–38

The Ten Commandments teach that love for and obedience to God are inseparable. The Father reveals His "lovingkindness to thousands, to those who love Me and keep My commandments" (Ex. 20:6). Jesus affirms this principle: "If you love Me, you will keep My commandments" (John 14:15), as does the apostle John: "By this we know that we have come to know Him, if we keep His commandments. For the one who says, 'I have come to know Him,' and does not keep His commandments, is a liar, and the truth is not in him; but whoever keeps His word, in him the love of God has truly been perfected" (1 John 2:3–5). A most beautiful description of a believer is one who loves "our Lord Jesus Christ with incorruptible love" (Eph. 6:24).

Although Christians don't always do what is right (cf. Rom. 7:15), they always love what is right and long to honor God. The Jewish leaders had the opposite outlook. They loved outward religious ceremonies and actions that supported their self-righteousness, pride, and hypocrisy.

Therefore the authentic saints are those who love God. Lost hypocrites are ones who hate Him (Ex. 20:5) and are His enemies (Prov. 8:36), as the Pharisees and scribes were.

ASK YOURSELF

How would you describe your hatred for the sins you continue to struggle with, the failings that seem inescapable at times even though you know God's power is sufficient to help you overcome them? Pray that He would deepen your grief over those things that dishonor Him.

THE GREAT COMMANDMENT, PART 3

"'You shall love the Lord your God with all your heart, and with all your soul, and with all your mind.' This is the great and foremost commandment."
—MATT. 22:37–38

Anyone who genuinely loves God with all his heart, soul, and mind is someone who trusts God and obeys Him. Such a disciple demonstrates this love by meditating on God's glory (Ps. 18:1–3), trusting in His power (31:23), seeking fellowship with Him (63:1–8), loving the divine law (119:165), loving what He loves (119:72), loving whom He loves (1 John 5:1), hating what He hates (Ps. 97:10), grieving over sin (Matt. 26:75), rejecting the world (1 John 2:15)—and he does it all with a wholehearted attitude of obedience (John 14:21).

Like Paul, the genuine follower of Christ knows his love and obedience are imperfect, but he presses "on so that [he] may lay hold of that for which also [he] was laid hold of by Christ Jesus," persevering "on toward the goal for the prize of the upward call of God in Christ Jesus" (Phil. 3:12, 14).

Our Lord's atoning death redeemed all who trust in it from their lack of love for God. And just as He forgives all past lack of love, Jesus provides believers' future love for God. Through our beloved Lord and Savior, "the love of God has been poured out within our hearts through the Holy Spirit who was given to us" (Rom. 5:5).

ASK YOURSELF

How do you typically respond to specific seasons or episodes of disobedience? Do they discourage you so deeply that you give in to even greater fits of unfaithfulness? How could you more immediately rush back into your Father's forgiving arms, seeking His restoration?

THE GREAT COMMANDMENT, PART 4

"The second is like it, 'You shall love your neighbor as yourself.'"
—MATT. 22:39

The second part of Jesus' great commandment is that we love our neighbors with the same love we have for ourselves. Not long after this occasion, Jesus reminded the crowds that the Jewish leaders "tie[d] up heavy burdens and [laid] them on men's shoulders, but they themselves [were] unwilling to move them with so much as a finger" (Matt. 23:4).

On the contrary, genuine love does not take advantage of one's fellow citizen or fellow believer. Love for a neighbor is by choice purposeful, intentional, and active, just as real love for God is—not simply sentimental or emotional. Jesus tells us this love is measured by love for ourselves. If we get hungry, thirsty, or sick, we seek to meet those needs appropriately. We don't merely talk about the food, water, or medicine necessary for those needs; we obtain the essential remedies for ourselves. We can't imagine simply telling ourselves, "Go in peace, be warmed and be filled," without doing something tangible to secure food, clothing, or shelter (see James 2:14–17).

Our Lord is not commanding us to love ourselves; He assumes we already do that. As Paul writes, "no one ever hated his own flesh, but nourishes and cherishes it" (Eph. 5:29). Just as people naturally seek to meet their own needs, they will also be sincerely considerate of others if they love them.

ASK YOURSELF

How could you more deliberately meet the needs of others in your home by making this significant shift in your thinking? How might this even apply to those who are particularly difficult for you to love, those who routinely make unwelcome demands on your time?

THE GREAT COMMANDMENT, PART 5

"'The second is like it, 'You shall love your neighbor as yourself.''"
—MATT. 22:39

Old Testament Judaism and New Testament Christianity both require people to love God and their fellow man. The apostle Paul later taught:

He who loves his neighbor has fulfilled the law. For this, "You shall not commit adultery, You shall not murder, You shall not steal, You shall not covet," and if there is any other commandment, it is summed up in this saying, "You shall love your neighbor as yourself." Love does no wrong to a neighbor; therefore love is the fulfillment of the law. (Rom. 13:8–10; cf. 1 John 4:7–8)

If people loved perfectly, we would not need any sort of law; people who truly loved others would never do them any harm. Similarly, Christians who loved God with all their being would never fail to obey, worship, and honor Him as Lord.

Mark's account (12:32–34) of this interchange reveals the lawyer's favorable response to Jesus:

"Right, Teacher; You have truly stated that He is One, and there is no one else besides Him; and to love Him with all the heart and with all the understanding and with all the strength, and to love one's neighbor as himself, is much more than all burnt offerings and sacrifices." When Jesus saw that he had answered intelligently, He said to him, "You are not far from the kingdom of God."

ASK YOURSELF

Do you ever notice a disconnect between the love, praise, and worship you extend toward God and the reciprocal sense of loving obligation you feel toward others in your life? What is missing when both of these things are not happening in tandem? How can you correct this linkage?

THE PHARISEES' INADEQUATE ANSWER, PART 1

Jesus asked them a question: "What do you think about the Christ, whose son is He?" They said to Him, "The son of David." —MATT. 22:41*b*–42

The world has never lacked an answer to the question "Who is Jesus Christ?" And as their many complimentary words indicate, a lot of people have ranked Jesus as the highest role model. For instance, poet/philosopher Ralph Waldo Emerson said He was the most perfect of all men, Napoleon believed Him to be better than a mere man, and author H. G. Wells said He left the most permanent impression on the world. However, many such people denied much of what Christ taught about Himself and His work.

Arguments over biblical Christianity so often come down to the issue of Jesus' divinity. All other matters are meaningless apart from this one, because if He were not God, He could not be the Savior of sinners, and people could not be reconciled to the Father. Yet many sects and religions accept Jesus as merely a prophet and great religious teacher, though not divine to any greater extent than other great men.

Jesus often had claimed to be Messiah and God's Son, but now He wanted the Pharisees to focus on what they already believed about His identity. He longed for them to answer His specific question, "Whose son is He?" In other words, "Who is the Christ, God's promised Anointed One?"

ASK YOURSELF

How often do you pose such a question to people within your daily reach? What do you think would be the most typical responses to it? Imagining them, how do you suppose you would go about defending His deity? Why not try inserting this question into an upcoming conversation?

THE PHARISEES' INADEQUATE ANSWER, PART 2

"What do you think about the Christ, whose son is He?" They said to Him,
*"The son of David." —*MATT. 22:42

Because the Pharisees were convinced Messiah was no more than a man, their obvious answer to Jesus' question was that Christ was "the son of David" (cf. Mark 12:35). Through Nathan the prophet, God had promised David,

> When your days are complete and you lie down with your fathers, I will raise up your descendant after you, who will come forth from you, and I will establish his kingdom. He shall build a house for My name, and I will establish the throne of His kingdom forever . . . (2 Sam. 7:12–13; cf. Ps. 89:3–4, 20–21, 24, 27–29; Amos 9:11; Mic. 5:2)

Christ, David's greater Son by extension of the ancestral name, will rule an everlasting kingdom. The Lord prophesied through Jeremiah: "'I will raise up for David a righteous Branch; and He will reign as king and act wisely and do justice and righteousness in the land'" (Jer. 23:5*b*).

However, as true as it was that the Messiah would be the Son of David, the Pharisees' answer to Jesus' question was inadequate. They no doubt considered their answer quite magnanimous, but "Son of David" was far too limited a title, for the Christ's greatness far exceeded His descent from David.

ASK YOURSELF

Is there anything inadequate in your own view of Christ? Who is He today that you never saw in Him before? What are some of the new insights He has revealed about Himself to you? As you pause to consider who He is and what He does, how do you expect your relationship with Him to grow and develop?

THE INFINITE REALITY OF JESUS CHRIST, PART 1

He said to them, "Then how does David in the Spirit call Him 'Lord,' saying,
'The Lord said to my Lord, "Sit at My right hand, until I put Your enemies
beneath Your feet"'? If David then calls Him 'Lord,' how is He his son?"
—MATT. 22:43–45

Jesus here presents a threefold argument in favor of His infinite reality as the Messiah, not merely the human descendant of David.

First, the Lord declares that David spoke under the Spirit's inspiration in Psalm 110:1, quoted here. "In the Spirit" emphasizes being under the Holy Spirit's control (cf. Rev. 1:10; 4:2). Christ's complete statement was actually, "David himself said in the Holy Spirit" (Mark 12:36). Thus Jesus did not merely refer to David's human spirit.

Second, the Jews accepted Psalm 110 as being from David and clearly messianic. Therefore it was inarguable that David was speaking of anyone but the Messiah, the second Lord mentioned in verse 1. When he said, "Sit at My right hand, until I put Your enemies beneath Your feet," David called the Messiah his Lord.

Finally, Christ declares the Messiah's deity. The Spirit revealed to David that God had told Messiah to sit at His right hand, a position of coequal rank and authority. When Jesus asked the Jews if David called Messiah Lord, He unquestionably made the point that "Son of David" alone is an insufficient title for Messiah. How could He be simply David's son? He is also Son of God.

ASK YOURSELF

How have you been slow to accept what the Word says to be true, whether about God's nature or about your own attitudes and lifestyle choices? What have been some of the worst costs of keeping yourself out of alignment?

THE INFINITE REALITY OF JESUS CHRIST, PART 2

He said to them, "Then how does David in the Spirit call Him 'Lord,' saying,
'The Lord said to my Lord, "Sit at My right hand, until I put Your enemies
beneath Your feet"'? If David then calls Him 'Lord,' how is He his son?"
—MATT. 22:43–45

Jesus does not mention the most important conclusion stemming from this passage: He Himself is the Messiah. But such a stated conclusion was unnecessary because He had been presenting true messianic credentials for three years. He had done and said so much to prove His deity that unbelievers, including the Pharisees, had to deny the obvious to conclude otherwise (cf. John 20:30–31; 21:25).

For certain, Jesus was not a phantom, as some heretics in the early church (such as the Gnostics) taught. He actually ate, drank, slept, felt pain, and died on the cross. He was even "tempted in all things as we are, yet without sin" (Heb. 4:15). He was the Son of Man in all respects, and He was specifically the Son of David, as clearly proved by the ancient temple records. But above all, our Lord was the Son of God and Messiah. We need look no further than the many miracles He did for the crowds of His day and for us to read about in the Gospels.

ASK YOURSELF

Because actions really do speak louder than words, would you say that your profession of Christ as Lord is backed up well by your behavior at home, at work, and in all of your relationships? Who needs to hear your apology for not living up to the standards of faith you claim? How do you intend to make changes?

THE INFINITE REALITY OF JESUS CHRIST, PART 3

"If David then calls Him 'Lord,' how is He his son?" —MATT. 22:45

The Son shares with the Father all the attributes of deity. For instance, He is the omnipotent Creator, the controller of the universe and all its creatures. He sees that we get food; He heals injuries and diseases; He can raise the dead, forgive sin, and grant eternal life. And He is the ultimate judge of all humanity and angels.

Furthermore, Christ is in all ways omniscient, as God is. He knew what the apostles and His opponents were thinking. "He did not need anyone to testify concerning man, for He Himself knew what was in man" (John 2:25).

The New Testament regularly and reliably presents Jesus as Messiah, Son of David and Son of God. The Father promised Paul's gospel message "beforehand through His prophets in the holy Scriptures, concerning His Son, who was born of a descendant of David according to the flesh, who was declared the Son of God with power by the resurrection from the dead, according to the Spirit of holiness, Jesus Christ our Lord" (Rom. 1:2–4). And the apostle exhorted his protégé Timothy to "remember Jesus Christ, risen from the dead, descendant of David, according to my gospel" (2 Tim. 2:8).

ASK YOURSELF

What are some of the deeper reasons why anyone or any church that refuses to accept the full divinity of Christ is trusting in a "gospel" that cannot save? What would be different about our faith in Christ if Jesus were not fully God? What would you say to anyone who claimed this to be an unimportant doctrine?

THE INFINITE REALITY OF JESUS CHRIST, PART 4

"If David then calls Him 'Lord,' how is He his son?" —MATT. 22:45

In his book *Protestant Christian Evidences*, Bernard Ramm lists a number of incisive answers to his own question: "If God became incarnate, what kind of man would He be?" In condensed form, six of his answers are: we would expect the God-man to be sinless; we would expect Him to be holy; His words would be the greatest ones ever uttered; He would exercise profound power over human personality; He could be expected to do supernatural feats; and we would see Him display the love of God. Of all the men who ever lived, our Lord as Messiah was the only one to perfectly meet all these criteria.

Paul describes the reality of who Jesus was and is this way:

> Christ Jesus, who, although He existed in the form of God, did not regard equality with God a thing to be grasped, but emptied Himself, taking the form of a bond-servant, and being made in the likeness of men. Being found in appearance as a man, He humbled Himself by becoming obedient to the point of death, even death on a cross. (Phil. 2:5c–8; see also vv. 9–11; John 1:14)

ASK YOURSELF

In response to some of the brief statements above, how does the holiness of Christ impact your life? Which of His words have been the most revolutionary for you? How does His dominance over human sin show itself in your own spiritual battles? How do His perfect expressions of both love and power intermingle to bring you comfort? Worship Him for these mighty acts of deity.

INAPPROPRIATE RESPONSE TO JESUS

No one was able to answer Him a word, nor did anyone dare
from that day on to ask Him another question. —MATT. 22:46

It's likely some of the Jewish leaders who heard Jesus' words that day later believed in Him. But when the Lord finished His short but irrefutable proof that He was Messiah, their response was hardly appropriate for the magnitude of that truth.

Essentially, all the religious leaders present on this occasion were flabbergasted and unconvinced, silenced but not convicted, humiliated but still arrogant, and grudgingly impressed but unbelieving. No doubt they realized Jesus had intimidated and embarrassed them, but they wanted to make sure the uneducated, unordained, and nonorthodox rabbi would do so for the last time.

A secular worldview has generally been indifferent to Jesus, whereas human religion has usually been hostile. Therefore religion like the Jews' will invariably be the greatest enemy of the gospel. In contrast, the Samaritan woman near the well of Sychar was open to the prospect of Messiah; thus Jesus revealed His messianic identity to her directly (John 4:25–26). That woman then trusted in Jesus, but the secular and religiously hostile Samaritans generally did not (vv. 39–42). Like so many people today, the Samaritans failed to believe the truth of Christ and His salvation, even though Scripture testifies so clearly to it.

ASK YOURSELF

What is your diagnosis for why the ones seemingly closest to understanding and embracing Christ's lordship would scorn Him, while those most in the dark would be drawn to the light? How do you see this happening in our own day? What barriers to faith seem almost inpenetrable, somehow innoculated against true belief?

FALSE SPIRITUAL LEADERS
HAVE NO AUTHORITY, PART 1

"The scribes and the Pharisees have seated themselves in the chair of Moses;"
—MATT. 23:2

The Jews viewed Moses as the chief lawgiver or supreme spokesman for God. Thus to sit in his chair was equivalent to being God's authoritative teacher, a claim many scribes and Pharisees made for themselves.

For this reason the Jewish leaders were envious of and opposed to our Lord's ministry. It angered them to see people discerning and claiming that Christ taught with an authority seemingly more genuine than theirs (Matt. 7:29). He was therefore a threat to the leaders' previously unchallenged position of religious authority.

False teachers also challenged the prophet Isaiah in his day. God warned him of "sons who refuse to listen to the instruction of the Lord; who say to the seers, 'You must not see visions'; and to the prophets, 'You must not prophesy to us what is right, speak to us pleasant words, prophesy illusions'" (Isa. 30:9–10; cf. Jer. 14:14; 23:21, 32).

Unregenerate people resist God's truth because it rebukes them, like Jesus did to the Pharisees. They would rather turn to the false doctrine of false teachers, even though it is without authority and far inferior to the gospel of Christ.

ASK YOURSELF

Do you recognize any hints of condescension in your own heart toward those of another race, another background, another family size, another income bracket (either up or down)? How do you perhaps lay claim to a "seat" of entitlement that enables you to see yourself as superior to others? What are some of the telltale signs that this is becoming a problem for you?

FALSE SPIRITUAL LEADERS
HAVE NO AUTHORITY, PART 2

"The scribes and the Pharisees have seated themselves in the chair of Moses;"
—MATT. 23:2

Jesus warns also that false leaders are lying shepherds who don't enter the sheepfold by the door (by Him) but come "only to steal and kill and destroy" (John 10:10; see also v. 1). They do not represent God or teach by His authority but are usurpers who want to subvert and destroy God's Word and work.

In marked contrast, those truly sent by the Lord as gospel ministers are like Timothy, divinely called and set apart by the laying on of hands as confirmation of their godly commission and biblical authority (1 Tim. 4:14). They follow the apostles' pattern, to whom Christ later said, "All authority has been given to Me in heaven and on earth. Go therefore and make disciples of all the nations" (Matt. 28:18–19; cf. John 20:22).

As in biblical times, the world still abounds with false teachers who claim to speak in God's name and power but do not. They are self-appointed ministers of human philosophies and traditions, obscuring God's truth and twisting His ways for their own selfish purposes. Believers need to be discerning of false prophets' evil intentions, false promises, deceptions, phony dreams and visions, and their unrighteous, immoral, arrogant, even greedy lifestyles.

ASK YOURSELF

Some people are spiritually skeptical of anyone who deviates even in minor points from their pet doctrinal stances, while others seem recklessly open to nearly everyone who sounds the least bit biblically reliable? How do you strike a healthy balance between these two extremes? What standards do you use to judge truth from error?

FALSE SPIRITUAL LEADERS LACK INTEGRITY, PART 1

*"Therefore all that they tell you, do and observe, but do not do according to their deeds; for they say things and do not do them." —*MATT. 23:3

By lack of integrity in false leaders, we mean they hypocritically demand practices of others that they themselves never do.

When Jesus said "all that they tell you, do and observe," He obviously referred only to that which conformed to Scripture (see Matt. 5:20). They were wrong about murder, divorce, adultery, praying, and nearly every other area of living (see 5:21–48 and 15:6). Our Lord's admonition is against discarding the baby with the bathwater—if false teachers sometimes teach the truth, we can and should obey it; God's Word is still God's Word.

Unbelieving false teachers, however, don't have the spiritual resources to keep God's law even if they want to. They live only in their unredeemed humanness (flesh) and by its power, and the flesh can't fulfill God's law (Rom. 3:20). The flesh can develop systems of external morality and conduct codes, but it cannot help people live up to them. It may talk much about God's love and humanity's need to be loving, but it can't change sinful hearts. Only the redeemed life, the life "created in Christ Jesus for good works" (Eph. 2:10; cf. Rom. 7:22) can actually do good works.

ASK YOURSELF

Is discernment lacking in your usual acceptance of the things others say? We know discernment is among the spiritual gifts, distributed supernaturally to some believers for use in the church. But according to Scripture, we all need to develop a shrewdness about us, not blindly taking everything at face value. How could you begin growing this trait in greater measure?

FALSE SPIRITUAL LEADERS LACK INTEGRITY, PART 2

"Therefore all that they tell you, do and observe, but do not do according to their deeds; for they say things and do not do them." —MATT. 23:3

Religious leaders without integrity often attempt to cover up their wicked behavior, but in so doing they merely trap it under the surface where it simmers and actually becomes more corrupt. Paul describes these hypocrites as being "seared in their own conscience as with a branding iron" (1 Tim. 4:2). In other words, they have lost all sensitivity to truth and holiness.

Jude goes on to call false teachers dreamers of wicked dreams, rejecters of authority, unreasoning animals, "clouds without water, carried along by winds; autumn trees without fruit, doubly dead, uprooted; wild waves of the sea, casting up their own shame like foam; wandering stars, for whom the black darkness has been reserved forever" (Jude 12–13; cf. vv. 8, 10; 2 Peter 2:1–3).

The best religious systems, fashioned by false teachers without integrity, even incorporating certain biblical standards, can't prevent sin and empower righteousness. That's because such an approach will never change hearts. Like what the pharisaical system produced, any false religion will doom people to hypocrisy and sham, manufacturing nothing more than outward righteousness and good works, external love and peace, while the sinful inner person remains unchanged.

ASK YOURSELF

Even as a believer, with a sin nature still in force, how often do you spot hypocrisy in your own external behaviors? What have you found to be the best remedies for putting pretense in its place, enjoying instead the freedom of living with openness and authenticity? What makes this such a challenge for us?

FALSE SPIRITUAL LEADERS
HAVE NO SYMPATHY, PART 1

*"They tie up heavy burdens and lay them on men's shoulders, but they themselves
are unwilling to move them with so much as a finger."* —MATT. 23:4

The Jewish leaders burdened people's shoulders with impossible loads
of religious requirements and rebuked them when they failed to fully
comply.

False teachers usually teach that if good works ultimately outweigh
the bad, then God will grant entrance into heaven. And, like the scribes
and Pharisees, false leaders offer people no real help in achieving any
goals.

By contrast, the Lord brings good news that He has taken away the
load of sin that always outweighs human good works. That's why the
Judaizers so angered Paul as they sought to pull the Galatians back into
legalism:

> But even if we, or an angel from heaven, should preach to you a
> gospel contrary to what we have preached to you, he is to be ac-
> cursed! As we have said before, so say I again now, if any man is
> preaching to you a gospel contrary to what you received, he is to be
> accursed! (Gal. 1:8–9)

In deciding between Christ's teachings or those of spurious teachers,
believers must remember "it was for freedom that Christ set us free;
therefore keep standing firm and do not be subject again to a yoke of
slavery" (5:1).

ASK YOURSELF

What makes this "freedom" the furthest thing from a license to sin, but
rather the blessed liberty enjoyed by one who is no longer a slave to sin?
How have you experienced this reality in your own life? Even in areas
where sin and temptation are particularly hard to fight, how does
Christ's freedom give you hope and power?

FALSE SPIRITUAL LEADERS
HAVE NO SYMPATHY, PART 2

"They tie up heavy burdens and lay them on men's shoulders, but they themselves are unwilling to move them with so much as a finger." —MATT. 23:4

The religious leaders were not interested in the gospel because it did not allow for human merit or good works. They could not comprehend a message that demanded, "Therefore humble yourselves under the mighty hand of God" (1 Peter 5:6).

The Jews thought they didn't need God's grace and didn't want it taught to others, because it provided spiritual liberation and undercut their enslaving, legalistic system. Peter writes about false prophets: "in their greed they will exploit you with false words" (2 Peter 2:3).

For hundreds of years Israel staggered and fell under the weight of unsympathetic, calloused religious leaders who neither loved God nor His people:

> Son of man, prophesy against the shepherds of Israel . . . "Thus says the Lord God, 'Woe, shepherds of Israel who have been feeding themselves! Should not the shepherds feed the flock? You eat the fat and clothe yourselves with the wool, you slaughter the fat sheep without feeding the flock.'" (Ezek. 34:2–3)

Such were the unsympathetic "teachers" who, as precursors of the scribes and Pharisees of Jesus' time, afflicted Israel.

ASK YOURSELF

How does legalism still linger in your own thoughts and attitudes? Does even the fact that you struggle with particular sins (whether you succumb to them or not) make you feel of less worth in God's sight? Are there any standards you apply to others that are more cultural and appearance-oriented than biblical? What is the unavoidable fruit of harboring legalism in your heart?

FALSE SPIRITUAL LEADERS
HAVE NO SYMPATHY, PART 3

"They tie up heavy burdens and lay them on men's shoulders, but they themselves
are unwilling to move them with so much as a finger." —MATT. 23:4

Today false leaders still build empires and amass fortunes by religiously swindling the people they pretend to serve. Like the false shepherds of ancient Israel, they prey on their own followers.

As Jesus surveyed the crowds, "He felt compassion for them, because they were distressed and dispirited like sheep without a shepherd" (Matt. 9:36). But the antidote for that situation is indicated by His refreshing words,

> Come to Me, all who are weary and heavy-laden, and I will give you rest. Take My yoke upon you and learn from Me, for I am gentle and humble in heart, and you will find rest for your souls. For My yoke is easy and My burden is light. (Matt. 11:28–30)

Following our Lord's example, Paul always ministered to his flock in the gentlest, most sympathetic fashion, like a caring mother. He reminded the Thessalonians,

> But we proved to be gentle among you, as a nursing mother tenderly cares for her own children. Having so fond an affection for you, we were well-pleased to impart to you not only the gospel of God but also our own lives, because you had become very dear to us. (1 Thess. 2:7–8)

ASK YOURSELF

Are you a person who responds best to confrontation and challenge, or are you better motivated by gentle reminders and assurances? How does Christ in His Word supply both of these to us? How have you experienced His perfect understanding of your nature by the way His Spirit draws you to repentance and leads you to obedience?

FALSE SPIRITUAL LEADERS HAVE NO SPIRITUALITY

"But they do all their deeds to be noticed by men; for they broaden their phylacteries and lengthen the tassels of their garments." —MATT. 23:5

You can also recognize false teachers by their lack of real spirituality—the absence of a genuine desire to please God. Like the Pharisees, they practice their religiosity "to be noticed by men." Such leaders do everything for outward show rather than from the heart. They don't care about godly character but only their own external façade (see Gal. 6:12).

Jude tells us false teachers are "worldly-minded, devoid of the Spirit" (Jude 19). They follow their carnal inclinations without restraint or shame, considering themselves the spiritual elite. To acquire prestige and amass wealth, such people might pastor a megachurch, direct media empires, and promote many self-serving activities as if spreading the gospel.

During Jesus' ministry, the means for gaining attention were more simple and limited, but even as today, false leaders did everything to promote themselves and gain respect. To those ends, the Jewish leaders would "broaden their phylacteries and lengthen the tassels of their garments." Both of these outward symbols were originally intended to be inward reminders and motivators to obey Scripture (Num. 15:38–40). But because the leaders misused them, they became marks of carnality rather than spirituality.

ASK YOURSELF

What makes religious pretension seem far more desirable than the hard work of developing true spiritual discipline, or even the hard work of settling down our impatient hearts to enjoy sweet relationship with Christ? What are some of the ways you mask a weak or undernourished faith with outward shows of spiritual awareness? What makes a deep, honest heart so much more appealing?

FALSE SPIRITUAL LEADERS HAVE NO HUMILITY

"They love the place of honor at banquets and the chief seats in the synagogues, and respectful greetings in the market places, and being called Rabbi by men."
—MATT. 23:6–7

As is true with their present-day counterparts, the Jewish religious leaders lacked humility and loved "the place of honor at banquets." False teachers nearly always glory in receiving positions of prestige and pre-eminence. Similarly, the scribes and Pharisees coveted the most important seats in the synagogues. Those places of worship often asked visiting teachers to read Scripture and present a homily. This custom afforded the Lord Jesus an invitation to read and expound Isaiah 61:1–2 in Nazareth (Luke 4:16–21). On that occasion Jesus displayed a truly humble spirit, unlike the Jewish leaders or any false teachers who would ostentatiously present themselves before the people.

Even pastors can sometimes be tempted to use their roles and activities for personal gratification and glory. Sadly, many local churches can encourage affectation and showiness by providing elaborate furnishings and showering excessive privilege and preference on their leaders. Congregations can avoid this pitfall by heeding Peter's teaching: "Be subject to your elders; and all of you, clothe yourselves with humility toward one another, for God is opposed to the proud, but gives grace to the humble" (1 Peter 5:5).

ASK YOURSELF

Humility is one of those traits you cannot really see in yourself without leaning toward pridefulness. But you can certainly see it in others. What are some of the leading indicators of humility that are most inspiring to you? Why is humility not dependent on a person's social class or economic level, but is rather a condition of the heart that supersedes externals?

True Spiritual Leaders Avoid Elevated Titles

"But do not be called Rabbi; for One is your Teacher, and you are all brothers."
—Matt. 23:8

We are to love, appreciate, and esteem true spiritual teachers who faithfully proclaim and interpret Scripture (1 Thess. 5:12–13). In that they shun the pretentions of false teachers, it makes it easier for us to receive them. Such leaders, unlike the Jewish leaders of Christ's day, know that He is our only elevated teacher. Christ is the exclusive source, through Scripture, of divine truth. Human spiritual teachers are mere channels of communication, utilizing God's Word and Spirit.

Real spiritual leaders are all brothers with every other believer, and no man can justify giving himself an elevated title of spiritual superiority. Thus Jesus said, "Do not call anyone on earth your father" (Matt. 23:9). This is in reference to spiritual fatherhood—anything suggesting a role as an elevated source of truth or religious superiority. The title of spiritual father is to be reserved for God alone, who is the ultimate source of spiritual life and blessing. When wrongly used, titles like Rabbi, Father, and Leader can be barriers between spiritual leaders and their followers. But even worse, they arrogate for men the honor and glory due only to God and thereby violate His Word.

ASK YOURSELF

Have you placed a spiritual authority figure onto a pedestal (whether he wants it for himself or not) that no human being can hope to maintain? What are the needs in our hearts that cause us to ascribe such preeminence to another person? What are the greatest dangers of allowing this misperception to continue? What will happen when this individual fails to meet your expectations?

TRUE SPIRITUAL LEADERS
ACCEPT LOWLY SERVICE, PART 1

"But the greatest among you shall be your servant. Whoever exalts himself shall be humbled; and whoever humbles himself shall be exalted." —MATT. 23:11–12

The greatest believers are the ones who are willing servants, and our Lord Himself was a supreme role model of this. During His earthly ministry, He was Servant of servants, even as in His deity He is King of kings and Lord of lords. Jesus' mission on earth was not to be served but to serve, "and to give His life a ransom for many" (Matt. 20:28).

In the upper room, Christ presented an object lesson to illustrate the principle of servanthood one last time:

So when He had washed their feet, and taken His garments and reclined at the table again, He said to them, "Do you know what I have done to you? You call Me Teacher and Lord; and you are right, for so I am. If I then, the Lord and the Teacher, washed your feet, you also ought to wash one another's feet. For I gave you an example that you also should do as I did to you. (John 13:12–15)

God does not approve so much of degrees, titles, or achievements, as He does of the one who is a selfless, humble servant.

ASK YOURSELF

What are the underlying weaknesses that lead us to make more of ourselves than we really are? What are the risks, indignities, and inconveniences of servanthood we hope to avoid? And yet how have you found a unique sense of joy and satisfaction—even a new depth of relationship with Christ—by choosing to be a selfless servant in your dealings with others, both at home and in the community?

TRUE SPIRITUAL LEADERS
ACCEPT LOWLY SERVICE, PART 2

*"Whoever exalts himself shall be humbled; and whoever
humbles himself shall be exalted."* —MATT. 23:12

Jesus' summary contrast between true and false teachers is the opposite
of the world's criterion for successful exaltation, which emphasizes looking out for number one and figuring that nice guys finish last.

But Jesus' sovereign wisdom expressed here says the arrogant, os-
tentatious, self-serving person eventually will experience humiliation and
failure, regardless of what unbelievers might think and accomplish. And
just as certainly, the person manifesting the opposite traits will one day
be exalted.

Peter exhorts all church elders:

Shepherd the flock of God among you, exercising oversight not
under compulsion, but voluntarily, according to the will of God; . . .
Therefore humble yourselves under the mighty hand of God, that he
may exalt you at the proper time. (1 Peter 5:2*a*, 6; see also vv. 2*b*–5)

Andrew Bonar, nineteenth-century preacher and author, knew believers were progressing when they spoke more of Christ than of themselves. They will also be in step with Thomas Shepherd, founder and
first president of Harvard University, who made this diary entry: "Today
I kept a private fast to see the full glory of the gospel and to seek the con-
quest of the remaining pride in my heart."

ASK YOURSELF

What are some of the practices that engender selflessness in your heart?
Even if these are difficult to embark upon, requiring a diligent
conquering of the stubborn self, how desperately do you desire the
benefits and changes they produce? Which of your attitudes and
perceptions toward life are in most need of maturity, because they
currently hinder you from seeing things biblically?

FALSE LEADERS AND THEIR
SPIRITUAL EXCLUSION, PART 1

"But woe to you, scribes and Pharisees, hypocrites, because you shut off the kingdom of heaven from people;" —MATT. 23:13a

No matter how appealing any false religion may be, its ultimate goal is to "shut off the kingdom of heaven from people." It may stimulate their minds, raise their moral standards, increase their economic success, and improve their social relationships, but it will ultimately damn their souls.

All sorts of false teachers today pretend to know God but do not, pretend to be His spokesmen but are not, and pretend to be in His kingdom but are not. Therefore many actually presume to be gatekeepers to God's kingdom when they, in fact, are not.

The scribes and Pharisees operated under the delusion that, just because they were descendants of God's chosen people who first received His law (Rom. 3:2; 9:4–5), they were automatically going to have God's favor and blessing. But in their boundless pride, which was actually spiritual darkness, these false teachers confused merely knowing the law with keeping it, and merely knowing about the truth with actually living it out.

What a precarious position to be in, compounded all the more by unlovingly excluding those from the kingdom who were sincerely seeking God and perhaps on the verge of true salvation.

ASK YOURSELF

Could there possibly be any aspect of your demeanor or behaviors that repel others from desiring relationship with Christ? How would you know if this were true? What kind of spiritual inventory is helpful for each of us to employ on a regular basis to ensure that we are not letting carelessness or indifference paint our faith in a bad light?

FALSE LEADERS AND THEIR
SPIRITUAL EXCLUSION, PART 2

"But woe to you, scribes and Pharisees, hypocrites, because you shut off the kingdom of heaven from people." —MATT. 23:13a

For the thoughtful believer, it's painful to consider, and immensely more so for the Lord Jesus, the thousands of Jews that Israel's false religious leaders helped to exclude from the kingdom of God. They removed from the people the key of knowledge by denying Jesus as Messiah, denying the need for repentance, and rejecting the gospel. Their works-oriented system rejected our Lord's gospel of sovereign grace, which is the only path into the kingdom. By turning people away from the Savior, the leaders confirmed their heresies; they kept people from salvation and helped seal their damnation.

The church's greatest battle is not against terrorism, secularism, wrong economic systems, or social injustice. Rather it's the battle for people's souls, which could be lost even if all the other battles were won. The great challenge for God's church in the twenty-first century is to clearly and boldly set forth His truth and likewise expose Satan's falsehoods, so often propagated by false leaders. A lost world needs to turn from those errors, hear and heed God's truth, and be converted.

ASK YOURSELF

What are some of the most common distractions that keep you from being interested in the spiritual condition of those around you? While God has called each of us to certain roles in His kingdom, He gives every one of us the tasks of sharing His gospel and becoming conduits of transformation. How could you refocus your heart on this Great Commission, reinvigorating your true love for others?

FALSE LEADERS AND THEIR SUBVERSION, PART 1

"Woe to you, scribes and Pharisees, hypocrites, because you travel around on sea and land to make one proselyte." —MATT. 23:15a

These false leaders traveled far and worked hard to make one proselyte, an outsider whom they brought into Judaism. Had this "outreach" effort been done in the right way and for the right reasons, it would have been commendable. After all, in the Abrahamic covenant God promised that through Abraham and his descendants "all the families of the earth will be blessed" (Gen. 12:3). And at Sinai, God set apart Israel as "a kingdom of priests and a holy nation" (Ex. 19:6), who, like her Messiah, was to be a light to the Gentiles (Isa. 49:6).

But for most of Israel's history (e.g., Jonah), she had no desire to bring Gentiles to God. However, by the time of Jesus' ministry many of the Jewish leaders were ardently trying to win Gentile converts. Partly because the Jews had such an unattractive reputation for elitism, proselytes weren't easy to make. Thus when a Gentile did convert, he was considered a prized person, even though he had now merely transferred from paganism to a subverted form of biblical religion.

These practices are certainly ones for genuine believers to avoid, but indicative of the kind of spiritually subversive approach false leaders take.

ASK YOURSELF

Do you know anyone who's been deceived by a spiritual charlatan into believing things that are counter to the Bible and ultimately destructive to their lives? What kind of responses have they given whenever you've expressed concern or raised an objection? How desperately are you praying that their eyes will be opened to the truth?

FALSE LEADERS AND THEIR SUBVERSION, PART 2

"Woe to you, scribes and Pharisees, hypocrites, because you travel around on sea and land to make one proselyte." —MATT. 23:15a

New converts, including those truly drawn to Christ, sometimes become very zealous for their new beliefs—even to the point of greater fervency than those who reached out to them. With the Jews' proselytes, because they entered a false religious system that had replaced biblical Judaism, each convert became "twice as much a son of hell" as the scribes and Pharisees. Because the proselytes' enthusiasm was not godly (cf. Rom. 10:2), it simply prepared them more certainly for hell.

As kingdom citizens, Christians must be ones who point others to the door of salvation. All believers have the keys of the kingdom, which is the gospel of their Lord Jesus Christ (Matt. 16:19), and every false teacher subverts the knowledge that leads to salvation (Luke 11:52).

How grateful God's children should be that at some time a spiritual door-opener confronted them with the truth, as opposed to a spiritual door-closer who would have shut them out of the kingdom. Even a drab presentation of the true gospel is superior to a fascinating presentation of a false gospel, and how grateful His children should be that they are now secure in His truth.

ASK YOURSELF

Who was the person who first opened the door of truth to you? Who are some of the others through the years who have guided you faithfully toward the realities of living with Christ, as well as the people in your life right now who continue to speak and demonstrate what Christianity is all about? How have you thanked these individuals for their impact on you?

FALSE LEADERS AND THEIR PERVERSION, PART 1

"You fools and blind men! Which is more important, the gold or the temple that sanctified the gold?" —MATT. 23:17

That the Pharisees had developed a double standard between gold and the temple regarding swearing is evidence that their concern was not for truth but for evasion, if the truth was inconvenient. The first part of the standard (the temple) allowed a person to lie with impunity, as long as he swore by the temple and not its gold.

The use of oaths in Jesus' day was so perverse as to even renege on promises to God. If the person decided later that for some reason a provision of the oath "wouldn't work," he then had an out.

Jesus had already prohibited all swearing of vows: "make no oath at all, either by heaven, for it is the throne of God, or by the earth, for it is the footstool of His feet. . . . But let your statement be, 'Yes, yes' or 'No, no'; anything beyond these is of evil" (Matt. 5:34, 37). A believing man or woman will always tell the truth; for them a simple yes or no is sufficient, because their character is their bond.

ASK YOURSELF

Have you perhaps developed a level of dishonesty in your life? Do you make up excuses to avoid accepting responsibilities? Do you hedge on details when asked to account for how you've been spending your time? Do even the people who know you best really know all about you? How could you correct any patterns of dishonesty and begin throwing off the burdens of living a shrouded life?

FALSE LEADERS AND THEIR PERVERSION, PART 2

*"You fools and blind men! Which is more important, the gold
or the temple that sanctified the gold?"* —MATT. 23:17

It was moral trickery and absurd logic for the Jewish leaders to claim that swearing by the temple was not binding but swearing by its gold was. Their perverse logic made a vow on something lesser more binding than a vow on something greater. The false teachers' double standards were simply pretenses to use holy things to disguise their unholy lies.

Jesus was not teaching some novel concept. He remembered the psalmist's principle, "Offer to God a sacrifice of thanksgiving and pay your vows to the Most High" (Ps. 50:14). In other words, if a believer makes a vow, he must keep it: "Your vows are binding upon me; O God; I will render thank offerings to You" (Ps. 56:12; see also 61:8; 66:13; 76:11). Notice how the psalmist connects the keeping of vows with praise and thankfulness to God, which we ought to consider the utmost of duty and privilege before Him. After all, since God is the Creator of everything, to make any kind of vow—swearing by anything—involves Him.

ASK YOURSELF

What are we failing to understand when we so easily make promises to God, then just as easily ignore or contradict them? What would help you realize more clearly that He is always here, that He is not kept in the dark when you revert to deception or disobedience? What keeps you from living with a healthy fear of God—a fear that produces lifestyles of wisdom, faithfulness, and gratitude?

FALSE LEADERS AND THEIR INVERSION, PART 1

"Woe to you, scribes and Pharisees, hypocrites! For you tithe mint and dill and cumin, and have neglected the weightier provisions of the law: justice and mercy and faithfulness; but these are the things you should have done without neglecting the others. You blind guides, who strain out a gnat and swallow a camel!"
—MATT. 23:23–24

In their inversion of biblical priorities, the Jewish teachers had reduced subjects like "justice and mercy and faithfulness" to the lighter (less weighty) rabbinic category, and lifted the tithing of herbs to the "weightier" category. But Jesus alluded to Micah when He identified the genuinely weighty matters: "And what does the Lord require of you but to do justice, to love kindness, and to walk humbly with your God?" (Mic. 6:8).

Our Lord did not oppose general tithing since tithing at that time was still valid under the old covenant. Because garden plants were not under Mosaic tithing, it's likely Jesus was referring to the general tithing principle in His exhortation. While the Pharisees had been faithful to certain tithing minutia, they had omitted God's weightier ethical demands.

The false Jewish leaders were unfair, unjust, unmerciful, unkind, greedy, and abusive toward the people. Such was completely opposed to "the weightier provisions of the law." These men displayed a most inverse example; they walked by sight rather than faith, and trusted their works rather than God's grace.

ASK YOURSELF

How do you find yourself giving excessive "weight" to certain acts and practices that come more easily for you, thereby feeling released from other spiritual obligations that are distasteful by comparison? What causes us to sort out such things by category rather than bringing our full lives into a state of surrender?

FALSE LEADERS AND THEIR INVERSION, PART 2

"Woe to you, scribes and Pharisees, hypocrites! For you tithe mint and dill and cumin, and have neglected the weightier provisions of the law: justice and mercy and faithfulness; but these are the things you should have done without neglecting the others. You blind guides, who strain out a gnat and swallow a camel!"
—MATT. 23:23–24

False teachers and their heresies, almost without exception, magnify the insignificant and minimize or ignore truly important spiritual themes. They idolize the worldly and disregard the spiritual.

Our Lord illustrated the Jews' inversion of priorities by noting that those leaders strained out gnats and swallowed camels. Those two creatures represent the smallest and largest, respectively, of ceremonially unclean animals (Lev. 11:4, 42). With their typical inversion of values and priorities, the Pharisees were more concerned about contamination from the tiny gnat than from the huge camel. They substituted external acts of religiosity for essential heart values.

Christians can also become ensnared by trivia. For example, some Scripture students seek to learn the meaning of every obscure sign and symbol in the Bible but pay almost no attention to its clearly stated moral truths.

ASK YOURSELF

Why is it often easier to give money to the church, to a missionary, or to a specific cause rather than getting actively involved in praying and serving others in a hands-on way? We cannot do everything—and are not called by God to do so—but what is one "camel"-sized task you could begin investing your heart and soul into? Aren't you ready to move beyond easy accomplishments to see what God could do if you really made an investment of yourself into His kingdom?

FALSE LEADERS AND THEIR EXTORTION

"Woe to you, scribes and Pharisees, hypocrites! For you clean the outside of the cup and of the dish, but inside they are full of robbery and self-indulgence. You blind Pharisee, first clean the inside of the cup and of the dish, so that the outside of it may become clean also." —MATT. 23:25–26

"Dish," as Jesus used it here, often denoted a platter that served exquisite delicacies. To illustrate the scribes' and Pharisees' hypocrisy, Christ's figure of speech suggests a lovely meal and fine wine served to a guest. However, even though the utensils are beautiful and clean, the food and drink they contain are spoiled.

Externally, false teachers can appear pious and devoted, but internally they are actually filled with moral and spiritual rubbish. "Robbery" connotes plundering and extortion, and self-indulgence essentially means lack of self-control, with the further indication of unrestrained self-gratification. They pillaged the souls and wallets of the people and used those gains for self-serving purposes.

Thus the Lord condemned the scribes and Pharisees, as He has all false teachers since, for their extortion of others and indulgence of themselves.

ASK YOURSELF

The battle to maintain inner cleanliness is certainly much more intense and costly than the relative ease of keeping the outer package pleasing in appearance. But what differences have you noticed in your public persona when your inner person is spiritually healthy and alive, submitted to Christ in private matters, pure even when others are not around to see? How much more vividly does your life shine with God's joy and peace when you have a deep-down clean?

FALSE LEADERS AND THEIR CONTAMINATION

"Woe to you, scribes and Pharisees, hypocrites! For you are like whitewashed tombs which on the outside appear beautiful, but inside they are full of dead men's bones and all uncleanness. So you, too, outwardly appear righteous to men, but inwardly you are full of hypocrisy and lawlessness." —MATT. 23:27–28

All false leaders, such as the scribes and Pharisees, spiritually contaminate everyone they touch. For this they should be condemned, as Jesus did the Jewish leaders.

Because people became ceremonially defiled or unclean for seven days if they touched a dead body or a grave (Num. 19:16), the Jews of Christ's day had all tombs washed carefully in the springtime to identify them for unsuspecting travelers. Thus they could prevent people from accidentally touching tombs, defiling themselves, and disqualifying themselves from participating in many Passover activities, including the important offering of sacrifices.

Similar to the whitewashed tombs, the Jews' false teachers appeared beautiful externally, but internally they were "full of dead men's bones and all uncleanness." The scribes and Pharisees were spiritually dead and disregarded God's law, even though they gave it lip service and claimed to be its true interpreters. In a far worse way than tombs polluting those who touched them, the religious leaders spiritually polluted all whom they touched. It has always been that way with all false teachers and those they seek to influence.

ASK YOURSELF

Have you confessed that some "dead men's bones" continue to take up storage space in your heart? How could you come to see the sin in your life with this same kind of repugnant image, wanting to get it away from you as quickly and completely as possible? What keeps you from seeing it this way?

JUNE 29

FALSE LEADERS AND THEIR PRETENSION

"For you build the tombs of the prophets and adorn the monuments of the righteous, and say, 'If we had been living in the days of our fathers, we would not have been partners with them in shedding the blood of the prophets.'"
—MATT. 23:29–30

Knowing that many Old Testament believers had been persecuted and killed by their forefathers, the scribes and Pharisees made a vehement disclaimer for themselves, smugly claiming that if they had been living in those days, they would not have participated in such sins. However, our Lord exposed their pretension, noting that they were the sons of those who murdered the prophets, which meant the false leaders testified against themselves (v. 31).

The Pharisees further revealed their wicked character in that they were at this time plotting to murder Jesus, the Messiah and true Prophet. They were so consumed by hatred of the truth and pretension toward God that they were blinded concerning what they were actually saying and doing.

At the start of John the Baptist's ministry, he called the unrepentant Jewish leaders who came to him a "brood of vipers" (Matt. 3:7), precisely the expression Jesus used now of these same false leaders (23:33). Neither the words of John nor those of the Lord Jesus had a positive effect on these men, but merely served to harden their hearts toward the gospel and reveal them as pretentious false leaders.

ASK YOURSELF

Having listened for many days to Jesus' admonition of these misguided religious leaders, does the harsh intensity of His rebuke surprise you? Does this sound like the gentle Jesus many today insist we all be like, all the time? What are some situations when stern directness is the most Christian of all acts?

FALSE LEADERS' JUDGMENT INEVITABLE, PART 1

"I am sending you prophets and wise men and scribes; some of them you will kill and crucify . . . so that upon you may fall the guilt of all the righteous blood shed on earth, from the blood of righteous Abel to the blood of Zechariah, the son of Bereciah, whom you murdered between the temple and the altar."
—MATT. 23:34, 35

Just as the "prophets and wise men and scribes," Christ's righteous messengers, would lead many to salvation, they would lead others to be confirmed in judgment. The false leaders would have additional chances to reject Christ and pile upon themselves even greater guilt and more severe judgment (cf. Rom. 2:5). This would be especially true for the hardened scribes and Pharisees.

It's not that God relishes people rejecting His grace and being condemned (2 Peter 3:9), but when ones such as false teachers persist in rejecting Him, they bring upon themselves His wrath and righteous judgment. The more they hear God's truth and reject it, the guiltier they become, with their judgment inevitable.

The Jewish leaders had access to Old Testament revelation and the perfect revelation of God's Son. The members of no generation in redemptive history have had more of the divine light, yet they accumulated God's judgment in direct proportion to their unbelief. These false leaders had the Son present, the source of all truth and light, yet they wouldn't receive Him.

ASK YOURSELF

Cry out to God today, asking Him to remove any barriers that keep you from seeing yourself as you truly are. How desperate are you to be delivered from the crippling effects of your own blind spots and carefully guarded sins? Make this a day of walking away from pretense and deception, marching into the freedom of truth.

FALSE LEADERS' JUDGMENT INEVITABLE, PART 2

*"I am sending you prophets and wise men and scribes; some of them you will kill
and crucify . . . so that upon you may fall the guilt of all the righteous blood shed
on earth, from the blood of righteous Abel to the blood of Zechariah, the son of
Bereciah, whom you murdered between the temple and the altar."*
—MATT. 23:34, 35

Twenty-first century humanity possesses the accumulated benefit of
two thousand years of gospel light, power, and blessing. Nevertheless,
each successive generation rejects the gospel more vigorously and amasses
to itself greater guilt and judgment. Paul asserted, "For we are a fragrance
of Christ to God among those who are being saved and among those who
are perishing" (2 Cor. 2:15). A gospel proclamation either drives people
further away from Christ or draws them to Him: "to the one an aroma
from death to death, to the other an aroma from life to life" (v. 16).

Because it runs contrary to many popular misunderstandings about
the gospel, the preceding truth is hard even for many believers to grasp.
But Scripture clearly shows us that the gospel is not only for bringing
men and women to salvation; sometimes it brings judgment on those, like
false leaders, who hear and reject it. God is both a Person of love and
grace *and* a Person of holiness and wrath—"the same sun that softens the
wax hardens the clay."

ASK YOURSELF

How have you seen the gospel scorned and resisted as you've sought to
express it to others? How have you seen it just ignored and minimized,
given very little weight, grossly misunderstood? How do you handle
this kind of rejection when the message you carry and seek to exhibit
through your life falls on such deaf ears?

FALSE LEADERS' JUDGMENT INEVITABLE, PART 3

"I am sending you prophets and wise men and scribes; some of them you will kill and crucify . . . so that upon you may fall the guilt of all the righteous blood shed on earth, from the blood of righteous Abel to the blood of Zechariah, the son of Berechiah, whom you murdered between the temple and the altar."
—MATT. 23:34, 35

Paul anticipated that some would reject the concept of God's prerogative in judgment and salvation: "He has mercy on whom He desires, and He hardens whom He desires. You will say to me then, 'Why does He still find fault? For who resists His will?'" (Rom. 9:18–19). Paul answered his own questions:

On the contrary, who are you, O man, who answers back to God? . . . What if God, although willing to demonstrate His wrath and to make His power known, endured with much patience vessels of wrath prepared for destruction? And He did so to make known the riches of His glory upon vessels of mercy, which he prepared beforehand for glory. (Rom. 9:20a, 22–23; see also vv. 20b–21)

The way people are at the end of life, believing or unbelieving, so they will be forever (see Rev. 22:11). Whatever God does is right because He is the measure of that standard. No matter if believers come to Him by His gracious redemption, or false teachers in His judgment refuse to come, He will be glorified forever.

ASK YOURSELF

What glory does God receive even when His message is treated badly and deemed unacceptable by others? How can you keep their low view of the gospel from discouraging you or making you feel timid about watching for opportunities to declare the hope of God's grace?

JESUS' COMPASSION FOR ISRAEL, PART 1

"Jerusalem, Jerusalem, who kills the prophets and stones those who are sent to her! How often I wanted to gather your children together, the way a hen gathers her chicks under her wings, and you were unwilling. Behold, your house is being left to you desolate!" —MATT. 23:37–38

Using Jerusalem to represent all Israel, Jesus here expresses His grief at the Jews' hardness and reminds them of their rebellion against Him. "Kills" and "stones" can be translated "killing" and "stoning," thus indicating that these harsh processes were ongoing as He spoke. The faithless and rebellious people had been killing God's servants, from Abel to Zechariah (v. 35). And they would continue this pattern by killing Jesus Himself and persecuting the apostles and teachers who followed after Him.

Our Lord did not desire that His people be punished but that they would turn to Him in genuine faith and devotion. He laments here that He longed to draw the Jews to Himself and protect them, "the way a hen gathers her chicks under her wings." Jesus' words contain a beautiful intimacy and tenderness, a tone that His voice likely conveyed as well. He had come "to His own, and those who were His own did not receive Him" (John 1:11).

ASK YOURSELF

How encouraged are you to read of Jesus' deep sense of passion for the lost, misguided children of Israel? How have you experienced His tender desire to draw you close and invite you into sweet fellowship with Him? When have you needed His forgiving embrace the most, and how has it changed your life?

JESUS' COMPASSION FOR ISRAEL, PART 2

"Jerusalem, Jerusalem, who kills the prophets and stones those who are sent to her! How often I wanted to gather your children together, the way a hen gathers her chicks under her wings, and you were unwilling. Behold, your house is being left to you desolate!" —MATT. 23:37–38

David exults, "How precious is Your lovingkindness, O God! And the children of men take refuge in the shadow of Your wings" (Ps. 36:7). It is God's desire that all people, especially His beloved people the Jews, take sanctuary under His wings (cf. 1 Tim. 2:3–4). The Lord Jesus often gave such generous and gracious invitations:

Come to Me, all who are weary and heavy-laden, and I will give you rest. Take My yoke upon you and learn from Me, for I am gentle and humble in heart, and you will find rest for your souls. For My yoke is easy and My burden is light. (Matt. 11:28–30)

Though God magnanimously offers Israel and all people the opportunity to receive and obey His Son, most nevertheless are unwilling. For the Jews, in the face of Christ's compassion for them and offer of salvation, their rejection of His kingdom meant they inherited divine judgment for their unbelief rather than the blessings associated with faith.

ASK YOURSELF

What are some of the means God is using today to draw people toward His promise of care and provision? Why are trouble and hardship such effective tools for opening our eyes to our great need for Him? What happens to us when we react to difficult circumstances by pushing Him even further away?

JESUS' COMPASSION FOR ISRAEL, PART 3

"Jerusalem, Jerusalem, who kills the prophets and stones those who are sent to her! How often I wanted to gather your children together, the way a hen gathers her chicks under her wings, and you were unwilling. Behold, your house is being left to you desolate!" —MATT. 23:37–38

In announcing, "Behold, your house is being left to you desolate!" the Lord indicated that, much as in earlier times (cf. Deut. 28:15–68; Isa. 5:1–7), God would leave Israel devastated and desolate. A few days earlier Jesus had called the temple His Father's house (Matt. 21:13), but it had been so long profaned that He now called it "your house," meaning the house of Israel, the faithless nation as a whole. The temple and all the Jews would soon be called Ichabod (cf. 1 Sam. 4:21) because the Father's glory and protective hand would depart from them. So now, while Israel is in that status, God's house is Christ's church, "the church of the living God, the pillar and support of the truth" (1 Tim. 3:15).

Although the Jews have suffered much because God withdrew His blessing from them, many individual Jews have turned and continue to turn to Christ in saving faith. Our compassionate Lord has never been completely without His chosen remnant (Isa. 10:22; Zech. 8:12; Rom. 9:27).

ASK YOURSELF

What is missing when we mistakenly believe we can take care of our own problems, that we can figure out what to do without God's help? What does this attitude reveal about our beliefs as well as our view of ourselves? Why is there no other alternative but desolation when we choose to rely on our inner strength and ingenuity rather than leaning on God's wisdom and sufficient supply?

ISRAEL'S SALVATION ENSURED

*"For I say to you, from now on you will not see Me until you say,
'Blessed is He who comes in the name of the Lord!'"* —MATT. 23:39

W ere it not for Christ's qualifying word here, "until," His words "from now on you will not see Me" would have marked the Jews' final moment in history. If so, biblical theology, both Old and New Testaments, would now be drastically altered. And people would no longer have trust in God's Word, because in fact He has repeatedly promised that His chosen people the Jews will ultimately be saved and blessed (see Jer. 23:5–6; Isa. 66:10–22).

Our Lord did not say "unless," making the Jews' future salvation only a possibility, but "until," making it a certainty. Even in this context of Jesus' severe diatribe and curses against the unbelieving false leaders, His words offered hope. One day the people of Israel will believingly utter the words "Blessed is He who comes in the name of the Lord!" and at that time they will be forever redeemed, restored, and blessed.

Writing of his own people the Jews, Paul says, "by their transgression salvation has come to the Gentiles, to make them jealous. Now if their transgression is riches for the world and their failure is riches for the Gentiles, how much more will their fulfillment be!" (Rom. 11:11*b*–12).

ASK YOURSELF

How have you repeatedly been blessed by the patience of the Lord? How would you describe its effects on you and the hopelessness that would dominate your life if not for His willingness to give you second chances? In what ways might He be calling you to exercise the same sort of patience toward others?

CHRIST COMES TO THE MOUNT OF OLIVES, PART 1

*As He was sitting on the Mount of Olives, the disciples came to Him privately,
saying, "Tell us, when will these things happen, and what will be the sign of
Your coming, and of the end of the age?"* —MATT. 24:3; see also vv. 1–2

For a long time, the apostles had believed God's kingdom would appear
very soon (Luke 19:11). Thus their use of "when" implies immediacy,
which from their standpoint could have meant tomorrow, the next day, or
the end of the coming Passover.

Jesus' men were poised for the final stages of His ministry to occur
in quick succession: He would swiftly defeat the rebellious nations, pu-
rify Jerusalem, regather the Jews, and set up His kingdom. But how
would they understand exactly when events would happen? They viewed
the events as a single continuum, with no church age coming between
His first and second comings.

For the Twelve, the imminence of Jesus' millennial kingdom would
be perhaps the most exciting part of their time with Him. They thought
surely the next time their Jewish opponents saw the Lord would be when
He revealed His glory, when even His enemies would concede, "Blessed
is He who comes in the name of the Lord!" (Matt. 23:39). More and more
the apostles were persuaded that an earthly kingdom could not be long in
coming.

ASK YOURSELF

What impact did the disciples' perspective likely have on their daily
decisions and priorities? What did their expectation of coming
deliverance perhaps cause them to consider unimportant in light of
Jesus' eternal kingdom? How might the same kind of outlook color our
own daily lives if our hearts were truly watchful and waiting?

CHRIST COMES TO THE MOUNT OF OLIVES, PART 2

As He was sitting on the Mount of Olives, the disciples came to Him privately, saying, "Tell us, when will these things happen, and what will be the sign of Your coming, and of the end of the age?" —MATT. 24:3; see also vv. 1–2

The apostles' expectancy for an immediate kingdom remained even after Christ's resurrection: "Lord, is it at this time You are restoring the kingdom to Israel?" (Acts 1:6). The "coming" they envisioned would not be a second coming but an unbroken, compressed, relatively brief series of events—Jesus' proclamation as King, destruction of His enemies, inauguration of His kingdom.

"Coming" here basically means presence and therefore turns the disciples' question as follows: "What will be the sign of Your manifesting Yourself as Messiah in full, permanent presence?" They weren't thinking of His return (e.g., 1 Thess. 3:13; 2 Thess. 2:8), because they could not conceive of His leaving.

The question Jesus' men wanted answered related to the ultimate end of the age—not simply to the end of an era in world history but to the termination of the current world system of sin and darkness, replaced by an age of righteousness and light. God would forever damn the ungodly and forever bless the godly. The apostles simply wondered when this would occur and what signs would signal its beginning.

ASK YOURSELF

What are the things you're most eager to live without when Jesus comes for His people? How could a fresh understanding of the temporary nature of such burdens as sin, turmoil, and sadness enliven your spirit today, causing you to hope even more enthusiastically for the joys of life eternal with Jesus?

INDICATORS OF THE END TIMES, PART 1

"What will be the sign of Your coming, and of the end of the age?"
—MATT. 24:3*b*

We can infer seven indicators from Jesus' end-times message (Olivet Discourse) that place the events in the more distant future. First is the figure of birth pangs (v. 8), which ancient Jewish writers frequently used, especially concerning the end times.

Labor pains occur shortly before the birth of a child, and with increasing frequency until the infant emerges. Similarly, events related to Christ's return will not begin until soon before that momentous event. Then they will occur with increasing rapidity, culminating with a cluster of catastrophic occurrences. In Revelation, the seal judgments likely unfold over a period of years (6:1–8:6), the trumpet judgments over a period of weeks (8:7–9:21; 11:15–19), and the bowl judgments during a time of days or hours (16:1–21).

Paul also looked to the more distant day when he used the same birth pang figure: "While they are saying, 'Peace and safety!' then destruction will come upon them suddenly like labor pains upon a woman with child, and they will not escape" (1 Thess. 5:3). This metaphor by Jesus' does not fit well when applied to Jerusalem's near-future destruction (close to the start of the church age) or the church age as a whole.

ASK YOURSELF

What are some of the disciplines and practices that keep you most aware of spiritual activity, most discerning of what certain events mean in God's kingdom schedule and economy? What distracts you the easiest from keeping your heart fully engaged in what matters from a kingdom perspective in these days?

INDICATORS OF THE END TIMES, PART 2

"What will be the sign of Your coming, and of the end of the age?"
—MATT. 24:3*b*

We can infer three more indicators from Jesus' Olivet Discourse, indicating that the events are future. First, He tells of believers who will endure birth pains to the end of the age (24:13–14). Since the apostles did not live that long, the events could not apply to them or any other Christians up to today. We will be raptured prior to the tribulation (1 Thess. 4:17), so Jesus' words apply to those who believe during the tribulation and endure to the end (Matt. 24:13).

Second, a worldwide proclamation of the gospel (v. 14) excludes the apostolic age when only part of the Roman Empire heard the gospel. Even today there are still millions, in spite of modern, technical outreach tools, who have not heard the evangel; thus Christ spoke of something for a future day (cf. Rev. 14:6–7).

Third, Jesus pointed to something from Daniel, "the abomination of desolation" (Matt. 24:15), a reference to events occurring during the time of Antichrist and before the messianic kingdom (Dan. 9:27). We have yet to witness these things, but can be certain they will happen in the future.

ASK YOURSELF

How are you currently involved in the carrying of gospel truth to the ends of the earth? Why does this remain a priority for the church, and how are we perhaps losing our focus on its importance amid the clamor of other activities? How has your own life been impacted by the courage required and the blessings derived from engaging other people and cultures with the hope of His good news?

INDICATORS OF THE END TIMES, PART 3

"What will be the sign of Your coming, and of the end of the age?"
—MATT. 24:3*b*

Three final indicators tell us that Jesus' discourse looked ahead to future events. First is Jesus' mention of the "great tribulation, such as has not occurred since the beginning of the world until now, nor ever will" (24:21). The horrific events associated with this happen at the very end of the present age (cf. Dan. 12:1–2).

Second, our Lord refers to phenomena that take place right after the tribulation—the darkening of the sun and moon, stars falling, and the Son of Man's sign appearing in the sky (Matt. 24:29–30). Obviously, such things have not yet occurred.

Finally is the indicator of the fig tree (vv. 32–35), applicable to the end of the summer season, as are all the Olivet events just before the end of the age. The indicators of the end times will occur within one generation, one that could be living only in the future when Jesus Christ returns.

It's not as though similar situations and conditions have never happened in recorded history. There have been many wars, famines, earthquakes, and the like since the fall, but the Olivet Discourse identifies in detail, sequence, and scale events that have to be unique to the future end times.

ASK YOURSELF

How does a genuine awareness of coming trouble on a grand scale impact your heart and outlook on the future? What might you be recognizing today that indicates a brewing mixture of end-times rumblings? What would you say to someone who thinks life will continually roll on unimpeded as it always has? How would you counteract their claim that Christianity is too focused on the hereafter?

DECEPTION BY FALSE CHRISTS

"For many will come in My name, saying, 'I am the Christ,' and will mislead many." —MATT. 24:5

Jesus here warns those living during the end times that the numbers of and deceptive influences by false Christs will greatly increase then. (There were false messiahs before Jesus' day, and there have occasionally been others since, including in our day, but the number of false teachers with their widespread deceptions will proliferate in the end as never before.) The deception of those days will grow and intensify so greatly because the Holy Spirit will withdraw His restraining power (see 2 Thess. 2:7). The world's systems and institutions will begin to self-destruct, suffering will become unbearable, sin will reach its maximum potential, and vulnerable people will desperately seek answers concerning the calamities (cf. 2 Tim. 3:13; 2 Peter 2:1–3).

The foremost of the deceivers will be the Antichrist. As Jesus Christ was righteousness incarnate, the Antichrist will be evil incarnate (see Dan. 8:23; 11:36). The New Testament calls him the man of lawlessness, son of destruction, and the Beast (2 Thess. 2:3; Rev. 11:7; 13:1–10). With assistance from other deceivers, he will point the world toward peace but a peace that's merely false and temporary (cf. 1 Thess. 5:3).

ASK YOURSELF

What are the primary causes for our culture's inability to determine truth from error? Why are false teachers and false gospels gaining such traction today, even in the guise of churches and ministries that claim to be Christian? How can we most effectively disciple our children and others to keep from being overcome and misled by untrue doctrine?

WARFARE AMONG THE NATIONS

"You will be hearing of wars and rumors of wars. See that you are not frightened, for those things must take place, but that is not yet the end. For nation will rise against nation, and kingdom against kingdom." —MATT. 24:6–7a

In this text Jesus mentions the second birth pain involving unprecedented warfare among the nations. There will be hot wars utilizing conventional combat, guerilla warfare, and terror tactics, as well as cold wars involving economics and politics. Our Lord implies that conflicts will increase not only in number but in intensity as His return nears, until there is an immense holocaust of carnage.

Christ seems not to distinguish between nation and kingdom, thus exempting no group of people from possible war. The future wars will include racial, ethnic, and cultural as well as national confrontations, as we see today, but on a vaster, more intense scale. The books of Daniel (7:24; 9:27; 11:40–45) and Revelation (9:14–16) provide many inspired details concerning end-times conflicts.

In Revelation, the apostle John sees additional details of the wars and rumors thereof in which the world will be embroiled during the end times. When Christ, depicted as a Lamb holding a scroll representing the Father's bequeathment of the world to the Son, opens each of the seven seals, He sets in motion each stage of His reclaiming the world for Himself (Rev. 6:1–8:5; cf. 16:13–14; 19:11–20).

ASK YOURSELF

How does the general inevitability of conflict affect you, as well as the present incarnations of warfare and bloodshed in our world today? Why is war so indicative of the human condition, and why is the power of God's grace so effective in bridging the barriers that exist between people and nations?

WORLD DEVASTATION

"And in various places there will be famines and earthquakes. But all these things are merely the beginning of birth pangs." —MATT. 24:7*b*–8

Throughout history the world has experienced many earthquakes, famines, plagues, and a few heavenly signs, but the birth pang of world devastation in the end times will overshadow all previous calamities. People will see the earth start to disintegrate from the powerful forces of evil during the future days Jesus looks to.

John foresaw some of the devastation after Christ broke the sixth seal:

> There was a great earthquake; and the sun became black as sackcloth made of hair, and the whole moon became like blood; and the stars of the sky fell to the earth, as a fig tree casts its unripe figs when shaken by a great wind. The sky was split apart like a scroll when it is rolled up, and every mountain and island were moved out of their places. (Rev. 6:12–14; cf. v. 8)

The trumpet judgments, revealed after the seventh seal of Revelation, preview more of the final devastation. A third of the earth and its trees will burn, a third of the sea will become blood and a third of its creatures will die, and many other devastations will occur (see Rev. 8:7–12; 16:1–11, 17–21). But all these things are "merely the beginning of birth pangs," as Jesus' continuing message demonstrates.

ASK YOURSELF

What do these glimpses of the awesome power of God stir in your heart? How does the immensity of His justified wrath toward unbelievers paint the surprising reality of His grace toward you in even bolder colors? How does it help you to reflect on what His mercy has, continues to, and will ultimately save you from?

BELIEVERS AND FUTURE TRIBULATION, PART 1

"Then they will deliver you to tribulation, and will kill you." —MATT. 24:9a

The next end-times labor pain Jesus identifies is persecution of the godly by the ungodly. More severely than ever, Christians will be treated in an unholy way and desecrated. Mark's parallel passage provides additional insight into what will take place for faithful believers: "They will deliver you to the courts, and you will be flogged in the synagogues, and you will stand before governors and kings for My sake, as a testimony to them" (13:9). The courts likely represent Gentile authority, and the synagogues represent Jewish authority—both groups will persecute believers.

Such persecutions will cost believers their freedom, their respect, and often their lives—and they will occur against those saved during the tribulation (Rev. 11:3, 11–13). The severe abuse will not be aimed as much against the tribulation saints as against God, whom they serve and represent. The reprobate world intensifies its hatred of God, and because it can't attack Him directly, it will savagely attack His people. When Paul said he wore "the brand-marks of Jesus" (Gal. 6:17), he testified to receiving wounds actually aimed at Jesus. The apostle represented the spirit of martyrdom that many will actually fulfill in the last days.

ASK YOURSELF

How does imagining the unmasked hatred and capabilities of human cruelty cause you to marvel that we have been spared its full onslaught so far? Even with atrocities a living reality for many today at the hands of others, why is the common grace of God the only true explanation for the hints of goodness and restraint we see among the people of the world?

Believers and Future Tribulation, Part 2

"Then they will deliver you to tribulation, and will kill you." —Matt. 24:9a

When the Holy Spirit withdraws His restraint of evil, Christians then on earth will suffer as never before. Satan's forces will not persecute and kill them so much for what they do as who they are. The saints will suffer because they identify with Jesus' name.

John saw a future picture of the martyred saints under the altar of incense:

> When the Lamb broke the fifth seal, I saw underneath the altar the souls of those who had been slain because of the word of God, and because of the testimony which they had maintained; and they cried out with a loud voice, saying, "How long, O Lord, holy and true, will You refrain from judging and avenging our blood on those who dwell on the earth?" (Rev. 6:9–10; cf. 7:9–10)

Later one of the elders in heaven explained to the apostle that "these are the ones who come out of the great tribulation, and they have washed their robes and made them white in the blood of the Lamb" (7:14).

In the end, unbelieving mankind will be unrepentant (9:21) of killing other unbelievers, but their most vicious attacks will be on Christians.

ASK YOURSELF

What indications do you see today that Christians are being singled out for ill treatment, whether in the media, in the courts, or in society at large? How does God expect us to react to this unfair, unjust conduct toward believers? What do you intend or expect your reaction to be if (or when) such hostile rejection is directed at you personally?

The Cost Too High for Unbelievers, Part 1

"At that time many will fall away and will betray one another and hate one another." —MATT. 24:10

Every noble cause has peripheral people who want to be part of it while the going is easy, but who depart when the cost of adherence gets too difficult. Christ's church is no exception. The phony Christians who fall away during the tribulation will not be genuine believers who become cowardly. In actuality they will be unbelievers who reveal their real character when they apostatize. They won't be like Peter, who in a period of weakness denied being a disciple, but rather like Judas, who because of his inner hatred for the Lord betrayed Him.

Of such pretenders, John writes, "They went out from us, but they were not really of us; for if they had been of us, they would have remained with us; but they went out, so that it would be shown that they all are not of us" (1 John 2:19). These deserters leave Christ's visible church because they were not and are not members of His invisible church. However, Jesus' true disciples are willing to suffer as He suffered, and no amount of affliction will cause them to fall away from their Lord (Matt. 10:32–33, 38; cf. John 8:31).

ASK YOURSELF

How has God used conflict and circumstances in your own life to confirm the trust you have in Him? How has any failure on your part to be true to Him caused you a grief you never want to experience again? Or how has your courage to stand in allegiance to Him shown you that He can be powerful in you no matter what the cost?

THE COST TOO HIGH FOR UNBELIEVERS, PART 2

*"At that time many will fall away and will betray
one another and hate one another."* —MATT. 24:10

The author of Hebrews warned the early church about apostasy: "Take care, brethren, that there not be in any one of you an evil, unbelieving heart that falls away from the living God" (Heb. 3:12). But Paul gave this guarantee to Timothy: "For if we died with Him, we will also live with Him; if we endure, we will also reign with Him; if we deny Him, He also will deny us; if we are faithless, He remains faithful, for He cannot deny Himself" (2 Tim. 2:11–13).

We can conclude from today's text that, just as now, many professing believers living during the tribulation will not be genuine. When the cost of discipleship becomes too high, these counterfeits will leave Jesus Christ and His church. They will be like those who told Jesus, "I will follow You wherever You go" and "Lord, permit me first to go and bury my father" and "I will follow You, Lord; but first permit me to say goodbye to those at home." Such people, although hesitating, seem to want to follow Christ, but they refuse to completely abandon the old life, and thus Jesus declares they are not "fit for the kingdom of God" (see Luke 9:57–62).

ASK YOURSELF

What gives you warning that some (perhaps many) who claim Christ as Savior will be exposed as faithless pretenders when the heat becomes too intense? How can we as believers and the churches we indwell become more effective in helping others anchor their faith deep in the sure, saving Word of God?

DECEPTION WILL BE TOO CONVINCING

"Many false prophets will arise and will mislead many." —MATT. 24:11

When the price of real, biblical, Christ-ordained discipleship gets too high, some will forsake the gospel, again proving that they were never true believers in the first place (cf. Heb. 6:4–8). However, others will renounce the kingdom simply because "false prophets" deceive them about the gospel.

During the tribulation, many heretical teachers will join the false christs (v. 5) in trying to deceive people about God. They will convincingly proclaim doctrines that seem true and godly but are, in reality, false and satanic. Overt evil such as the world has never before experienced will permeate the end times, and false religions will also abound as never before. The Devil will seek to be an angel of light (2 Cor. 11:14) right up to the very end.

The great harlot of Babylon (Rev. 17) symbolizes the flourishing presence of false religion in the end times. The vast religious system of the world will prostitute itself before humanity, attempting by bogus gospels and other spurious means to shield people from the authentic gospel of salvation. These efforts will have a common characteristic: hatred for the saints, the genuine, sanctified brethren of the Lord Jesus Christ.

ASK YOURSELF

Are there any untrue or cleverly distorted doctrines that have seemed plausible to you at some point in your life? What caused you to fall victim to such error? How was its deception later exposed to you, and how painfully was your lesson learned? What of value have you gleaned from your experience of grappling with this matter? How can this help you in parenting, in discipling, in sharing Christian life with others?

SIN WILL BE TOO ATTRACTIVE, PART 1

"Because lawlessness is increased, most people's love will grow cold. But the one who endures to the end, he will be saved." —MATT. 24:12–13

The lawlessness prevalent in the end times will surely include the ignoring of human laws. But lawlessness will be revealed most forcefully in increased disobedience of God's law. Evil will be growing so rapidly that people who initially seem interested in the gospel will ultimately reject it because of sin's many new enticements.

In this time of lawlessness, people will stop trying to hide their sins but will flaunt them, which then will draw many (including some professed believers) away from whatever interest they might have had in the things of God. Paul lists some sins that will mark this period: "lovers of self, lovers of money, boastful, arrogant, revilers, disobedient to parents, ungrateful, unholy, unloving, irreconcilable, malicious gossips, without self-control, brutal, haters of good, treacherous, reckless, conceited, lovers of pleasure rather than lovers of God, holding to a form of godliness, although they have denied its power" (2 Tim. 3:2–5).

But the Lord Jesus promises us that those who endure to the end will be saved. Their endurance will not produce salvation but will be Spirit-empowered proof that they truly are saved. None of the challenges and temptations of these difficult last days will cause true Christians to renounce Christ, because He will protect them from defection.

ASK YOURSELF

How have you experienced the clouding, confusing effects of sin, distorting your hold on reality and your confidence in Christ? What has typically been the result when coming out of a season of sin? How has truth appeared to you whenever it has come clearly back into view?

SIN WILL BE TOO ATTRACTIVE, PART 2

*"Because lawlessness is increased, most people's love will grow cold. But the one who endures to the end, he will be saved." —*MATT. 24:12–13

Spiritual endurance always characterizes true salvation. Jesus taught, "You will be hated by all because of My name, but it is the one who has endured to the end who will be saved" (Matt. 10:22). The person who resists sin's attractiveness and endures all hardships that may come because of his relationship to Christ proves that he belongs to the Savior. Jesus assures this man or woman that they will eventually be delivered from this evil world system into God's righteous, eternal kingdom.

The perseverance of the saints is a basic component of the biblical doctrine of salvation. It asserts that true believers in Jesus' atoning work will not depart from the faith (see John 8:31; Col. 1:21–23; Heb. 4:14; James 1:2–4). The apostle Paul assures us of salvation's divine completion in us: "For I am confident of this very thing, that He who began a good work in you will perfect it until the day of Christ Jesus" (Phil. 1:6; cf. John 10:27–29).

"The one who endures to the end" is the overcomer, the Christian who does not fear suffering or death and will receive the crown of life, the one who will "not be hurt by the second death" (see Rev. 2:10–11).

ASK YOURSELF

How has the joyful amazement of seeing godliness at work in your thoughts and actions encouraged your heart at times when you may have doubted God's hand on your life? How does such an experience transform any idea that good works are a means of salvation, when they are actually the blessed result?

THE GOSPEL DECLARED TO THE WHOLE WORLD

"This gospel of the kingdom shall be preached in the whole world as a testimony to all the nations, and then the end will come." —MATT. 24:14

In spite of all the end-time birth pains and what they indicate—deceiving false christs and false teachers; widespread warfare, pestilence, and disaster; vicious persecution of believers; and defection of counterfeit Christians— proclamation of Jesus Christ's gospel will continue to occur. In the face of Antichrist's tyranny and hell's demons wreaking havoc, our Lord will not be without witness.

Prior to the final holocaust of the bowl judgments, and before the increasingly rapid birth pangs leading to the kingdom, God will send an angel

> having an eternal gospel to preach to those who live on the earth, and to every nation and tribe and tongue and people; and [saying] with a loud voice, "Fear God, and give Him glory, because the hour of His judgment has come; worship Him who made the heaven and the earth and sea and springs of waters." (Rev. 14:6–7)

Following that final and complete evangelization of the earth, mankind's day will be over, its rebellion at an end, and the opportunity for salvation closed, because "then the end will come."

ASK YOURSELF

How has the rapid integration of different cultures and people groups into our once fairly homogenous cities and towns changed the face of international missions? How are you and your church responding to the presence of other nationalities in your neighborhoods? Why might God have allowed such changes to occur in our cultural makeup? What might revival look like in the modern-day church, and how would your church probably respond to it?

RESPONSE TO FUTURE TROUBLES

"But pray that your flight will not be in the winter, or on a Sabbath."
—MATT. 24:20

Today's text is part of Jesus' call for urgency, in which He stresses the need for saved Jews to flee immediately when the second half of the tribulation looms. Anyone who is on his rooftop when he hears of the abomination of desolation should not waste even a few minutes to retrieve possessions from his house before fleeing (vv. 15, 17). No material items are worth the risk of the slightest delay.

This dreaded moment will not be the time even to take a stand for Christ—only a time for fleeing into His arms. The time for testimony will be gone, and the believer's only sensible response will be to take immediate flight.

Although Palestinian winters are comparatively mild, even slightly inclement weather can be a hindrance to travel. Thus Jesus said, "pray that your flight will not be in the winter." And those Jews fleeing should also pray that it not be on the Sabbath, when Jews remaining might try to impede their flight because of the belief that the Sabbath was being profaned.

To the Lord, no hindrance to flight should be overlooked on that day, and no possession considered worth retrieving. Because of the terrifying enormity of the great tribulation, immediate, undeterred flight will be the only right response.

ASK YOURSELF

Have you ever been in a situation in which the only thing you could do was simply react? How can you more confidently ensure that your first response to calamity or emergency is the same one you would make if you had time to measure it out? How often is Jesus the first place you run when you need help?

A Severe Calamity

"For then there will be a great tribulation, such as has not occurred since the beginning of the world until now, nor ever will." —MATT. 24:21

The Lord's message to Israel is that things will get much worse before they get better. At the direction of Antichrist, the Jews will suffer treachery, desecration of the rebuilt temple, severe persecution, and vicious slaughter—all unlike anything in previous history. During that time God will supernaturally shorten the daylight hours to provide His fleeing people the extra protection of more darkness.

In fact, at least three times during the great tribulation, God will radically alter the light-producing heavenly bodies to progressively reduce the amount of daylight until the forces of evil must work in total darkness (cf. Rev. 6:12–14; 8:12; 16:10). God will use the darkness "for the sake of the elect" (Matt. 24:22), allowing them to hide from their would-be destroyers.

"The elect" can represent both Israel (Isa. 45:4) and people who become believers during the tribulation (Rev. 17:14). The first New Testament use of "elect" occurs in Matthew 24:22. By this term Jesus introduces the concept that believers have been divinely chosen and called out to be His very own children. And when God has a chosen people, He will, if necessary, restructure the whole universe to protect the elect and fulfill His promises for them.

ASK YOURSELF

How have you experienced God's supernatural protection over your life, whether by keeping you from making an unwise decision, or preventing someone else from carrying out harmful plans against you, or giving you insight about a dangerous situation before it happened? How has this deepened your trust and confidence in Him for the future?

SUBTLE CONFUSION IN THE FUTURE, PART 1

"Then if anyone says to you, 'Behold, here is the Christ,' or 'There He is,'
do not believe him. For false Christs and false prophets will arise and will
show great signs and wonders, so as to mislead, if possible, even the elect."
—MATT. 24:23–24

Christ's words "if possible" make it clear that Antichrist and his cohorts will not be able to deceive the elect. This has always been impossible for Satan: "My sheep hear My voice, and I know them," Jesus said, "and they follow Me; and I give eternal life to them, and they will never perish; and no one will snatch them out of My hand" (John 10:27–28). The saints will be able to discern and avoid even the most subtle deception because they always have the Spirit-inspired knowledge of the true Messiah within them.

Satan will nevertheless forcefully attempt to use the turmoil of the final days to undermine the confidence of believing refugees and convince them to follow a false messiah or prophet. These deceivers would instantly betray them to Antichrist once they were without God's sanctuary. With the cosmos being radically torn apart—stars falling, sun and moon diminishing, millions dying, and thousands of Jews having been slaughtered—the refugees from tribulation will be exhausted and vulnerable to the schemes of false leaders, were it not for God's gracious provision.

ASK YOURSELF

How fearful are you of the future? What does your outlook reveal about your confidence in God and His ability to carry out His plans to the end of this age and beyond? How do you truly desire to approach the turmoil of tomorrow, and what can help you live up to the courage you want to possess?

SUBTLE CONFUSION IN THE FUTURE, PART 2

"Behold, I have told you in advance. So if they say to you, 'Behold, He is in the wilderness,' do not go out, or, 'Behold, He is in the inner rooms,' do not believe them. For just as the lightning comes from the east and flashes even to the west, so will the coming of the Son of Man be." —MATT. 24:25–27

Jesus' words "I have told you in advance" indicate He was speaking to the tribulation fugitives prophetically across the intervening centuries. Our Lord in essence said, "Beware of all claims about My identity and whereabouts. Heed only what I'm teaching you now, not anything else you will hear or see during the tribulation."

But how will the Lord's protected ones know when He really appears to set up His kingdom? How can they discern those events from the many spurious ones? Jesus assures them His coming will be sudden, quick, publically visible, universal, and glorious, "as the lightning comes from the east and flashes even to the west." An angel told John, "Behold, He is coming with the clouds, and every eye will see Him, even those who pierced Him; and all the tribes of the earth will mourn over Him" (Rev. 1:7). Our Lord's appearance will be unmistakable to everyone on earth, including His most implacable foes (cf. Rev. 6:15–16).

ASK YOURSELF

Imagine if Jesus had not chosen to tell us "in advance" what His coming would be like. Is it possible you are facing another situation that seems full of mystery and unknowns? Yet what has He told you "in advance" that can be of enough help to get you through the uncertainties? What will your trust look like?

FUTURE SCENE IN THE HEAVENS

"The sun will be darkened, and the moon will not give its light, and the stars will fall from the sky, and the powers of the heavens will be shaken."
—MATT. 24:29b

Christ here describes the cosmic scene when He appears. The entire universe will start to disintegrate very rapidly (see also Luke 21:25–26). Things will be so catastrophic that people will faint (literally die) from sheer terror. No single or combination natural disaster in recorded history will approach the extreme disruption of these end-time events.

During this time "the powers of the heavens will be shaken" by the Lord Jesus, the One who "upholds all things by the word of His power" (Heb. 1:3). When He chooses to withdraw part of His power from the created order, gravity will weaken, planetary orbits will fluctuate, and all navigational aides will be futile or highly unreliable. That's because all the forces of natural energy, here called "the powers of the heavens," will be in dysfunction, with all stable reference points and uniform forces ceasing.

Christ's divine control, along with His Father, of even these chaotic and disintegrating processes will prevent the complete disappearance of the earth. His sovereign power will preserve and restore the planet and its people for our Lord's millennial kingdom.

ASK YOURSELF

How many unseen, uncontrollable elements are at play in our world and universe, maintaining our survival through the sheer grace of almighty God? In what way does such dependence affect how completely you trust in Him for everyday issues? How foolish does this make our doubts of Him appear by contrast? Why do we often choose to ignore this One we need so desperately?

FUTURE SIGN IN THE SKY, PART 1

"The sign of the Son of Man will appear in the sky, and then all the tribes of the earth will mourn, and they will see the Son of Man coming on the clouds of the sky." —MATT. 24:30a

Many of the early church fathers believed "the sign of the Son of Man" would be a giant, fiery cross, visible to the entire world and piercing the sky's profound end-time darkness. But the sign will likely be the Shekinah glory as the unveiled Christ makes His appearance.

However, the sign will indeed also be the Son of Man Himself—revealing Himself in His infinite, undiminished glory as the supreme sign of that future coming. And this ultimate sign will bring many to their knees in repentance as they acknowledge their need of divine salvation. Among those who confess their sins will be many Jews (Zech. 12:10–11; Rom. 11:25–26; cf. Isa. 59:20). But there will also be people from "all the tribes of the earth" who finally "will mourn" because of their rebellion against God and their rejection of His Son. Having heard the gospel proclaimed (Matt. 24:14; Rev. 14:6), these sinners will in brokenness turn from sin and embrace Jesus as Lord and Savior.

ASK YOURSELF

Knowing that some will not believe in Christ until they're faced with the most dire, most extreme circumstance, how ready and open do you intend to remain for your friends and family members who have not yet placed their faith in Christ? How do you know this is true—that no hour prior to His return is ever too late for anyone to call out to Him?

FUTURE SIGN IN THE SKY, PART 2

"The sign of the Son of Man will appear in the sky, and then all the tribes of the earth will mourn, and they will see the Son of Man coming on the clouds of the sky." —MATT. 24:30a

Precisely as the Lord ascended to heaven in the clouds, He will return "in just the same way" (Acts 1:11; cf. Dan. 7:13–14). The psalmist says God uses clouds as His chariot (Ps. 104:3), and Isaiah depicts "the Lord . . . riding on a swift cloud" (Isa. 19:1). No matter what the exact nature of these clouds, Christ, in the midst of dark calamity, will use them to unveil Himself in His total majesty (cf. Zech. 14:6–7).

Although all saints before the tribulation will have left earth (1 Thess. 1:10), they will witness Christ's glorious appearance on earth. In fact, they "will be revealed with Him in glory" (Col. 3:4), having already been clothed as the bride of Christ (Rev. 19:8–9). It seems that the church, along with Old Testament believers, will accompany their Master as "the armies which are in heaven, clothed in fine linen, white and clean," following Him "on white horses" (v. 14). Instead of peering up to the sky, as those on earth will do, when Jesus appears (cf. Luke 21:28), they will be looking down from the heavens as they return with Him.

ASK YOURSELF

Remembering the unspeakable joy of those special seasons when God's Spirit has seemed especially real to you, try to imagine the exhilaration of being with Him, safe and secure, His glory visible to your eyes. What does this coming reality motivate in you as you labor for a little while, by faith, on this earth?

THE STRENGTH AND GLORY OF CHRIST

"With power and great glory." —MATT. 24:30*b*

Incredible demonstrations of His divine power over the entire created order will accompany Christ's return. He will conquer and destroy all His enemies, including sin and satanic forces (Dan. 9:24; Rev. 19:20), and will demonstrate ultimate mastery over the earth's ecosystems (Isa. 11:6–9; Zech. 14:8).

Along with the many examples of our Lord's divine power will be astounding revelations of His "great glory" (see also Matt. 25:31). Peter, James, and John had already glimpsed a preview of this glory at the transfiguration when "His face shone like the sun, and His garments became white as light" (17:2). Years later, Peter recalled and commented on that unforgettable event:

> We were eyewitnesses of His majesty. For when He received honor and glory from God the Father, such an utterance as this was made to Him by the Majestic Glory, "This is My beloved Son with whom I am well-pleased"—and we ourselves heard this utterance made from heaven when we were with Him on the holy mountain. (2 Peter 1:15*c*–18)

No person has yet seen Christ's unveiled glory, and no one will see it until His future appearance. But on that day there will be no mistaking His identity as there was during His first advent. All humanity will see the Son in His total glory and recognize Him as God—though all will not honor Him as divine.

ASK YOURSELF

How is it imaginable that some could see Christ in all His glory yet still not believe? But what should people already be able to see of God's goodness, though they refuse to attribute it to Him and continue on in their stubborn rebellion?

THE ANALOGY OF THE FIG TREE, PART 1

"Now learn the parable from the fig tree: when its branch has already become tender and puts forth its leaves, you know that summer is near." —MATT. 24:32

When our Lord presented a parable to the apostles and explained it, it was a graphic illustration that clarified a teaching. In view of that, it's evident that He told this parable of the fig tree to further elucidate His instruction about His second coming.

In the context of what Jesus had just been teaching, this parable should be easy to discern. The surrounding region had many fig trees, grown commercially but also in many family yards for the fruit and shade they provided during the hot summers.

The disciples would have known of other biblical fig tree illustrations: Jotham and the inhabitants of Shechem (Judg. 9:10–11); Jeremiah's vision of two baskets of fig trees (Jer. 24:1–10); the fig tree in Hosea's prophecy about Israel (Hos. 9:10); and Joel's splintered fig tree to depict Judah's devastation by locusts (Joel 1:4–7). Christ Himself had used the fig tree on several other occasions to assist His teaching (see Matt. 7:16; 21:19; Luke 13:6–9). Therefore the usage in today's text presented the apostles with an uncomplicated, easy to grasp analogy.

ASK YOURSELF

What are some of the most descriptive examples from nature that have taught you deep truths about God? How has He brought them repeatedly to mind throughout your life as visual reminders of biblical, eternal realities? Which of these have you been faithful to teach to your children and to others? Which of them perhaps represent special communication between you and God that have a very personal meaning, one that frequently encourages you?

THE ANALOGY OF THE FIG TREE, PART 2

"Now learn the parable from the fig tree: when its branch has already become tender and puts forth its leaves, you know that summer is near." —MATT. 24:32

Jesus reminded the disciples of the fig tree's nature: "when its branch has already become tender and puts forth its leaves, you know that summer is near." When tender young leaves appear on the tree, we know that summer approaches and at the end of that season figs will be ready for harvest.

Throughout Matthew the figure of harvest symbolizes judgment—the separation of unbelievers from believers, and the condemnation of unbelievers to hell (see Matt. 3:12; 13:30). The approach of final judgment is why Jesus, seeing the crowds who came out to hear Him, exhorted the apostles, "The harvest is plentiful, but the workers are few. Therefore beseech the Lord of the harvest to send out workers into His harvest" (9:37–38). Without saving faith, those people and millions more like them were and are destined to experience God's eternal judgment. The fields of "ripened" people are ready for harvesting, just as are groves of ripening fig trees.

So here and elsewhere Jesus used the harvest to represent a time of rewarding believers and punishing unbelievers. The analogy of the fig tree simply illustrates to us that, when certain signs begin to occur, the time of Christ's return will be very near.

ASK YOURSELF

What kind of reaction and response should the believer make toward the reality of impending judgment? What should it motivate in you? What should it affect in your typical day? How might you expect the Enemy to use God's coming judgment as a weapon in seeking to place false guilt upon you?

AN UNMISTAKABLE APPLICATION

*"So, you too, when you see all these things, recognize
that He is near, right at the door."* —MATT. 24:33

Our Lord's application of the fig tree parable is very unmistakable. "All
these things" refers unquestionably to all the calamitous events involved
with the final days (Matt. 24:4–29). Those circumstances will denote
"that He is near," just as the budding fig tree shows that the summer har-
vesttime is near.

Luke's narrative quotes Jesus as saying here, "So you also, when you
see these things happening, recognize that the kingdom of God is near"
(Luke 21:31). The premier event of the final day will be Christ's personal
coming to establish His kingdom on earth. When all the indicators He
just described occur, our King will be "right at the door," as it were,
knocking and ready to enter.

Jesus' mention of the fig tree gives us a simple and reasonable interpretation that the tree's leaves represent the aforementioned signs of His
coming and that "this generation" (Matt. 24:34) refers to those living and
witnessing the signs unfolding at the end. The Lord tells the disciples He
will return very soon after people witness all the signs, before the generation who sees them can pass away. Jesus spoke as if He were standing directly in front of future generations (cf. Isa. 66:10–14; Zech. 9:9), about
to reveal Himself in full glory.

ASK YOURSELF

Knowing that being "right at the door" has meant at least two
thousand years of waiting for Christ's return, what promises of
God toward you are still as certain as His Word, though you must
patiently watch and wait a little longer? In what way do you
attempt to hustle God along in fulfilling His plans?

An Unprecedented Alteration, with Unchanging Authority

"Heaven and earth will pass away, but My words will not pass away."
—Matt. 24:35

In Matthew 5:18 Jesus says, "Until heaven and earth pass away, not the smallest letter or stroke shall pass from the Law until all is accomplished." There He uses the expression about heaven and earth as an analogy for the enduring quality of God's Word, which is how He uses the similar phrase here. Even though the universe will pass away, our Lord's prophetic words about the end times will completely come to pass. Other Scriptures predict that God's judgment will dramatically affect the universe, but this will not happen until at the end of the millennial kingdom when the creation as we know it will end (2 Peter 3:10; Rev. 21:1).

On yet another occasion, concerning the durability of His words, Jesus said, "It is easier for heaven and earth to pass away than for one stroke of a letter of the Law to fail" (Luke 16:17; cf. John 10:35). The psalmist had already declared the same certainty when he wrote that Scripture is "clean, enduring forever" (Ps. 19:9). Whatever sin affects, such as the created order, must pass away, but the Word of God is not so affected. Like silver highly refined in the furnace, Scripture is utterly pure (Ps. 12:6).

ASK YOURSELF

Would you say your confidence in God's Word approaches the level of trust that the Word Himself declares in it? Is there any room for doubt in your heart that He will accomplish what He says? How could you develop an even more secure relationship with His Word, truly seeing it as iron—imperishable, unbreakable?

CHRIST'S RETURN: DATE UNKNOWN, PART 1

"But of that day and hour no one knows, not even the angels of heaven, nor the Son, but the Father alone." —MATT. 24:36

Even though people will see many tangible, unmistakable signs of Christ's coming just before it occurs, God will not reveal the precise time in advance. Once the indicators Jesus describes in Matthew 24 start to appear, observers can know the general time period of His return. However the exact day and hour of that return won't be known, a truth He repeats several times (24:42, 44; 25:13).

Thus no human beings, not even tribulation believers, will know in advance the exact date for the Lord Jesus' return. Although Christ gives no reason for their not knowing, it's easy to surmise some of the problems such knowledge could cause. For instance, if unbelievers knew precisely the date Jesus would return, they would be tempted to procrastinate, turning to Him only at the last moment, minimizing the importance and urgency of embracing salvation.

Even if people knew the hour and date when Jesus appears in the sky, they would have no guarantee they'd live until that moment. Like the rich farmer (Luke 12:16–20), they would have no assurance of their length of life and therefore no certainty they'd still be alive to exercise faith as the Lord returns. No one, Christian or non-Christian, could function normally knowing the precise date of Christ's future appearance.

ASK YOURSELF

It is wise of God to leave some of our questions unanswered, knowing the frailty and self-centeredness of human nature. What are some of the other questions He has not chosen to answer for you? How might He be exercising fatherly love and wisdom in withholding such information?

CHRIST'S RETURN: DATE UNKNOWN, PART 2

"But of that day and hour no one knows, not even the angels of heaven, nor the Son, but the Father alone."—MATT. 24:36

It's amazing to us that not even the Lord Jesus at this time knew when He would return. Although He was fully God and fully man (John 1:1, 14), on earth He voluntarily restricted the use of certain divine attributes. "Although He existed in the form of God, [Christ] did not regard equality with God a thing to be grasped"—that is, to be held on to during His incarnation (Phil. 2:6).

Christ of His own choice restricted His knowledge to that which His Father wanted Him to know. "All things that I have heard from My Father I have made known to you" (John 15:15; cf. 4:34; 5:30). Certain things God revealed to His Son simply as He does to all people: through Scripture, through divine working in His life, and through general revelation (Rom. 1:19–20). But for Jesus, His Father did reveal certain things directly to Him. However, Jesus' human understanding was always limited by what God wanted to provide Him.

Therefore, even at the end of His earthly ministry, the Son still did not know the exact day and hour of His future return to earth. During Christ's incarnation, only the Father had omniscience of such matters.

ASK YOURSELF

Great power resides in Christ's ability to understand us, to know exactly what we're going through and how it feels to be finitely human. How does His total understanding of you affect the way you communicate with Him, believe in Him, respond to His silences, worship Him through difficulty and confusion?

CHRIST'S RETURN: ALERTNESS NEEDED, PART 1

"Therefore be on the alert, for you do not know which day your Lord is coming."
—MATT. 24:42

As the end of the age approaches, people will not be expecting Christ's return and will be apathetic about it. Despite the many signs and wonders, they will be unconcerned about the things of the Lord, especially His imminent return to judge them. No matter how compelling the evidences will be that Jesus is coming soon, hypocritical and godless humanity will make every effort to deny them. They will seek to link scientific and natural causes for the end-times cataclysms; they'll look everywhere for answers except to God's Word.

During the tribulation, the Holy Spirit and His righteous restraint will leave the earth (2 Thess. 2:6–7), people will become hardened in sin and ungodliness as never before (cf. 2 Tim. 3:13), and evil and Satan will be unchecked. In this frenzy of ungodliness, sinners will be increasingly impervious to truth and resentful of the divine standards of holiness. Rather than alertly waiting and welcoming the return of the King of kings and Lord of lords, and turning to Him in repentance and faith, they will curse Him (Rev. 9:21).

ASK YOURSELF

What are your most difficult temptations when it comes to being alert and watchful for Christ's fulfillment of His Word? What have you learned about yourself in those moments and seasons when staying diligent in prayer is most called for, and yet your attention span falls victim to distractions that make you quickly tire of faithful waiting? What needs to be defeated or eliminated from your life in order for your devotion to Christ to remain secure?

CHRIST'S RETURN: ALERTNESS NEEDED, PART 2

"Therefore be on the alert, for you do not know which day your Lord is coming."
—MATT. 24:42

In the days prior to the flood, people were either oblivious to what was approaching (Matt. 24:37–39) or mocking of Noah at his divinely revealed notion of a flood coming to cover the earth. Only after it was too late did that generation realize its tragic destiny.

That is much the way it will be just before our Lord returns in future glory and judgment. All the calamitous events, the disruption of the heavens, and the preaching of God's witnesses will have no effect on the majority of people. They will disregard or reject the warnings and appeals from God right up until His Son appears in righteous judgment to confront them.

During the tribulation, multitudes will come to faith in Christ (Rev. 7:1–14), and there will be a wonderful revival in the nation Israel (Rom. 11:26). But nonetheless, belief, not unbelief, will dominate that period, as will ungodliness rather than godliness, and spiritual lethargy rather than alertness. Secularism and false religion will dominate the world, much like today, only in a far greater degree, whereas mankind should have an alertness toward its Lord's return.

ASK YOURSELF

What are some of the ways that individuals and churches could counteract the malaise of our age, exhibiting a strength of will, faith, and character that challenges the prevailing shallowness of modern culture? What might others see in you if you forsook the safe and generally acceptable path, choosing instead a bold, adventurous, determined lifestyle unwilling to be consumed by wastes of time? How might it help them see themselves and their outlook more seriously?

CHRIST'S RETURN: ALERTNESS NEEDED, PART 3

"Therefore be on the alert, for you do not know which day your Lord is coming."
—MATT. 24:42

When the Lord Jesus Christ finally appears again in judgment, "Then there will be two men in the field; one will be taken and one will be left. Two women will be grinding at the mill; one will be taken and one will be left" (Matt. 24:40–41). When He returns, one person will be taken in judgment and the other will remain to enter His kingdom. This parallels the figures of the sheep and goats our Lord uses in 25:32–46. The ones left will be His sheep, believers who will reign with Him during the millennium.

Right up until the consummation of history, just "before the great and glorious day of the Lord shall come . . . it shall be that everyone who calls on the name of the Lord will be saved" (Acts 2:20–21). In those final moments, everyone who sincerely calls on Christ in faith and repentance will be set apart as His chosen ones and will inherit the kingdom prepared for them.

Therefore the Lord exhorts all of us to be alert and live faithfully in anticipation of the day of His return. The phrase "be on the alert" is a present imperative in the original, indicating a call for continual expectancy.

ASK YOURSELF

How do you deal with the reality that earth's final moments are coming, that your mortal life will come to an end? What great comfort do you draw from knowing that you are His, certain to be rescued forever? What great anguish of soul do you experience for those who are rejecting so great a salvation?

CHRIST'S RETURN: READINESS REQUIRED, PART 1

"For this reason you also must be ready; for the Son of Man is coming at an hour when you do not think He will." —MATT. 24:44

Even though the people living during the tribulation will not know the exact time of Christ's appearing, His words give them detailed information regarding the extraordinary signs occurring just before He returns. So, using a symbol Jesus employs, men and women in the final days will know for sure that the thief (Matt. 24:42) will break into the house soon and they should be ready accordingly.

Obviously, our Lord does not equate His character to that of a thief; He simply compares His return with the stealth and unexpectedness a thief usually employs. Elsewhere the New Testament frequently makes this same comparison (Luke 12:35–40; 1 Thess. 5:2; 2 Peter 3:10). Obviously, thieves and burglars don't seek to rob places where they know they're expected. Nor do they carry out their actions at times when people would most expect them.

In one sense, however, the Lord will assume the role as well as the unexpectedness of a thief when He appears. For unbelievers, who will not be ready, He will arrive and take away everything they have—all they cherished and trusted in instead of Him.

ASK YOURSELF

What are the most common ways we prepare for the unexpected elements of life, everything from computer crashes to car repairs? Are you one who is more carefully cautious, thinking ahead, or have you learned most of your lessons the hard way, caught unaware and unready? How well do you apply this level of concern and attention in training your heart to be ready for Christ's return?

CHRIST'S RETURN: READINESS REQUIRED, PART 2

"For this reason you also must be ready; for the Son of Man is coming at an hour when you do not think He will." —MATT. 24:44

In this verse Jesus seems to use being "ready" to primarily denote being saved and being spiritually prepared to greet Him as Lord, Savior, and King rather than as Judge. The readiness of salvation is the indispensable element in preparedness for our Lord's return. Without it, elements such as expectancy will be meaningless, and faithfulness will be impossible. Without redemption through Christ's blood, people will face only judgment and damnation after His return.

Readiness for Christ's final appearance will be crucial because, as He reminds us again, "the Son of Man is coming at an hour when you do not think He will." Even the saints who are looking to that day with preparedness will still be astonished when He arrives because they won't know the precise day. They will be pleasantly surprised and filled with joy, but their readiness won't give them insight into the exact time of Jesus' arrival.

When the Lord does return, faithful believers will find themselves in Christ's gracious presence and also find themselves being served by His divine hand (see Luke 12:35–37).

ASK YOURSELF

How have you noticed the unsaved hedging themselves against the possibility that this coming day might occur? What actions and avoidances do they take, trying to stay somewhat acceptable to God? How are you sometimes guilty of treating your faith in God with the same manner of superstition and selective appearances? What have you learned about the emptiness of such expressions?

CHRIST'S RETURN:
FAITHFULNESS NECESSARY, PART 1

"Blessed is that slave whom his master finds so doing when he comes."
—MATT. 24:46

Here is another analogy and familiar image to underscore Jesus' point about preparedness for His return. The specific responsibility of the household slave is incidental to the Lord's main point, which is that every believer is a slave to Him and therefore obligated to serve and obey in every respect. Every saint has received a stewardship and responsibility to use his life, energy, spiritual gifts, and every good thing to serve God and glorify Him (cf. Matt. 25:19–23); this is the essence of faithfulness.

Faithful believers, who look forward to their Lord's coming, will obtain charge of all that belongs to Christ, having inherited the fullness of God's kingdom as fellow heirs with the Son (Rom. 8:17). In addition, when Jesus returns He promises, "He who overcomes, I will grant to him to sit down with Me on My throne, as I also overcame and sat down with My Father on His throne" (Rev. 3:21).

God will also hold unbelievers, represented by the evil slave (Matt. 24:48), responsible for how they handle the divine stewardship. Some, aware of their need for salvation, will nevertheless postpone trusting in Christ, thinking they have time for that later. In so behaving, they reveal unfaithfulness concerning our Lord's return ("My master is not coming for a long time," v. 48).

ASK YOURSELF

How does your life show that you are a servant of God? In what ways do you fail to exemplify this dynamic of relationship? What attitudes and actions do you adopt that are not in keeping with this understanding? How would acknowledging your grateful position help you serve with greater freedom?

CHRIST'S RETURN:
FAITHFULNESS NECESSARY, PART 2

"Blessed is that slave whom his master finds so doing when he comes."
—MATT. 24:46

The truth that God holds everyone who has ever lived accountable for what he or she possesses appears in the parable of the king (Matt. 18:23–34). Even the prodigal son (Luke 15:11–17) shows that an unbeliever can squander his divinely given stewardship. And in the end times, many such people will be honest about their unbelief—their lack of faithfulness—even wearing such openness as a badge of moral and intellectual integrity. But truthful non-Christians will be equally guilty and damned as any hypocrites they might disdain or feel superior to.

People who mince no words about their unfaithfulness and unbelief and those who are hypocrites or deceive themselves into thinking they'll eventually believe will equally suffer the torments of hell. Both groups will know inconsolable grief and unremitting pain for all eternity.

When everyone sees "the Son of Man coming on the clouds of the sky with power and great glory" (Matt. 24:30), it will draw the faithful, Christ's people, to Him in loving gratitude. But it will repel the unfaithful, unbelievers, away from Him in hateful indignation. It will be final reception and redemption for some, and final rejection and judgment for many others.

ASK YOURSELF

What have you learned in dealing with those who reject Christian faith with carefully reasoned honesty? Do they seem harder to reach than those who feign belief? How has conversing with them and hearing their arguments caused you to dig deeper, affirming again the validity of your faith? What do these individuals truly seem to be wrestling with the most?

CHRIST'S RETURN:
FAITHFULNESS NECESSARY, PART 3

"Blessed is that slave whom his master finds so doing when he comes."
—MATT. 24:46

One factor that tests believers' faithfulness in awaiting Christ's return is that it has been centuries since He first outlined the signs of His return. But why is He waiting so long to come again? One reason is that God is waiting for evil to run its course. The apostle John heard the angel shout to Christ, "Put in your sickle and reap, for the hour to reap has come, because the harvest of the earth is ripe" (Rev. 14:15). Not until an angel notifies the Son of Man that the harvest of judgment on unbelievers is completely ready will He execute that judgment. God's sovereign purpose is to allow sin to reach its evil limits.

Second, our Lord is awaiting the salvation of all whose names are in the Lamb's Book of Life. He must gather into the church all Gentile saints during the present age (Rom. 11:25), as well as all Jews who believe (v. 26).

What seems to us like a long time is but a moment to God. We must not use our finite perceptions to question the Lord's promises or to falter in our faithfulness leading to His appearance. God is simply, in His sovereign patience and love, allowing the fullest possible period for people to repent and believe (see 2 Peter 3:3–9).

ASK YOURSELF

What kind of patience are you exercising yourself as you pray for and share truth with the unsaved people within your reach? How often do your interactions with them turn into arguments and accusations? How should we manage the seriousness of salvation with the perfect timing of God in bringing it about?

CHRIST'S RETURN:
FAITHFULNESS NECESSARY, PART 4

"Blessed is that slave whom his master finds so doing when he comes."
—MATT. 24:46

Christians today need to be faithfully prepared for Christ's coming in the rapture of the church, even as end-times believers will need to be prepared for His return to set up His millennial kingdom. Many passages encourage us to these ends, such as:

> [You know] the time, that it is already the hour for you to awaken from sleep; for now salvation is nearer to us than when we believed. The night is almost gone, and the day is near. Therefore let us lay aside the deeds of darkness and put on the armor of light . . . put on the Lord Jesus Christ, and make no provision for the flesh in regard to its lusts. (Rom. 13:11–12, 14)

Paul also commended the Corinthians for "awaiting eagerly the revelation of our Lord Jesus Christ" (1 Cor. 1:7), and reminded the Philippians that "our citizenship is in heaven, from which also we eagerly wait for a Savior, the Lord Jesus Christ" (Phil. 3:20). Hebrews' author further encourages us, "Let us consider how to stimulate one another to love and good deeds, not forsaking our own assembling together, as is the habit of some, but encouraging one another; and all the more as you see the day drawing near" (Heb. 10:24–25; see also James 5:8; 1 Peter 4:7; 1 John 2:18; Rev. 22:20).

ASK YOURSELF

What makes the end of time no longer a thing of dread and fear but rather a cause for great celebration and excitement? How eager are you, as the day draws ever closer, to relinquish your hold on this world and to embrace with joy the promise of life forever with your Lord and Savior?

PARABLE OF THE TEN VIRGINS: BRIDESMAIDS, PART 1

"Then the kingdom of heaven will be comparable to ten virgins, who took their lamps and went out to meet the bridegroom." —MATT. 25:1

The message of this parable simply illustrates truths Jesus has been teaching about His return: He will judge and reward; the date will be unexpected, so people must be ready. Once Christ appears at the end of days, the opportunity for salvation will be gone forever.

This story is not an allegory; every little aspect does not have a mystical meaning that we should speculate about. Not every detail, mentioned or unmentioned, has a bearing on Jesus' main point. For Him, the parable is clear and complete.

The word translated "to meet" literally means "a meeting" and often designated the official welcoming of a dignitary. In the context of the parable's portraying the coming of Christ's kingdom, and in the midst of His ongoing teaching about His return, "the bridegroom" obviously refers to the Lord Himself. The "ten virgins" or bridesmaids represent His professed followers, and the "lamps" depict their external identity with His church. The lamps further symbolize an expectation of Jesus' imminent return, and they illustrate the preparedness and readiness of the young women to receive their divine bridegroom, the Lord Jesus, when He arrives to take them into His wedding feast, "the kingdom of heaven."

ASK YOURSELF

What are some of the "lamps" you are failing to keep ablaze and effective as you wait for the end of life and the coming of Christ? What are you choosing to keep lit in their place, and how is the light from such substitutes proving inadequate for what you truly need?

Parable of the Ten Virgins: Bridesmaids, Part 2

*"Five of them were foolish, and five were prudent. For when the
foolish took their lamps, they took no oil with them, but the prudent
took oil in flasks along with their lamps." —*Matt. 25:2–4

In appearance the ten virgins are the same, each wearing an appropriate
wedding garment and carrying the required lamp for the wedding procession. But they were not all identical; half were foolish (unprepared)
and half were prudent (prepared). Proof that half of the bridesmaids, in
spite of their garments, were unprepared is that they brought along no
oil. Their lamps had nothing to burn in them—nothing to produce light
and meaning. A torch with no fuel is worthless, even as a profession of
faith in Christ with no real relationship to Him is infinitely more worthless, because a person remains in spiritual darkness.

Similar to the man without proper clothes in the parable of the wedding feast (Matt. 22:11–13), five of the young women were without correct lamps. They had a form of godliness but no spiritual power because
they didn't belong to God (cf. 2 Tim. 3:5). Outwardly they seemed committed to the Lord, but they had no heart commitment because His saving grace had not regenerated them, and their faith was dead (James
2:17). The five were in darkness rather than light.

ASK YOURSELF

How have you experienced spiritual darkness in your own life?
How do you typically respond when you find yourself disappointed
with the direction God has taken you and confused about where
to go next? What are the lights that have held out hope and
encouragement for you in the midst of despair?

PARABLE OF THE TEN VIRGINS: BRIDESMAIDS, PART 3

*"Now while the bridegroom was delaying, they
all got drowsy and began to sleep." —*MATT. 25:5

The statement "the bridegroom was delaying" reminds us again that we can't know precisely when our Lord will return. At this point much time will have passed since His first coming, and most people will be conducting business as usual when Christ does return (Matt. 24:28, 43). (Jesus may also have been telling the apostles that His return would be later than they anticipated; see Luke 19:11.) Even the short period in the end times between signs of His coming and His actual appearance will make some think Christ is delaying His return.

We can support that notion by noting that all the bridesmaids became drowsy and sleepy. In greater or lesser preparedness, they were all waiting for the bridegroom with some sense of expectancy. Our text does not say for sure that sleep represents a lazy lack of readiness or faithlessness. That the prepared, faithful women also fell asleep shows that true believers will not know exactly when Christ will come again. In fact, the sleep of the foolish might indicate a false sense of security, whereas the sleep of the wise bridesmaids could indicate the real sense of security in their Lord.

ASK YOURSELF

What keeps you from being able to rest securely in the Lord, feeling doubtful or impatient in the face of situations in which the reality of God's ever-present involvement is disguised from view? What would be the greatest benefits of letting your faith in Christ determine your outlook and opinions, even when visual signals indicate no reason for such faith?

Parable of the Ten Virgins: Bridesmaids, Part 4

"Then the kingdom of heaven will be comparable to ten virgins, who took their lamps and went out to meet the bridegroom." —MATT. 25:1

Normal life should continue for the believer who eagerly looks for Christ's return. Christians do not prove they are ready for the Lord's appearance by reclusively and idly waiting for Him somewhere but by enthusiastically and faithfully serving Him. But this will not exclude such normal earthly activities as eating, drinking, working, and sleeping.

It will not be their involvement and faithful responsibility in the mundane activities of life that will distinguish the prepared from the unprepared when Jesus Christ returns. Rather, the distinguishing factor will be the supernatural, heart-motivated, faithful obedience to God that only believers will possess.

Commentator William Arnot observed more than a century ago:

> There is not a more grand or a more beautiful spectacle on earth than a great assembly reverently worshipping God together. No line visible to human eye divides into two parts the goodly company; yet the goodly company is divided into two parts. The Lord reads our character and marks our place. The Lord knows them that are his, and them that are not his, in every assembly of worshippers.

ASK YOURSELF

Make this a day to recommit yourself to looking forward to His return, engaging in ongoing worship that encompasses the whole of your life—your churchgoing, your errand making, your business calendar, your downtime. What would watchfulness look like at any point of your morning, afternoon, or evening? If inattentiveness and complacency have been given room to rule in your heart, resolve to devote the rest of your life to more significant things.

Parable of the Ten Virgins: the Bridegroom, Part 1

"But at midnight there was a shout, 'Behold, the bridegroom!
Come out to meet him.'" —MATT. 25:6

All the ten virgins knew the bridegroom would come soon, so they waited for him at the bride's house. They knew the final wedding festivities were imminent, but until the shout announcing his arrival, they didn't know the exact time the groom would come. Likewise, people alive at the end of the tribulation will have seen all the signs of Christ's coming and will realize His appearance is very near (cf. Matt. 24:30).

As soon as they heard the shout of arrival, all the bridesmaids trimmed their lamps (25:7), probably by cutting off the ragged edges of cloth on their torches and soaking the cloth with oil to make the lamp ready for lighting. Then the foolish bridesmaids realized they should have brought oil. Previously unconcerned about that, perhaps they had believed they could run to the shop and purchase more oil at any time. Or maybe they had thought they could borrow some from the other women (v. 8). The reason for their negligence is really irrelevant. Since they had much warning of the bridegroom's coming and plenty of opportunity to be prepared, nothing could excuse their failure to be ready.

ASK YOURSELF

What could be causing the "oil" of your preparedness to be in short supply, not readily available when a crisis or question arises that demands faith to be on cue at a moment's notice? What do you notice to be different about those who are strong and prayerful and encouraging to others when life most demands it? How could God transform you into someone who operates with that kind of faith?

Parable of the Ten Virgins: the Bridegroom, Part 2

"The foolish said to the prudent, 'Give us some of your oil, for our lamps are going out.'" —MATT. 25:8

When Christ comes at the end of the tribulation, many professed believers will be panicked on realizing they actually have no spiritual life. They will be self-deceived, having thought that mere association with church and religion would make them part of Christ's body of believers, or that many good works were sufficient (cf. Matt. 7:22–23). Certainly they will have ignored Paul's admonition: "Test yourselves to see if you are in the faith; examine yourselves! Or do you not recognize this about yourselves, that Jesus Christ is in you—unless indeed you fail the test?" (2 Cor. 13:5).

That the prudent bridesmaids refused to share oil with the foolish (Matt. 25:9) was not merely because the prudent were selfish and uncaring, but because they didn't have enough oil to share. Just as one cannot transfer a segment of his physical life to another, neither can he share spiritual life, which is distinct to each person. Spiritual life is a gift from the Holy Spirit—the saved can't themselves become saviors. When unbelievers must appear before God's judgment seat, whether at death or the Lord's coming, the intercession of all the believers who ever lived will do them no good. Then there will be no second chance, no hope.

ASK YOURSELF

Who might you be tempted to blame for your faith being less strong and vibrant than it ought to be? What have people done to you, what have your circumstances set in motion that has made your ability to trust in God a challenge? But what never gets dealt with when passing blame supersedes personal responsibility?

PARABLE OF THE TEN VIRGINS:
THE BRIDEGROOM, PART 3

"Go instead to the dealers and buy [oil] for yourselves." —MATT. 25:9*b*

Genuine salvation can't be purchased. The buying of oil from the dealers simply refers to obtaining redemption from its only source, God. Jesus taught a similar concept in His parables of the treasure and the pearl of great price (Matt. 13:44–46). There the discoverer sold everything to acquire that which was worth more than all else. The price for salvation is the complete giving up of our own merit, which has no intrinsic value anyway but must be surrendered so as not to block God's grace.

Even the apostle Paul wished he could give up his own salvation if that would save his fellow Jews (Rom. 9:3–4). But he knew that was impossible, because saving faith in Jesus Christ must be individually appropriated. Our Lord Himself stressed the necessity of such careful faith:

> Everyone who comes to Me and hears My words and acts on them, I will show you whom he is like: he is like a man building a house, who dug deep and laid a foundation on the rock; and when a flood occurred, the torrent burst against that house and could not shake it, because it had been well built. (Luke 6:47–48; cf. v. 49)

ASK YOURSELF

What does the solid foundation of God's grace mean when you are bombarded with guilt over past sins? What does it provide when others give you the impression that you are not doing as much for God as you should? What peace of mind could be yours if you were always totally convinced His grace is all you need?

PARABLE OF THE TEN VIRGINS: THE BRIDEGROOM, PART 4

"And while they were going away to make the purchase, the bridegroom came, and those who were ready went in with him to the wedding feast; and the door was shut." —MATT. 25:10

The tragedy for the foolish bridesmaids was that there was no further opportunity to buy oil for their lamps because all the shops were closed.

In another of Jesus' many illustrations of lost salvation opportunity, He said,

> Once the head of the house gets up and shuts the door, and you begin to stand outside and knock on the door, saying, "Lord open up to us!" then He will answer and say to you, "I do not know where you are from." Then you will begin to say, "We ate and drank in Your presence, and You taught in our streets"; and He will say, "I tell you, I do not know where you are from; depart from Me, all you evildoers." In that place there will be weeping and gnashing of teeth when you see Abraham and Isaac . . . in the kingdom of God, but yourselves being thrown out. (Luke 13:25–28)

It will be terrifying in the last day when unbelievers face God and realize they are eternally lost. Surely it will replicate the feelings the scoffers of Noah's day had when they faced rising floodwaters knowing they would drown, with no chance to enter the closed door of the ark.

ASK YOURSELF

As a believer, you have absolute assurance that a heavenly reception awaits you at the end of your earthly life. But is there any uncomfortable choice or action before you today that you've put off longer than you should? What if this day represented your last real chance to act on it?

PARABLE OF THE TEN VIRGINS: THE WARNING

"Be on the alert then, for you do not know the day nor the hour." —MATT. 25:13

Once again Jesus calls on those living at the end of the tribulation to be alert because they won't know the exact date or hour of His return. The catastrophic signs would indicate only generally the nearness of His appearing.

Our Lord had issued a more detailed warning just a day earlier in the temple:

> Be on guard, so that your hearts will not be weighted down with dissipation and drunkenness and the worries of life, and that day will not come on you suddenly like a trap; for it will come upon all those who dwell on the face of all the earth. But keep on the alert at all times, praying that you may have strength to escape all these things that are about to take place, and to stand before the Son of Man. (Luke 21:34–36)

Tennyson's epic *Idylls of the King* borrows figures from this parable to rebuke Queen Guinevere about the cost of sin:

> No light, so late, and dark and chill the night!
> O let us in, that we may find the light.
> Too late, too late, ye cannot enter now.
> Have we not heard the Bridegroom is so sweet?
> O let us in, tho' late, to kiss His feet!
> No, no, too late! Ye cannot enter now.

ASK YOURSELF

How do you tend to react after you've let a deadline pass without handling your responsibility well or on time? What could anyone have done to spare you the shame and anxiety? How could you perhaps do the same for others, as it relates to their own salvation?

PARABLE OF THE TALENTS: RESPONSIBILITY, PART 1

"To one he gave five talents, to another, two, and to another, one, each according to his own ability; and he went on his journey." —MATT. 25:15

Reference to the man's slaves supports the idea that Jesus here illustrated the organizational church, composed of professed disciples, and not humanity in general. The Gospels refer to many as Christ's disciples, even though some were false—"disciples" offended regarding eating Jesus' flesh and drinking His blood (John 6:42–66). Judas Iscariot was known as a disciple and an apostle. Because they are attached to the outward church, Christ entrusts even false followers with certain of His possessions.

The term rendered "slaves" (Matt. 25:14) denoted all kinds of bondservants. This included ordinary laborers and household servants as well as skilled tradesmen and educated professionals. Masters owned all slaves as property, and often had the power of life and death over them.

The numbers of talents given to the slaves in this parable have no significance other than to illustrate a variety of responsibilities, from the greater to the lesser. But it's notable that the owner granted responsibilities to "each according to his own ability." The man knew each slave well and entrusted to them only the responsibility he expected each could handle well—no unreasonable expectations were imposed.

ASK YOURSELF

What are the specific investments God has made in you, whether by virtue of your family background, or your natural abilities, or your relationships with others? How are you utilizing each of these in contributing to His kingdom? Which, however, have you chosen to use for your own selfish ends and wants?

PARABLE OF THE TALENTS: RESPONSIBILITY, PART 2

"To one he gave five talents, to another, two, and to another, one, each according to his own ability; and he went on his journey." —MATT. 25:15

Here "talents" refers to money, although the word itself defines a simple measure of weight. A coin's weight and composition determined its value. For instance, a gold talent had great value, a silver talent less, and a bronze or copper one considerably less value. But the actual worth of the coins given to each slave is beside Jesus' main point, which is the common accountability for differing levels of responsibility, based on individual ability.

The Lord depicts just three levels of responsibility, but this implies a wide range of abilities among people. Men and women also differ a great deal in opportunity and privilege. Some church members have known scriptural truth since childhood, whereas others know only the basics of the faith. Genuine believers also receive spiritual gifts that differ widely from one person to another (1 Cor. 12:4–11). Some Christians are around other saints regularly and continually learn and grow. Others, however, are the only Christians in their families or communities. Our Lord sovereignly knows everyone's gifts, abilities, and situations, and He graciously assigns responsibilities accordingly.

ASK YOURSELF

How have you perhaps heaped upon yourself a level of responsibility that is not yours to carry? How much of the load you bear is measured not by what God has tasked you to manage, but rather by what others are expecting and demanding of you— or that you are demanding of yourself? How well are you able to resist and say no to things that are not within your scope?

PARABLE OF THE TALENTS: RESPONSIBILITY, PART 3

"To one he gave five talents, to another, two, and to another, one, each according to his own ability; and he went on his journey." —MATT. 25:15

Different levels of responsibility existed even among the apostles. Clearly, Peter, James, and John were the inner circle, with Peter the most prominent of the three. In the Jerusalem church, Jesus' half brother James became the recognized leader, with commensurate influence and responsibility. The parable of the talents seems to imply that, even through the millennial kingdom and into eternity, the saints will continue to possess different levels of responsibility.

For our Lord the issue here is what each slave does with the appropriate responsibility he has divinely received. Ideally the faithful servant should have the heart motivation to accomplish as much as possible during his master's absence. And the master desired equal effort according to each one's ability, not necessarily the same quantitative return from each slave.

The slaves with five and two talents did not produce equal profits but equal percentages of the respective talents they'd received (Matt. 25:16–17). Similarly, believers with different capabilities and opportunities might produce differing results while ministering with equal faithfulness. As the apostle Paul instructs, "each will receive his own reward according to his own labor" (1 Cor. 3:8).

ASK YOURSELF

What are some of our common motivations for taking on the responsibilities that belong to others? More recognition or verbal thanks? Less effort or time involvement? What does God uniquely know about you that makes you perfectly suited for the jobs He has called you to perform? Why would you be insufficient or unsatisfied doing anything else?

PARABLE OF THE TALENTS: THE REACTIONS

"Immediately the one who had received the five talents went and traded with them, and gained five more talents. In the same manner the one who had received the two talents gained two more. But he who received the one talent went away, and dug a hole in the ground and hid his master's money." —MATT. 25:16–18

The man with five talents represents the disciple whose highest desire is to serve God, obeying what Jesus called the greatest commandment, to "love the Lord your God with all your heart and with all your soul and with all your might" (Deut. 6:5; cf. Matt. 22:37).

Even though the slave with two talents had less to work with than the first, he worked just as diligently and faithfully. Like his fellow servant, he doubled his master's money. Both men maximized the opportunities they had received.

The third man's reaction was radically different, however. Hiding valuables in the ground was common in the ancient world; it was an easy and practical way to protect jewelry and coins. But burying your talent as he did was no way to conduct business and earn a profit. The third slave, instead, should have responded as the other two. Like the believer with modest resources who makes the most of what he has, this man had the obligation to invest his single talent and realize the optimum results.

ASK YOURSELF

How could you begin to appropriate a skill, possession, or capability that you've largely dismissed as unimportant before, something you've resisted exposing to public use for fear it might embarrass you or call forth more than you wanted to sacrifice? Do you believe God can still wring value from this?

PARABLE OF THE TALENTS: OUR RECKONING, PART 1

*"Now after a long time the master of those slaves came
and settled accounts with them."* —MATT. 25:19

In telling his master that he had gained five more talents (Matt. 25:20), the first slave was not boasting but simply reporting the facts. He knew he had merely done what was expected of him, and had followed Jesus' teaching: "when you do all the things which are commanded you, say, 'We are unworthy slaves; we have done only that which we ought to have done'" (Luke 17:10).

Late in his life, Paul told Timothy:

I am already being poured out as a drink offering, and the time of my departure has come. I have fought the good fight, I have finished the course, I have kept the faith; in the future there is laid up for me the crown of righteousness, which the Lord, the righteous Judge, will award to me on that day; and not only to me, but also to all who have loved His appearing. (2 Tim. 4:6–8)

Paul, like any faithful servant, was confident God knew his integrity and would reward him according to His gracious promises. And in this parable the master commends the first slave's attitude more than his accomplishment (25:21). God's priority for us is excellent character that expresses itself in excellent service.

ASK YOURSELF

Who do you need to recognize for the faithful way they have ministered to you, or performed a work task, or shown Christlikeness in their everyday lives? Are you quick enough to notice these qualities in your spouse, your children, the people you deal with on a routine basis? Would they see this same kind of quality in the work you do and the way you do it?

PARABLE OF THE TALENTS: OUR RECKONING, PART 2

*"Now after a long time the master of those slaves came
and settled accounts with them."* —MATT. 25:19

The master highly rewards his first slave: "You were faithful with a few things, I will put you in charge of many things; enter into the joy of your master" (Matt. 25:21*b*). Not only will our Father give more earthly responsibility to saints who are faithful, but He will give them greater opportunity for eternal service. Both in the millennial and eternal aspects of the kingdom, faithful believers will receive greater responsibilities over more significant things.

For certain, heaven will not be boring for us. It will be an infinite period of ever-expanding and increasingly joyous service. And this will be most evident for those who served their Lord most unswervingly on earth. Everyone in heaven will have eternal life and will be equally righteous, Christlike, and glorious. Perfection there will have no degrees. The distinctions will be in opportunities and levels of service. The redeemed will possess ranks, similar to the angels, and God will determine those ranks and resulting service by the saint's devotedness in this life.

Everything done in heaven will be perfectly right and satisfying. Whatever one's status there, it will be according to God's perfect will and therefore will be enjoyed and lived out forever in perfect, harmonious fashion.

ASK YOURSELF

How could we begin to appropriate more of this heavenly dynamic
in our experience today? At least from your perspective, could
you care less about comparing yourself to others? Could you
do your work simply for the joy of pleasing the Lord? Could
you serve without worrying what it will cost you?

PARABLE OF THE TALENTS: OUR RECKONING, PART 3

*"Now after a long time the master of those slaves came
and settled accounts with them." —*MATT. 25:19

The master in the parable also gives a second reward to the faithful first slave: "enter into the joy of your master" (v. 21c). In addition to the heavenly opportunity for greater service, believers will share the divine joy of their Lord, and that on top of the divine sinlessness and holiness they will acquire.

Imagine the ecstasy we as saints will experience when we realize that our sinfulness is forever abolished and our righteousness forever established. It was the wonderful prospect of securing this gracious redemption that motivated the Lord Jesus: "for the joy set before Him [He] endured the cross, despising the shame, and . . . sat down at the right hand of the throne of God" (Heb. 12:2).

The second faithful slave makes the same report of doubling his talents, and the master's response parallels that to the first slave: "Well done, good and faithful slave. You were faithful with a few things, I will put you in charge of many things; enter into the joy of your master" (Matt. 25:23).

The unfaithful slave, by contrast, did not give the master any talent earnings but only excuses (vv. 24–25). Jesus identifies this man as belonging to the master (v. 14), but the reckoning for him is drastically different from that for his fellow slaves.

ASK YOURSELF

How does the possibility of greater reward distress you, either by confusing you about heaven or leaving you concerned that you will not measure up at the final reckoning? How does it rather motivate you to surrender yourself even more devotedly to your calling in Christ while on earth?

PARABLE OF THE TALENTS: OUR RECKONING, PART 4

*"Now after a long time the master of those slaves came
and settled accounts with them."* —MATT. 25:19

In two distinct ways the third slave reveals a superficial relationship to the Lord and a lack of genuine regeneration.

First, he did not even attempt to use his talent for his master's profit. He did recognize the master as his legal owner and probably pretended to honor him while he was gone. Thus he did not behave immorally or selfishly like the prodigal son (Luke 15:11–32) or the unmerciful servant (Matt. 18:21–35). He simply neglected the stewardship the master gave him.

Second, he manifested a counterfeit loyalty by denouncing his master's character, accusing him of being "a hard man" (25:24), essentially of being unmerciful and dishonest. This false view proves that the third slave had no true knowledge of or relationship with his owner. Like the unregenerate church member with no spiritual fruit or worship, the man was blind to God's grace, mercy, kindness, and glory because he had never surrendered himself to divine sovereignty and saving grace.

Similarly, unconverted churchgoers reside in the realm of the Lord's redeemed community and have exposure to teaching from the Word and fellowship with His people. Nevertheless, people like the third slave make no positive, saving response to the gospel and thus render no truly fruitful service.

ASK YOURSELF

How have you reacted over the years to this story Jesus told, one you have likely heard often? Which of the three characters most closely resembles the person you are today? How do you intend to learn from this lesson and apply it to your life going forward?

PARABLE OF THE TALENTS: OUR RECKONING, PART 5

" 'Then you ought to have put my money in the bank, and on my arrival
I would have received my money back with interest.' " —MATT. 25:27

The culture of Jesus' day had a banking system that was similar in many respects to our contemporary system. The top rate someone could charge on a loan was probably about 12 percent simple interest, and the percentage you could earn on a deposit was about half that. The disobedient slave could have therefore, without much effort, earned at least 6 percent by depositing his one talent. That he didn't even make an attempt illustrates his complete irresponsibility and indifference to his master.

Even if this slave's accusation, "I knew you to be a hard man, reaping where you did not sow and gathering where you scattered no seed" (25:24), had been valid, it wouldn't have excused his indolence toward his owner's concerns. Actually the man didn't care at all for his master one way or the other, and his excuse was probably more spur of the moment than planned. He didn't expect any reckoning with the master, and when the owner's return caught him by surprise, the third slave simply made an outrageous, illogical charge. His own rhetoric and previous inaction left him guilty.

ASK YOURSELF

Is there an area in your life where you're failing to produce even a minimum amount of obedience to God's command? What could be the root cause of this disregard, especially since you sincerely seek to follow the Lord in most respects? How do you seek to justify your indifference to this one point of difficulty?

PARABLE OF THE TALENTS: OUR RECKONING, PART 6

*"Now after a long time the master of those slaves came
and settled accounts with them."* —MATT. 25:19

The first two slaves in the parable served the Lord with their talents before His return, which they looked for, and thereby proved the genuineness of their salvation. But the third slave laid aside his talent and did
only what he wanted. He claimed to be God's servant but definitely
proved otherwise.

The third servant received the displeasure of the master not merely
for losing profit but because the man squandered his opportunity. According to our Lord, having little to work with is no excuse for not investing what's available. Even someone who knows little Scripture and
has few talents and service opportunities must use those blessings for
God's service.

The profits earned by the first two slaves represent the achievement
and enjoyment of lives faithfully dedicated to God's kingdom. The third
slave's failure to properly use his talent depicts a useless, worthless life in
which profession of faith in Christ turns out to be false and a careless
waste of opportunity and blessing.

The first two men were genuinely alive spiritually with resultant
faithful service; however the third had merely the appearance of spiritual
life with no accompanying good works. Two built their houses on solid
rock; the other built his house on shifting sand (see Matt. 7:24–27).

ASK YOURSELF

How do you help yourself maintain an awareness of God's right
to hold you accountable for your daily actions and decisions?
What are the first kinds of safeguards you ignore or avoid
when you're not serving Him wholeheartedly?

PARABLE OF THE TALENTS: THE REWARD

"For to everyone who has, more shall be given, and he will have an abundance; but from the one who does not have, even what he does have shall be taken away."
—MATT. 25:29

Every local church contains tares that, except to God, are indistinguishable from the wheat (Matt. 13:24–30). We can't determine the true character of fellow church members by their outward deeds, because unbelievers can be quite active and seemingly interested in the church's mission. But God sees whatever "ministry" they do as of no service to Him or benefit to His kingdom. In the realm of God's sovereign kingdom, the only acceptable service offered to Him will be that rendered by genuine saints.

Jesus presents the third servant as not simply an unfaithful Christian but a faithless non-Christian. A weak believer who fails to make the best use of his abilities, spiritual gifts, and service opportunities will have his work "burned up, [and] he will suffer loss; but he himself will be saved, yet so as through fire" (1 Cor. 3:15). Someone like the third servant, however, has no saving faith at all, and his seeming good works and church ministry will count for nothing. That person one day hears Christ's devastating words "I never knew you; depart from Me, you who practice lawlessness" (Matt. 7:23).

ASK YOURSELF

Why are some unbelievers more diligent in serving, helping, caring, and showing loyalty than a noticeable number of Christians? On the other hand, why are many of the valuable ministries performed by faithful believers deemed of little importance to the vast majority of the world? Why is the practice of comparing good works such a fruitless exercise?

THE VINE AND VINEDRESSER

"I am the true vine, and My Father is the vinedresser." —JOHN 15:1

By Jesus' time, Israel's apostasy had made her an empty vine and disqualified her as a channel of God's blessings. Such blessings now derive solely from union with Christ, "the true vine." "True" describes the real as distinct from the type (cf. Heb. 8:2), and the genuine as opposed to the counterfeit (cf. Rev. 3:7, 14). The Son is the true vine in the same sense as He's the true light (John 1:9), the ultimate revelation of spiritual truth, as well as being the true bread from heaven (6:32), the sole source of spiritual sustenance.

Jesus' designation of the Father as "the vinedresser" while He, the Son, is the vine does not at all diminish Christ's deity or full equality with God. During His earthly ministry, Jesus often assumed a subordinate role to His Father. Besides, the purpose of this analogy is to underscore the Father's care for the vine and the branches.

The word translated "vinedresser" designates someone who tills the soil—in other words, a farmer (2 Tim. 2:6) or vine-grower (Mark 12:1–2). In addition to the planting, fertilizing, and watering of a vine, a vinedresser had to remove branches that didn't bear fruit and prune ones that did, enabling them to produce more fruit. Using these two types of branches, the Lord's analogy instructs us about the bearing of spiritual fruit.

ASK YOURSELF

How have you experienced the work of the "vinedresser" in your own life? What has He been wisely willing to remove from you in order to keep you growing in a fruitful, productive manner, free from distraction and deception?

BLESSINGS OF THE ABIDING BRANCHES, PART 1

*"I am the vine, you are the branches; he who abides in Me
and I in him, he bears much fruit."* —JOHN 15:5a

Three distinguishing traits of true branches are notable in Jesus' analogy. First, they bear fruit, which most clearly contrasts them from false branches. Second, they abide (remain, continue) in His love. And third, they live according to the source of life, obeying God's commandments by following the Son's obedient example. As our Lord had earlier instructed those who would follow Him, "If you continue in My word, then you are truly disciples of Mine" (John 8:31). Consistent obedience always proves that our love for Christ is real (14:15, 21, 23).

This doesn't mean, however, that we as believers will always obey the Lord perfectly; there are times when we fall short and behave immaturely. As Paul told the Corinthians:

I, brethren, could not speak to you as to spiritual men, but as to men of flesh, as to infants in Christ. I gave you milk to drink, not solid food; for you were not yet able to receive it. Indeed, even now you are not yet able, for you are still fleshly. For since there is jealousy and strife among you, are you not fleshly, and are you not walking like mere men? (1 Cor. 3:1–3)

The exhortation to abide thus applies to unbelievers, *and* to believers who are not abiding to the fullest.

ASK YOURSELF

What are some of the works Christ has produced in you that could only be coming from His righteousness empowering you, never from anything you could work up on the inside? How have you proven your own feeble inadequacy time and again?

BLESSINGS OF THE ABIDING BRANCHES, PART 2

"And every branch that bears fruit, He prunes it so that it may bear more fruit."
—JOHN 15:2*b*

God prunes the true branches by removing whatever keeps them from righteous and fruitful results. Pruning includes divine discipline, as Scripture reminds us, "It is for discipline that you endure; God deals with you as sons; for what son is there whom his father does not discipline?" (Heb. 12:7; cf. vv. 8–11; 1 Cor. 11:32).

But discipline, which might involve trials and pain, is only the handle of God's knife; the blade is His Word. Scripture is crucial in believers' initial cleansing at salvation (cf. Rom. 1:16), and it continues to prune, purge, and cleanse them. The writer of Hebrews sets this out clearly: "For the word of God is living and active and sharper than any two-edged sword, and piercing as far as the division of soul and spirit, of both joints and marrow, and able to judge the thoughts and intentions of the heart" (4:12). God uses adversity and suffering to prepare His own for Scripture's pruning: "Before I was afflicted I went astray, but now I keep Your word. . . . It is good for me that I was afflicted, that I may learn Your statutes" (Ps. 119:67, 71; cf. 94:12).

ASK YOURSELF

What is your usual reaction to the Lord's discipline? How are you able to discern, recognize, and respond to it, rather than automatically considering it something to rebuke and run from? What are some of the most profound lessons you've learned from His fatherly pressure in recent days, and what might keep Him from having to exert His corrective hand concerning this issue again?

BLESSINGS OF THE ABIDING BRANCHES, PART 3

"Abide in Me, and I in you. As the branch cannot bear fruit of itself unless it abides in the vine, so neither can you unless you abide in Me." —JOHN 15:4

Jesus' words on the vine and branches emphasize significant truths concerning Christian conduct. First, every true branch believer who abides in Christ, the true vine, will bear spiritual fruit—there's no such thing as a fruitless believer. John the Baptist challenged people to "bear fruit in keeping with repentance' (Matt. 3:8). In Luke 6:43 our Lord declares, "There is no good tree which produces bad fruit, nor, on the other hand, a bad tree which produces good fruit" (cf. Matt. 3:10; 17:17–20).

Second, Jesus' true disciples can't bear fruit on their own, just as He taught, "apart from Me you can do nothing" (John 15:5). There are times when they will have lapses of unfaithfulness, but genuine spiritual branches attached to the true vine will ultimately produce fruit (cf. Ps. 92:12–14; Matt. 13:23). And the apostle Paul describes such fruit by spiritual qualities: "The fruit of the Spirit is love, joy, peace, patience, kindness, goodness, faithfulness, gentleness, self-control" (Gal. 5:22–23).

Praise is also another key spiritual fruit: "Through Him then, let us continually offer up a sacrifice of praise to God, that is, the fruit of lips that give thanks to His name" (Heb. 13:15).

ASK YOURSELF

Have you been frustrated lately by your lack of faithfulness, your apparent inability to resist temptation and translate your love for God into grateful obedience? What encouragement do you draw from knowing that your ability to follow is ordained by God, that He is already enough to give you what you need?

BLESSINGS OF THE ABIDING BRANCHES, PART 4

"Abide in Me, and I in you. As the branch cannot bear fruit of itself unless it abides in the vine, so neither can you unless you abide in Me." —JOHN 15:4

Scripture without doubt classifies sacrificial love in meeting others' needs as spiritual fruit. As Paul recognized the Philippians' financial support of his ministry, he reported to them, "Not that I seek the gift, but I seek the fruit that abounds to your account" (Phil. 4:17 NKJV; cf. Rom. 15:28).

We may also define righteous, God-honoring behavior in general as spiritual fruit (see Matt. 3:8; 13:23). Paul urged the Colossians to be "bearing fruit in every good work" (Col. 1:10), because all believers were "created in Christ Jesus for good works, which God prepared beforehand so that we would walk in them" (Eph. 2:10; cf. Phil. 1:11).

Finally, Scripture calls converts to the gospel another type of spiritual fruit—not the artificial fruit of so-called converts who make shallow "decisions for Christ" but true disciples who abide obediently in the true vine. Jesus said of His sacrificial death, "Truly, truly, I say to you, unless a grain of wheat falls into the earth and dies, it remains alone; but if it dies, it bears much fruit" (John 12:24; cf. 4:36; Rom. 1:13).

ASK YOURSELF

Why are such good works as these often a sacrifice? What are some of the costs and inconveniences you must undergo personally in order to be kind toward others, to remain sensitive to their needs, to invest yourself in sharing the message of Christ with one who still questions His truth and grace? In what ways have you sometimes decided that the sacrifice is more than you want to make?

BLESSINGS OF THE ABIDING BRANCHES, PART 5

*"If you abide in Me, and My words abide in you, ask
whatever you wish, and it will be done for you."* —JOHN 15:7

This sweeping promise of blessing by Jesus presupposes that one has
met three conditions. First, the prayer He promises to answer must be offered in His name—consistent with His person and will and so that His
answer might show forth His glory.

Second, the promise applies only to those who abide in Him. God has
not promised to answer the prayers of unbelievers. However, He may
choose to do so sometimes in accordance with His sovereign purposes.

The third condition for realizing Jesus' promise is that His words must
abide in the person offering prayer. "Words" refers to the individual utter-
ances of our Lord. Answered prayer comes only to people whose lives are
guided and directed by Scripture's specific commands (cf. Ps. 37:4).

True branches also have the blessing of living lives that glorify God
(John 15:8). God's glory is the greatest theme in the universe, and it is
our highest duty and privilege as believers to live lives that contribute to
that glory. Paul expressed it this way: "I will not presume to speak of
anything except what Christ has accomplished through me" (Rom. 15:18;
cf. Gal 2:20).

ASK YOURSELF

What makes "abiding" in Christ such a challenge at times? What are
some of the first signals that indicate you are beginning to pull away
from the Lord and pursue other things as your top priority at the
moment, or to find your release and fulfillment in substitute
pleasures? How has God chosen in times past to draw you back
toward fellowship with Himself, and how have you responded?

BLESSINGS OF THE ABIDING BRANCHES, PART 6

"If you abide in Me, and My words abide in you, ask whatever you wish, and it will be done for you." —JOHN 15:7

A further blessing Christ promises to those who abide in Him is His divine love: "If you keep My commandments, you will abide in My love; just as I have kept My Father's commandments and abide in His love" (John 15:10). Faithful obedience is essential to experiencing God's gracious and merciful love.

The culminating blessing for all abiding branches, and the one to which all the others contribute, is full and complete joy. Jesus promises to convey to Christians that same joy He already shares with His Father: "These things I have spoken to you so that My joy may be in you, and that your joy may be made full" (v. 11). This divine joy will permeate and guide the lives of all who live in communion with their Lord. In His High Priestly Prayer shortly after this instruction, Christ repeated this promise: "these things I speak in the world so that they may have My joy made full in themselves" (17:13). And as David learned tragically after his sin with Bathsheba, only the obedient experience this joy: "Restore to me the joy of Your salvation" (Ps. 51:12). On the other hand, obedient saints receive "joy inexpressible and full of glory" (1 Peter 1:8).

ASK YOURSELF

In what times have you experienced the deepest sense of joy in Christ, when the reality of His grace, presence, and provision have rested most tangibly on your heart? Out of what painful circumstances have you been the most surprised to possess this joy? Why is it unlike anything an unbeliever can know?

BURNING OF THE NONABIDING BRANCHES, PART 1

"If anyone does not abide in Me, he is thrown away as a branch and dries up; and they gather them, and cast them into the fire and they are burned." —JOHN 15:6

These nonabiders are not believers losing their salvation, nor are they fruitless believers. All genuine believers bear fruit, so these fruitless believers (v. 2*a*) have to be unbelieving, false disciples. And we know the Lord promised He wouldn't discard any true followers: "All that the Father gives Me will come to Me, and the one who comes to Me I will certainly not cast out" (John 6:37).

In this context, the phrase "in Me" does not refer to believers' union with Christ, as Paul often used the expression; here it simply denotes those who only outwardly attach themselves to Him (cf. Matt. 13:20–22; Rom. 11:16–24). The New Testament has many descriptions of those kinds of people who will always be around the true church. Our Lord called them tares among the wheat (Matt. 13:25–30); bad and discarded fish (13:48); goats who are condemned (25:33, 41).

Nonabiding branches eventually leave the church's fellowship (1 John 2:19), and in so doing reveal unbelieving hearts (Heb. 3:12; cf. 10:26, 39). Although such branches often think they are headed for heaven, they are in reality traveling the broad path leading to hell (Matt. 7:13–14).

ASK YOURSELF

Why do you think Christ is so readily claimed by those who have no real intention of submitting to His lordship? How has the church contributed to painting a version of Christian faith that downplays the cost of discipleship? Why is this much different from declaring that a person's good works lead to salvation?

BURNING OF THE NONABIDING BRANCHES, PART 2

"If anyone does not abide in Me, he is thrown away as a branch and dries up; and they gather them, and cast them into the fire and they are burned." —JOHN 15:6

The eventual fate that awaits all nonabiding branches is to be "cast . . . into the fire and . . . burned." Jesus had warned that "at the end of the age the angels will come forth and take out the wicked from among the righteous, and will throw them into the furnace of fire" (Matt. 13:49–50*a*). The stunned questions of such people, "Lord, Lord, did we not prophesy in Your name, and in Your name cast out demons, and in Your name perform many miracles?" (7:22), will prompt this unnerving reply from Christ: "I never knew you; depart from Me, you who practice lawlessness" (v. 23).

To truly abide in Christ produces spiritual fruit resulting in eternal joy and blessing. But those who don't abide, in spite of what they profess, will be fruitless and ultimately find themselves in hell. Christ's sober declaration regarding Judas Iscariot, "Woe to that man by whom the Son of Man is betrayed! It would have been good for that man if he had not been born" (Matt. 26:24; cf. 2 Peter 2:20–21), applies to all counterfeit disciples and false prophets. Thus the choice for everyone between living the world's way and abiding in the Lord is clear.

ASK YOURSELF

Have you ever appealed to God for mercy and pain reduction based on your dutiful pattern of following Him? What is the great fallacy in trying to hold up our personal acts as collateral in bargaining with God? What do we as believers know about ourselves that prohibits us from overestimating our sacrifice?

FRIENDS OF JESUS LOVE EACH OTHER, PART 1

"This is My commandment, that you love one another, just as I have loved you.
Greater love has no one than this, that one lay down his life for his friends."
—JOHN 15:12–13

Here Jesus gives for the second time on that evening in the upper room a command that His disciples love one another (cf. John 13:34). Love is the fulfillment of the commandments He spoke of in 15:10. Paul also expounded this principle to the Roman believers:

> Owe nothing to anyone except to love one another; for he who loves his neighbor has fulfilled the law. For this, "You shall not commit adultery, you shall not murder, you shall not steal, you shall not covet," and if there is any other commandment, it is summed up in this saying, "You shall love your neighbor as yourself." Love does no wrong to a neighbor; therefore love is the fulfillment of the law. (Rom. 13:8–10)

Only those who abide in the Lord have the ability to love as He loved. At salvation, the "love of God [was] poured out within [their] hearts through the Holy Spirit who was given to [them]" (Rom. 5:5; cf. Gal. 5:22). What the apostle told the Thessalonian Christians, "Now as to the love of the brethren, you have no need for anyone to write to you, for you yourselves are taught by God to love one another" (1 Thess. 4:9), applies to all believers.

ASK YOURSELF

How have you seen Christian love on vibrant display in your home, in your church, in acts of service and ministry and genuine compassion? Wherever it is lacking, what is the likely cause for a deficiency of love in the believer's life?

FRIENDS OF JESUS LOVE EACH OTHER, PART 2

"This is My commandment, that you love one another, just as I have loved you. Greater love has no one than this, that one lay down his life for his friends."
—JOHN 15:12–13

Christians must strive to love sacrificially, just as Jesus did. To that end, Paul taught the Ephesians, "Walk in love, just as Christ also loved you and gave Himself up for us, an offering and a sacrifice to God as a fragrant aroma" (Eph. 5:2). The love believers have for one another should be a selfless effort to meet each other's needs—in a way that lets the world know who we really are (John 13:35).

We see Jesus' love manifested in His substitutionary atonement: "We know love by this, that He laid down His life for us" (1 John 3:16*a*; cf. Rom. 5:6–8; 2 Cor. 5:21; 1 Peter 3:18).

John expressed brotherly love's practical implications: "But whoever has the world's goods, and sees his brother in need and closes his heart against him, how does the love of God abide in him? Little children, let us not love with word or with tongue, but in deed and truth" (1 John 3:17–18). True friends of Christ will display their mutual love by humbly meeting one another's needs.

ASK YOURSELF

From whom have you possibly withheld love in recent days, whether from fear of being asked to get more involved than you wanted, or from an unwillingness to forgive, or from prearranged plans you didn't want to give up? What might have happened if you had made the choice to love in a costly way? How have you been blessed before by allowing the Lord's love to shine through?

FRIENDS OF JESUS OBEY HIM, PART 1

*"You are My friends if you do what I command you." —*JOHN 15:14

Because all sin is rebellion against God (Matt. 7:23; 2 Cor. 6:14; 1 John 3:4), repenting from sin and turning in faith to Christ and becoming His friend necessarily imply obedience (Rom. 6:17). Therefore, throughout its pages, Scripture closely connects faith and obedience (1 Sam. 15:22–23; Acts 6:7; 1 Peter 1:1–2; 1 John 3:6). The apostle Peter, by contrast, defines unbelievers as "those who do not obey the gospel of God" (1 Peter 4:17).

Paul's chief ministry goal was "to bring about the obedience of faith among the Gentiles" (Rom. 1:5). The heroes of faith celebrated in Hebrews 11 proved their faith was real by their obedience to God. Hebrews 5:9 even uses obedience as a synonym for faith: "Having been made perfect, [Jesus] became to all those who obey Him the source of eternal salvation" (cf. John 3:36). When people told Jesus His mother and brothers were looking for Him, He answered, "'Who are My mother and My brothers?' Looking about at those who were sitting around Him, He said, 'Behold My mother and My brothers! For whoever *does the will of God*, he is My brother and sister and mother'" (Mark 3:33–35, emphases added).

ASK YOURSELF

In times when obedience is lacking in your life, what are the usual background issues that cause it? What are some of the most common deceptions you choose to believe, or the misjudgments you make in setting priorities, which inevitably lead you toward an apathetic or perhaps openly resistant heart? How have you been jarred from such errors, returning to Christ in full submission?

FRIENDS OF JESUS OBEY HIM, PART 2

"You are My friends if you do what I command you." —JOHN 15:14

Genuine friends of Jesus realize that obedience, as important as it is, does not earn them salvation. Redemption is solely "by grace . . . through faith . . . not as a result of works, so that no one may boast" (Eph. 2:8–9). God "saved us, not on the basis of deeds which we have done in righteousness, but according to His mercy by the washing of regeneration and renewing by the Holy Spirit" (Titus 3:5). And Paul also instructs us, "By the works of the Law no flesh will be justified in His sight. . . . For we maintain that a man is justified by faith apart from the works of the Law" (Rom. 3:20, 28; cf. Phil. 3:9).

Whereas obedience is not the basis of salvation, it is the inevitable result; it is the major outward evidence that a person has a saving relationship with Christ. The true branches that abide in Him, the true vine, will certainly bear spiritual fruit (see again John 15:1–11). Our Lord's sheep hear His voice and follow Him (10:27); genuine disciples obey His Word (8:31). Although good works save no one, a faith without them is dead and can't really save anyone (James 2:14–26; cf. Eph. 2:10).

ASK YOURSELF

How do you come the closest to serving Christ freely, without expectation of reward based on your obedient acts, able to allow the Spirit to bear fruit in you for His own good and glory? What makes this the greatest freedom of all, as opposed to the presumed freedom of giving oneself over to sin and selfish living? What causes the greatest barrier to serving God with such pure simplicity?

FRIENDS OF JESUS KNOW THE TRUTH, PART 1

"I have called you friends, for all things that I have heard from My Father I have made known to you." —JOHN 15:15b

The Old Testament calls some of its greatest characters slaves: Moses (Num. 12:7), David (2 Sam. 7:5), and Isaiah (Isa. 20:3). Likewise, New Testament figures Paul (Rom. 1:1) and John (Rev. 1:1) called themselves slaves of Christ. The Greek term denotes their complete submission to God and always refers to slavery, even though the word is often rendered "servant" or "bond-servant." Jesus is Lord; believers are His slaves.

Although Scripture calls Christians slaves, the term doesn't sufficiently convey their relationship to Christ. Amazingly, the Word also calls believers God's friends—a loftier title even than "disciple." The Old Testament calls only Abraham by the privileged title "friend of God" (see 2 Chron. 20:7; Isa. 41:8; James 2:23). William Barclay tells why a friend of the king (God) was so special:

> This phrase is lit up by a custom practised at the courts both of the Roman emperors and of kings in the middle east. At these courts, there was a very select group called the friends of the king, or the friends of the emperor. . . . He talked to them before he talked to his generals, his rulers and his statesmen. The friends of the king were those who had the closest and the most intimate connection with him.

Jesus grants this kind of access to His friends.

ASK YOURSELF

Do you perhaps have a hard time seeing yourself in such intimate terms with God? What causes you to doubt that He truly desires to relate to you in this way? How do you balance this level of closeness with an appropriate awe and fear of His greatness and grandeur?

FRIENDS OF JESUS KNOW THE TRUTH, PART 2

*"I have called you friends, for all things that I have heard
from My Father I have made known to you." —*JOHN 15:15*b*

Jesus promised that His friends, believers, "will know the truth, and the truth will make [them] free" (John 8:32; cf. 17:6–8).

When the apostles asked Jesus why He spoke to the people in parables, He replied, "To you it has been granted to know the mysteries of the kingdom of heaven, but to them it has not been granted" (Matt. 13:11; cf. Luke 10:23–24).

The friends of Christ have insight into "the mystery which has been kept secret for long ages past, but now is manifested, and by the Scriptures of the prophets, according to the commandment of the eternal God, has been made known to all the nations, leading to obedience of faith" (Rom. 16:25–26). The New Testament reveals much about these previously hidden mysteries, or truths (Matt. 13:11; Eph. 3:4–6; 5:32; 6:19; Col. 2:2; 1 Tim. 3:9).

That believers understand truth indeed distinguishes them as Jesus' friends:

> Now we have received, not the spirit of the world, but the Spirit who is from God, so that we may know the things freely given to us by God, which things we also speak, not in words taught by human wisdom, but in those taught by the Spirit, combining spiritual thoughts with spiritual words. (1 Cor. 2:12–13; cf. vv. 14–16)

ASK YOURSELF

What is God's purpose for revealing elements of His wisdom and reality to us as His "friends"? What does He intend us to do with what He is showing us? How have you experienced the fact that "knowledge makes arrogant, but love edifies" (1 Cor. 8:1)?

FRIENDS OF JESUS ARE CHOSEN BY HIM, PART 1

*"You did not choose Me but I chose you, and appointed you that you would go and bear fruit, and that your fruit would remain." —*JOHN 15:16*a*

The apostles did not choose Jesus as their rabbi, rather He chose them (contrary to the usual Jewish practice in which potential disciples asked if they could follow a certain teacher). Knowing that Christ chose the apostles, and by extension all believers, to salvation apart from human merit (John 6:44; Acts 13:48; Rom. 8:28–30) eliminates all pretense for spiritual pride we might otherwise have (cf. 1 Cor. 1:26–31; Eph. 2:9).

After the Lord called the disciples to salvation, He appointed them to ministry. "Appointed" here has the connotation of setting someone apart or ordaining the person for special service (cf. Acts 20:28; 1 Tim. 1:12; 2:7).

After choosing and training the apostles, our Lord commanded them, and indeed all Christians, to proclaim the gospel and bear fruit. He did not select us to be mere spectators while the world continues on its way to hell. On the contrary: "Go therefore and make disciples of all the nations, baptizing them in the name of the Father and the Son and the Holy Spirit, teaching them to observe all that I commanded you; and lo, I am with you always, even to the end of the age" (Matt. 28:19–20).

ASK YOURSELF

How is your daily struggle of faith and obedience altered by realizing that your faithful fruit-bearing for Christ is an appointment, an assigned task? How have you perhaps neglected to understand the importance, the privilege, in fact, of being called to such a lofty and responsible position?

FRIENDS OF JESUS ARE CHOSEN BY HIM, PART 2

"You did not choose Me but I chose you, and appointed you that you would go and bear fruit, and that your fruit would remain, so that whatever you ask of the Father in My name He may give to you." —JOHN 15:16

When friends of Jesus make known the good news of salvation and some sincerely respond in faith, those people become fruit that remains. The fact that Jesus repeats His promise of John 15:7, "whatever you ask of the Father in My name He may give to you," underscores how important prayer is to effective evangelism (cf. Luke 10:2; 2 Thess. 3:1).

While the friends of Christ Jesus possess many privileges and blessings, they also have many related responsibilities. Scripture commands them to "fervently love one another from the heart" (1 Peter 1:22). They must study the truth diligently (2 Tim. 2:15) to know it even better. They have been called out of the world, so they must take care not to love it (1 John 2:15). As we have seen, they must yield to God's pruning so they might bear more spiritual fruit (John 15:2). The anticipation of answered prayer requires Jesus' friends to pray effectively (James 5:16) and unceasingly (1 Thess. 5:17). In summary, genuine believers must "walk in a manner worthy of the calling with which [they] have been called" (Eph. 4:1).

ASK YOURSELF

Does your calling in Christ feel too heavy for you to carry, too ambitious for you to undertake? What would keep you from starting afresh today or in the morning, remembering that His Spirit is at work in you to accomplish these things, knowing that eternal investments yield a return nothing else can match?

THE WORLD HATES CHRISTIANS, PART 1

"Because you are not of the world, but I chose you out of the world, because of this the world hates you." —JOHN 15:19b

The word translated "world" (from which we get "cosmos") in this context means the fallen, demonic world system (see John 12:31; Eph. 2:1–3; 1 John 5:19). The Devil hates God and His people and therefore aims his wrath at them as he "prowls around like a roaring lion, seeking someone to devour" (1 Peter 5:8).

The world despises Christians because their righteous lives condemn its unrighteousness: "he who is upright in the way is abominable to the wicked" (Prov. 29:27). John further illustrates this principle by mentioning the first human murder: "Cain . . . was of the evil one and slew his brother. And for what reason did he slay him? Because his deeds were evil, and his brother's were righteous" (1 John 3:12).

Though we must live in the world (1 Cor. 5:9–10), we are to stand apart from it so we might indict its sin. Paul admonished, "Prove yourselves to be blameless and innocent, children of God above reproach in the midst of a crooked and perverse generation, among whom you appear as lights in the world" (Phil. 2:15). Likewise, the apostle exhorted the believers in Ephesus, "Do not participate in the unfruitful deeds of darkness, but instead even expose them" (Eph. 5:11).

ASK YOURSELF

What do you consider the greatest costs and unpleasantries about being out of step with the prevailing culture, choosing to live without others' acceptance? What happens in a believer's life when he or she determines this is too high a price to pay, that the approval of friends and associates is worth more than the smile of God?

THE WORLD HATES CHRISTIANS, PART 2

"Because you are not of the world, but I chose you out of the world, because of this the world hates you." —JOHN 15:19

While worldly people hate Christians, they love each other. They are comfortable with and supportive of fellow unbelievers (cf. Rom. 1:32). Concerning believers' relationship to the world, Jesus said, "If you were of the world, the world would love its own" (John 15:19*a*). This conditional clause assumes the situation to be false and could be rendered, "If you were of the world (and you are not). . . ." If the apostles or any other believers were of the world, they would experience the world's imperfect love for its own. But those who know Christ are not part of the world because He chose them out of it (cf. 2 Tim. 2:26; Heb. 2:14–15). All credit for salvation belongs to Him.

The truth of election indeed silences human pride and ought to make us supremely grateful to be loved by God and not the world. Ephesians 1:4, 6 reminds us that the Father "chose us in Him before the foundation of the world, that we would be holy and blameless before Him. . . . to the praise of the glory of His grace, which He freely bestowed on us in the Beloved" (cf. Rom. 3:27–28; 4:2).

ASK YOURSELF

How have you experienced the cold shoulder of worldly rejection? What is the difference between making ourselves annoying and unpleasant to others, as opposed to being maligned simply because of our association with Christ and His truth? What are some of the other forms of "hate" that may not be as overtly hostile, yet express a subtle disdain for the faith your life represents?

THE WORLD HATES BELIEVERS: IT HATED CHRIST

"You know that it has hated Me before it hated you . . ." —JOHN 15:18*b*

The saints should not be surprised if the world hates them, inasmuch as it hated Jesus before it despised them (cf. John 17:14). The gospel of John reveals much regarding this hatred. For instance, "the Jews were seeking all the more to kill Him, because He not only was breaking the Sabbath, but also was calling God His own Father, making Himself equal with God" (5:18; cf. 7:1, 32; 8:59; 11:47–53). When we face adversity and suffering, Hebrews calls on us to "consider Him who has endured such hostility by sinners against Himself" (12:3).

Jesus earlier told the apostles, "A slave is not greater than his master" (John 13:16), and here in 15:20 He repeats that statement. In chapter 13, when He washed the disciples' feet, the Lord referred to the humblest service of a slave. But here His point is that believers should expect to follow His (their Master's) example of suffering (cf. 1 Peter 2:21), they have no right to expect the world to treat them any better than it did Jesus (see also Matt. 10:24–25). If anyone truly knows Him and strives consistently to obey Him, he understands that he identifies with the Lord Jesus in the "fellowship of His sufferings" (Phil. 3:10; cf. Col. 1:24).

ASK YOURSELF

Rehearse some of the ways Jesus was mistreated and misunderstood while serving His Father on earth. If you do not see similar reactions mirrored in your own life, what might be the cause? What is indicative of someone who has few if any enemies? Could it be that your behaviors and attitudes are more acceptable to the world than they ought to be?

THE WORLD HATES BELIEVERS: IT DOESN'T KNOW GOD, PART 1

"But all these things they will do to you for My name's sake, because they do not know the One who sent Me." —JOHN 15:21

The world's hostility toward Christians is mainly because believers know the Lord. He taught the saints, "Blessed are you when people insult you and persecute you, and falsely say all kinds of evil against you because of Me" (Matt. 5:11; cf. 24:9). Concerning the newly converted Saul of Tarsus, He said, "I will show him how much he must suffer for My name's sake" (Acts 9:16). "If [believers] are reviled for the name of Christ, [they] are blessed, because the Spirit of glory and of God rests on [them]" (1 Peter 4:14). Thus enduring hostility for Jesus' sake is a recurring New Testament theme (cf. Mark 8:35; Luke 21:12–17; Rom. 8:36).

Ultimately, the world hates Christ and His disciples because it does "not know the One who sent" Him. Because "the mind set on the flesh is hostile toward God" (Rom. 8:7), "those who are in the flesh cannot please God" (v. 8; cf. Eph. 2:1; 4:18). Everyone who hates God is responsible for that sin, "because that which is known about God is evident within them; for God made it evident to them. For since the creation of the world His invisible attributes . . . have been clearly seen . . . so that they are without excuse" (Rom. 1:19–20; cf. vv. 18, 21).

ASK YOURSELF

What might others learn about Christ's nature by seeing how He operates in you on a regular basis? How much of an awareness toward outsiders should you feel obliged to maintain as you go about the duties and demands of your day?

THE WORLD HATES BELIEVERS: IT DOESN'T KNOW GOD, PART 2

"But all these things they will do to you for My name's sake, because they do not know the One who sent Me." —JOHN 15:21

The world's hatred of our Lord, though despicable and inexcusable, was within the Father's sovereign plan. "They have done this," Jesus said, "to fulfill the word that is written in their Law, 'They hated Me without a cause'" (John 15:25). This is a quote from Psalm 35:19 and 69:4, with the point being that if a mere human like David could be so hated, how much more the innocent Son of God? A lost world hated Christ because He exposed its sin and showed it who He really is. However, in view of what He said and did, there's no valid reason to hate Him. That the world's hatred continues is evidence of sin's vileness.

But for believers who eventually encounter opposition for their faith, there is much joy in Jesus' promise:

> Blessed are those who have been persecuted for the sake of righteousness, for theirs is the kingdom of heaven. Blessed are you when people insult you and persecute you, and falsely say all kinds of evil against you because of Me. Rejoice and be glad, for your reward in heaven is great; for in the same way they persecuted the prophets who were before you. (Matt. 5:10–12)

ASK YOURSELF

What are the elements of Christ's sacrifice and ministry that should resonate with anyone who truly longs to know significance in life? How are you looking for opportunities to speak of His character and His influence on you, especially with those who seem the most open to receiving His grace themselves?

CHRISTIAN WITNESS IS TO THE WORLD

"And you will testify also, because you have been with Me from the beginning."
—JOHN 15:27

In this postmodern age of relativism and cynicism, nothing is more essential than confronting the unbelieving world with a clear presentation of the truth of Christ's gospel. We know unbelievers will generally receive the message with hostility and opposition, yet the Lord demands Christians to speak with bold conviction, enabled by the Holy Spirit's power. Paul told the Ephesians,

> pray on my behalf that utterance may be given to me in the opening of my mouth to make known with boldness the mystery of the gospel, for which I am an ambassador in chains; that in proclaiming it I may speak boldly, as I ought to speak. (Eph. 6:19–20)

We as Christians can't effectively confront the world if we are part of it. Although we live in the world, we must not be "of the world" (cf. John 15:19; 17:14). James warns us, "Do you not know that friendship with the world is hostility toward God? Therefore whoever wishes to be a friend of the world makes himself an enemy of God" (James 4:4; cf. 1 John 2:15).

Despite the world's animosity, we must witness to the lost with compassion and love, being "kind to all, able to teach . . . with gentleness correcting those who are in opposition, if perhaps God may grant them repentance" (2 Tim. 2:24–25).

ASK YOURSELF

Being very honest, is there any prevailing, consistent aspect of your life that would discount the message of Christian faith and belief if you were to share the gospel with others? What would help you realize the seriousness and urgency of dealing with this matter before it restricts your witness any further?

CHRISTIAN WITNESS IS FROM THE FATHER

*"When the Helper comes, whom I will send to you from the Father,
that is the Spirit of truth who proceeds from the Father."* —JOHN 15:26a

God the Father testified to His Son Jesus in several ways. For example, He testified to Jesus through the divine works Christ did. The Savior told His enemies, "The works which the Father has given Me to accomplish—the very works that I do—testify about Me, that the Father has sent Me" (John 5:36; cf. Acts 2:22).

The Father's direct statements also testified to Jesus. Twice, at Christ's baptism and transfiguration, God said, "This is My beloved Son, in whom I am well-pleased" (Matt. 3:17; 17:5). Of the transfiguration, Peter later wrote, "we ourselves heard this utterance made from heaven when we were with Him on the holy mountain" (2 Peter 1:18).

Finally, the Father testified to Christ through the Holy Spirit. The apostles told the Sanhedrin, "We are witnesses of these things [concerning Christ]; and so is the Holy Spirit" (Acts 5:32; cf. 1 John 5:6). The book of Hebrews teaches us:

> How will we escape if we neglect so great a salvation? After it was at the first spoken through the Lord, it was confirmed to us by those who heard, God also testifying with them, both by signs and wonders and by various miracles and by gifts of the Holy Spirit according to His own will. (Heb. 2:3–4)

ASK YOURSELF

How has the Lord most clearly demonstrated Himself to you throughout the course of your life? How does His revelation of Himself to you prove how specifically and personally He reaches out to redeem those He is drawing to Himself? How could you be part of this process in others' lives?

CHRISTIAN WITNESS IS ABOUT THE SON, PART 1

"He will testify about Me." —JOHN 15:26b

The objective of Christian witness is to testify about Jesus. Peter boldly declared in his Pentecost sermon, "This Jesus God raised up again, to which we are all witnesses" (Acts 2:32; cf. 3:15; 5:30–32). Paul affirmed, "I determined to know nothing among you except Jesus Christ, and Him crucified" (1 Cor. 2:2), and Peter called himself a "witness of the sufferings of Christ" (1 Peter 5:1).

Yet in spite of Scripture's clear emphasis on believers' being witnesses of Christ, much of contemporary evangelistic methodology focuses on political and social activism and meeting people's felt needs. It also softens the New Testament emphasis on Jesus' person and work and the critical importance of confronting sinners with their sin and its consequences unless faith in the atoning work of Christ rescues them. Such inadequate gospel presentations can leave men and women loving their iniquity and ignorant of real justification by faith and with a false and temporary profession. But Christian witness must follow Paul's pattern:

> I was with you in weakness and in fear and in much trembling, and my message and my preaching were not in persuasive words of wisdom, but in demonstration of the Spirit and of power, so that your faith would not rest on the wisdom of men, but on the power of God. (1 Cor. 2:3–5; cf. vv. 1–2; 1:18–25)

ASK YOURSELF

What causes us to lighten our descriptions of Christian faith, making it easier to sell and less demanding of the whole self? How have you seen God's power on display in someone who was truly putting their sin to death at the cross? What tempts us to want and expect freedom any other way?

CHRISTIAN WITNESS IS ABOUT THE SON, PART 2

*"He will testify about Me." —*JOHN 15:26*b*

Along with the truth about God's Son, repentance is at the heart of the gospel witness. John the Baptist challenged his audience to "repent, for the kingdom of heaven is at hand. . . . bear fruit in keeping with repentance" (Matt. 3:2, 8). From the beginning of His public ministry, our Lord's message was "Repent, for the kingdom of heaven is at hand" (Matt. 4:17). When the Jewish leaders rebuked Him for spending time with society's dregs, Christ answered, "I have not come to call the righteous but sinners to repentance" (Luke 5:32). After His resurrection He announced that "repentance for forgiveness of sins would be proclaimed in His name to all the nations, beginning from Jerusalem" (Luke 24:47).

The early church obeyed Jesus' command to preach repentance. On Pentecost Peter exhorted his listeners, "Repent, and each of you be baptized in the name of Jesus Christ for the forgiveness of your sins; and you will receive the gift of the Holy Spirit" (Acts 2:38; cf. 3:19). Paul characterized his ministry as one of "solemnly testifying to both Jews and Greeks of repentance toward God and faith in our Lord Jesus Christ" (20:21), and his witness was that people "should repent and turn to God, performing deeds appropriate to repentance" (26:20; cf. 17:30).

ASK YOURSELF

How might God be calling you to repentance today, not as a requirement for the salvation He has already provided but in opening your heart to deeper, truer, more honest relationship with the Father? What have you learned about the power of repentance that should help you lay aside any resistance you feel in returning to Him with all your heart?

CHRISTIAN WITNESS IS ABOUT THE SON, PART 3

"He will testify about Me." —JOHN 15:26*b*

A memorable example of how a biblical witness must focus on Jesus and a repentant, submissive surrender to Him is the story of the rich synagogue ruler (Luke 18:18–27). Although the young man was outwardly religious, he knew his life lacked something vital. Thus he asked, "Good Teacher, what shall I do to inherit eternal life?" (v. 18). This was no academic, rhetorical question; he sincerely felt his need and diligently pursued an answer. Oblivious to the crowds, the young ruler "ran up to [Jesus] and knelt before Him" (Mark 10:17). He came to the right person, since Christ is the only true source of eternal life (John 14:6). And the man asked the right question, namely, how he might obtain eternal life.

However, this seemingly certain prospect for conversion walked away unsaved. He proudly valued his earthly treasures more than Jesus' promise of heavenly riches. His superficial faith prevented him from confessing his sin and forsaking all to enter the kingdom.

The Lord Jesus refused to ignore the man's genuine spiritual issues for an expedient "decision" from him. Christians today must not ignore such issues either. The essentials of sin, judgment, repentance, and discipleship can't be watered down or the cross removed from our witnessing (Gal. 5:11). Those who divert the focus of evangelism away from Jesus and these essentials actually present a false gospel (1:8–9).

ASK YOURSELF

How has the oppressive weight of sin hindered your freedom and enjoyment of Christ? Why should we ever expect to be at rest in Him while carrying such a load? As you experience anew His liberating grace today, share what He has done for you with others who need to hear.

CHRISTIAN WITNESS IS THROUGH BELIEVERS

*"And you will bear witness also, because you have
been with Me from the beginning."* —JOHN 15:27

As a believer, your witness is inseparably linked to the witness of the
Holy Spirit (v. 26), since He enables you to testify effectively to the
world about Jesus Christ. So vital is the Spirit's empowering of Christian
witness that the Lord told His disciples to remain in Jerusalem until the
coming of the Spirit on the day of Pentecost (Luke 24:49). It was "in the
power of the Spirit" that Paul "fully preached the gospel of Christ"
(Rom. 15:19).

The apostles were qualified to testify about Christ because they had
been with Him from the beginning of His earthly ministry (an essential
prerequisite in replacing Judas, cf. Acts 1:21–22). Christians today are
not eyewitnesses of Jesus Christ as the apostles were, but we point people
to the apostolic testimony recorded in Scripture.

God's people are His chosen means to reach the elect among the
lost. That wonderful promise of Romans 10:13—"whoever will call on
the name of the Lord will be saved"—finds its fulfillment only when
believers proclaim the saving truth of the gospel (vv. 14–17).

ASK YOURSELF

How faithfully are you telling others, even in routine
conversation, about the things God has done, the peace He
provides, the purpose you've found in following Him? What keeps
this from being an easy, natural undertaking? How has talking about
Christ become increasingly (and ironically) taboo, even in our
culture of tolerance and acceptance of others' viewpoints?

JESUS PRAYS TO HIS FATHER, PART 1

*Jesus spoke these things; and lifting up His eyes to
heaven, He said, "Father, the hour has come."* —JOHN 17:1a

Jesus began His prayer by lifting up His eyes to heaven. That was a familiar posture, acknowledging God's throne in heaven, and for Jesus, it reflected the confidence of His pure heart. To address God as Father meant that Jesus recognized His submission and dependence, and at the same time it revealed His essential equality with God ("making Himself equal with God," John 5:18).

Though equal with the Father, Jesus was also distinct from the Father—*clearly* He wasn't praying to Himself! That's an important theological truth: the Son is equal to the Father yet distinct from Him. Jesus is essentially equal to the Father, sharing in divine glory (17:5), and at the same time, He's a distinct person within the Godhead. Jesus is no mere mode or manifestation of the Father, as some erroneously teach.

When Jesus addressed God as Father, He not only underscored fundamental realities of the Trinity, He revealed the intimacy of fellowship He shared with God. This kind of relationship, completely foreign to the Jews of Jesus' day, is what God grants to everyone who believes (17:20, 26). In Christ, we have received the right to become children of God (1:12).

ASK YOURSELF

What are some of the most notable parallels of the father-child relationship that are most important to you as a child of God? How does He fulfill these roles in your life? In what ways, however, have you projected onto God any of the difficulties you've experienced in your relationship with your earthly father? How has God surpassed your expectations or compensated for your lack?

JESUS PRAYS TO HIS FATHER, PART 2

*Jesus spoke these things; and lifting up His eyes to heaven, He said, "Father, the hour has come." —*JOHN 17:1a

We see in Jesus' dramatic statement ("the hour has come") that the unfolding drama of redemptive history was on the verge of fulfillment. It was time for a sweeping victory. Christ would crush the serpent's head, triumphing over the prince of this world and the kingdom of darkness (Gen. 3:15; John 12:31; 16:11; Col. 2:14; Heb. 2:14).

The hour had come for the Son of Man to offer Himself as the perfect and only atoning sacrifice for sin; for the man of sorrows (Isa. 53:3) to be "pierced through for our transgressions . . . crushed for our iniquities" (v. 5); for "the chastening for our well-being [to fall] upon Him [so that] by His scourging we are healed" (v. 5).

The hour had come for the sinless One to be made sin for us, so we "might become the righteousness of God in Him" (2 Cor. 5:21); for God to cancel "the certificate of debt consisting of decrees against us," taking "it out of the way, having nailed it to the cross" (Col. 2:14).

For every believer, Christ's darkest hour has given way to profound joy, providing an enduring reason to praise and worship our great God and Savior, Jesus Christ.

ASK YOURSELF

What are some of the examples in your own life when God seemed to say, "The hour has come"? It was time for a season of suffering to end. Time for a certain sin to lose its mastery over you. Time for your worry and regret to cease so you could live in the freedom of your relationship with Christ. What now needs to come to a close in your life?

THE RELATIONSHIP JESUS OFFERS

"This is eternal life, that they may know You, the only true God, and Jesus Christ whom You have sent." —JOHN 17:3

Eternal life is available only to those who know, in a deep, intimate love relationship, the only true God through Jesus Christ. "Eternal" doesn't merely refer to longevity but more profoundly to the kind of life true believers have received. If you know Christ, you should see evidence of His divine life in you—perfect peace, sacrificial love, and abiding joy—the marks of shared communion with Him.

Understood in this way, eternal life is both a future possession and a present reality. In John 5:24 Jesus says, "Truly, truly, I say to you, he who hears My word, and believes Him who sent Me, *has* eternal life" (emphasis added).

As a believer, you enjoy eternal life *right now* as you experience the rich blessings of a personal and intimate fellowship with Christ (John 15:1–11; 1 Cor. 1:9; Eph. 1:3; Phil. 3:8–11; 1 John 1:3; 5:20). And you look forward to the consummation of your joy, the full expression of eternal life, when you see Christ face-to-face (1 John 3:2) and worship Him in the perfect, unending glory and joy of heaven (Rom. 8:19–23, 29; 1 Cor. 15:49; Phil. 3:20–21; Rev. 22:3–4).

ASK YOURSELF

What are the main obstacles to experiencing abundant, eternal life in your here and now? Knowing what these are, how diligent are you in eliminating the ones you can control, or standing firm against the ones that must still be dealt with and confronted? How has God's Spirit helped you conquer these in the past?

THE REQUIREMENT JESUS MEETS

*"I glorified You on the earth, having accomplished
the work which You have given Me to do."* —JOHN 17:4

To save those whom the Father had given Him (Matt. 1:21; Luke 19:10), Jesus had to be absolutely sinless and perfectly righteous. He succeeded.

Though "tempted in all things as we are," Jesus was "yet without sin" (Heb. 4:15). He had to be "holy, innocent, undefiled, [and] separated from sinners" (Heb. 7:26), for God would accept only a *sinless* sacrifice. Jesus was "a lamb unblemished and spotless" (1 Peter 1:19) who "committed no sin" (2:22).

The other side of accomplishing His Father's work was "to fulfill all righteousness" (Matt. 3:15). By living a life of perfect obedience, Jesus fulfilled *all* of God's righteous requirements. He was perfectly holy (Lev. 19:2), became the final sacrifice for sin (cf. Heb. 10:1–18), and now gives eternal life to all who believe in Him.

If you are united to Christ, God has imputed that sinless, perfect life to you. On the cross, God treated Jesus as if He had committed all *your* sins, so He could treat you as if you had lived Christ's perfect life (cf. 2 Cor. 5:21). It's the ultimate expression of love: submission to His Father (John 15:10) and compassion for sinners (v. 13).

ASK YOURSELF

What does Christ's sacrifice and determination inspire in you?
If you have placed your faith in Him and submitted to Him as
Lord, how strongly does His perfect righteousness counteract
any fears you may possess, anything that causes you to feel
as though your salvation is still in question? What is God
calling you to face with this kind of steady resolve?

THE REVERENCE JESUS DESERVES

"Now, Father, glorify Me together with Yourself, with the glory which I had with You before the world was." —JOHN 17:5

Jesus looked beyond the Valley of the Shadow of Death, which lay immediately before Him, to the glory of His exaltation. The full revelation of His eternal glory was the "joy set before Him," for which He "endured the cross, despising the shame" (Heb. 12:2; cf. Matt. 27:46). He was eager to lay aside the fleshly robe of humiliation, the suffering and shame of the cross (Phil. 2:5–8), to reveal His true, divine glory (John 1:14).

Jesus is currently and forever enthroned at the right hand of His Father (cf. Mark 16:19; Eph. 1:20), His rightful place, by virtue of who He is (John 1:1) and as reward for what He accomplished (Phil. 2:9–11). Having fulfilled His role as the Suffering Servant, He is now King of kings and Lord of lords (1 Tim. 6:15; Rev. 17:14; 19:16).

The significance of John 17:5 for the believer is monumental: Christ's exaltation secures future redemption. His resurrection and exaltation mean the Father has accepted the sacrifice of His Son for your sins (Eph. 1:6). Jesus' exaltation brings repentance and forgiveness (Acts 5:30–31); His resurrection guarantees your resurrection and full redemption (Rom. 8:23; 1 Cor. 15:20–22, 45–49); and in union with Him, you'll see Him one day in the fullness of His glory.

ASK YOURSELF

It's hard for our minds to imagine the "glory" experienced among the members of the Godhead. But how does thinking about it help you transcend the problems and concerns of your everyday? What do we gain by seeking to worship God in all His glory?

DISCIPLES RECEIVE, BELIEVE, AND PERSEVERE

"The words which You gave Me I have given to them; and they received them and truly understood that I came forth from You, and they believed that You sent Me."
—JOHN 17:8

The Gospels are quite candid about the disciples' shortcomings and misunderstandings, and yet Jesus' words reveal a genuineness of faith that isn't always obvious. The disciples understood, embraced, and believed significant truths, giving clear evidence of divine grace at work within them (Matt. 16:17; John 6:70).

The disciples watched Jesus' power and compassion in action, as He healed the sick, cast out demons, and forgave sinners. They listened to Jesus pray, eavesdropping on His intimate relationship with His Father. They responded positively to His authoritative teaching, knowing He had words of eternal life (John 6:68).

Jesus' life and ministry produced faith in the disciples' hearts; they came to a settled conviction about who Christ was (Matt. 16:16; John 1:14; 16:29–30) and continued when others departed (John 6:66–69). After Pentecost, their powerful witness confounded the most learned of men (Acts 4), which brought conflict, persecution, and even martyrdom.

Simply stated, the disciples had come to know that Jesus spoke words from the Father; they received them, believed them, and persevered in them. These are the marks of true discipleship.

ASK YOURSELF

What does it mean to persevere in the truths God has revealed to you from His Word? What are some of the biblical teachings you have repeatedly clung to, even in times when your feelings, fears, and doubts were working hard against the Spirit's reminders? How has God's truth kept you going?

SPECIAL GIFT, SPECIAL LOVE

"I ask on their behalf; I do not ask on behalf of the world, but of those whom You have given Me; for they are Yours." —JOHN 17:9

God loves every person in the world without exception, even people who reject the gospel (cf. Mark 10:21). Theologians call this love common grace. "He causes His sun to rise on the evil and the good, and sends rain on the righteous and the unrighteous" (Matt. 5:45; cf. Acts 14:17). God pleads with sinners to repent (Ezek. 18:32; Acts 17:30), and extends the gospel invitation to all (Matt. 11:28–30). But God also has a special grace, a particular love reserved for His elect (1 Tim. 4:10).

Christ's intercessory work as High Priest is only for those who belong to Him, those whom the Father gave. In fact, Jesus prayed for unbelievers only once, when He cried out on the cross, "Father, forgive them; for they do not know what they are doing" (Luke 23:34). That's a model for us as believers (cf. Matt. 5:44), but it also shows that Jesus did not intercede for the unredeemed world.

Jesus' intercession and advocacy are inextricably linked to the atonement He provided for the elect (cf. 1 John 2:1–2). His special, particular love is reserved for all whom the Father has given Him.

ASK YOURSELF

How encouraging is it to you that your Father has a divine plan, an eternal purpose, one that He is carrying forth even today in your life and in the lives of many others? How has He hounded you with His grace, seeking your heart, pursuing a relationship with you, proving again and again His great love for you?

Jesus Sends Sanctified Disciples

"Sanctify them in the truth; Your word is truth." —John 17:17

Disciples throughout the ages need to be conformed internally, increasingly, and completely to Jesus Christ. Jesus had completely cleansed His disciples (i.e., justification; John 15:3), and He continued to wash their feet as they walked in the filth of this world (i.e., sanctification; John 13:10; cf. 1 John 2:1–2). And though the Evil One would aggressively try to derail their sanctification, the Father Himself guaranteed their growth through the Word of truth (v. 17) and the Spirit of truth (14:17; 15:26; 16:13).

Just as the Father sent Christ into the world, so He also sends sanctified believers into the world. This was His pattern with the first disciples. They went out to "make disciples" of Christ in "all the nations, baptizing them in the name of the Father and the Son and the Holy Spirit, teaching them to observe all that [Christ] commanded [them]" (Matt. 28:19–20).

Having been set apart from the world and transformed by God's grace, the disciples became heralds of this same grace to the world that hated them. Through their witness, the world would be exposed to the gospel, and many (including us) would come to saving faith.

ASK YOURSELF

What has Christ accomplished in you—in your attitudes, in your confidence, in your character and ability—that would never have happened without His work of grace in your heart? What parts of your life continue to need the touch of His transforming, sanctifying power in order for you to be strong and effective? How do you intend to surrender even more of yourself to His control?

THE ROOT OF TRUE UNITY, PART 1

"I do not ask on behalf of these alone, but for those also who believe in Me through their word." —JOHN 17:20

As Jesus prayed, He looked ahead through the centuries to intercede for all who would believe. You can observe a profound theological balance in His prayer. On the one hand, Jesus prayed for those the Father had given Him; they were guaranteed to come to Him because of divine election (v. 6; cf. 6:44). On the other hand, their salvation does not happen apart from faith (cf. Rom. 10:9–10). Everyone who hears the gospel is personally responsible to believe.

The vast majority of these future believers had yet to be born (like us) and yet, these precious people had been on the Lord's heart from eternity past. Our Savior has known each one of us. Our names have "been written from the foundation of the world in the book of life" (Phil. 4:3; Rev. 13:8; 20:15; 21:27). And His intercession ministry, which includes this two thousand-year-old prayer, continues to this day. "He always lives to make intercession for [us]" (Heb. 7:25).

ASK YOURSELF

How did you come to believe on the Lord Jesus? In the months and years since, how has your belief in Him grown and matured, deepening with each new piece of understanding about His nature? What have you experienced in life or observed in others that continues to affirm the reliability of Scripture and the validity of its Author, anchoring your faith ever deeper in the Savior of your soul? How might you have opportunity to express these things to someone you know who does not yet believe?

THE ROOT OF TRUE UNITY, PART 2

"I do not ask on behalf of these alone, but for those also
who believe in Me through their word." —JOHN 17:20

The apostles and their associates were the earliest gospel preachers and the human authors of the New Testament (John 14:26; 16:13–15). Their word would become the channel through which salvation would flow to all future believers. But when Jesus prayed this prayer, the immediate future didn't look too promising.

Judas Iscariot, one of the most trusted members of the Twelve (John 12:6), was betraying Jesus at that very moment. Peter, their impetuous and seemingly fearless leader, was about to cower before a servant girl's accusations, denying the Lord repeatedly (John 18:17; cf. vv. 25–27). The rest of the disciples would scatter, abandoning Jesus to His arrest and crucifixion (Matt. 26:56). They were hardly ready to make an impact on the world.

But their witness turned the world upside down (Acts 17:6). In spite of their weaknesses, worldly persecution, and satanic opposition, the Holy Spirit empowered the disciples to begin the chain of believing that has continued unbroken to the present day (cf. 2 Tim. 2:2). And Jesus ensured the unstoppable growth of the church, built on the promise of Christ and the foundation laid by the prophets and apostles (Matt. 16:18; Eph. 2:20), in this very prayer.

ASK YOURSELF

Thinking of the various personalities and shortcomings of the early disciples, how are you encouraged that God can use your church for mighty works as well, despite the odd fits and noticeable blemishes of your congregation? What do you find most refreshing in knowing that Christ can unify His people?

THE REQUEST FOR TRUE UNITY

". . . that they may all be one." —JOHN 17:21

Some have the mistaken tendency to look for the appearance of Christian unity based on external forms and structures (e.g., denominations, cobelligerency), rather than the essence of Christian unity, based on spiritual realities. But outward appearance doesn't always tell the whole story (cf. 1 Sam. 16:7).

Jesus' prayer has already been, and continues to be, fulfilled. It started with the birth of the church on the day of Pentecost when the Holy Spirit united believers in Christ, making them one with Him and each other (Acts 2:4). Since then, every believer has been added to the universal and invisible body of Christ, the church (1 Cor. 12:13).

Ephesians 4:4–6 depicts this spiritual unity, created by the Holy Spirit. *One body* describes the church, composed of all believers since the church's inception on the day of Pentecost. *One Spirit* unites the church in Christ through baptism (1 Cor. 12:13). *One hope* is the promised eternal inheritance (Eph. 1:13–14). *One Lord* is Jesus Christ, head of the body (Col. 1:18). *One faith* is the objective body of apostolic doctrine, "once for all delivered to the saints" (Jude 3). *One baptism* is the common, public confession of faith in Jesus Christ. And *one God and Father* is the sovereign Lord of all, including the church.

ASK YOURSELF

Where have you seen some of the most inspiring evidences of unity among believers? Why is it unthinkable that anything like this could happen without the overseeing role of the Holy Spirit? What could you do (or choose not to do) in order to engender a greater sense of unity with the believers you know?

REFLECTING PERFECT UNITY, PART 1

*"As You, Father, are in Me and I in You . . . that
they may be perfected in unity."* —JOHN 17:21–23

The unity of believers on earth should reflect the unique, intra-Trinitarian unity between Jesus Christ and His Father. First, they are fundamentally united in motive. Jesus had prayed, "Father, glorify Your name"; His Father replied, "I have both glorified it, and will glorify it again." Jesus' ultimate desire was to glorify the Father (John 7:18; 8:50, 54; 17:1, 4, 5, 24), and that's to be the motive for all believers as well. "Whether, then, you eat or drink or whatever you do, do all to the glory of God" (1 Cor. 10:31).

Second, the Father and the Son are united in their *mission* to redeem lost sheep. God purposed and planned the mission of redemption. Christ carried it out; He came to die as a sacrifice for sins, redeeming His elect for eternity. And the church is united in this mission as heralds of the gospel (Matt. 28:19–20).

Third, the Father and the Son are united in *truth*. The Father gave words of truth to the Son, and He gave them to His apostles (John 17:8). The apostles preached and wrote the truth to be handed down through the ages (2 Tim. 2:2). This intra-Trnitarian unity in the truth must unify the church as well (cf. Rom. 15:5–6).

ASK YOURSELF

How would you describe the motive you carry into each day?
Is it the kind of mission befitting a follower of Christ? Does
your place in His kingdom have a significant impact on your
usual business and practice? How might your sense of unity
within the body be affected by a shift in your goals and thinking?

REFLECTING PERFECT UNITY, PART 2

*"As You, Father, are in Me and I in You . . . that
they may be perfected in unity."* —JOHN 17:21–23

The church should reflect the perfect unity of the relationship between Jesus and His Father. Besides unity in motive, mission, and truth, there are two more considerations.

The Father and the Son are united, fourthly, in *holiness* (John 17:11, 25). The throne room of heaven echoes with the angelic cry, "Holy, Holy, Holy, is the Lord of hosts, the whole earth is full of His glory" (Isa. 6:3; cf. Rev. 4:8). Likewise Jesus, bearing the divine nature, is "holy, innocent, undefiled, separated from sinners" (Heb. 7:26).

This aspect of divine holiness, separation from sin, is how believers unite in holiness. They shun evil (1 Peter 3:10–12) and pursue holiness. Hebrews 12:14 says, "Pursue peace with all men, and the sanctification without which no one will see the Lord." Tolerating sin obscures the glory of divine holiness we're meant to display.

Finally, the Father and the Son are united in *love*. Intra-Trinitarian love is an unbroken reality, and one of Jesus' favorite themes (e.g., John 3:35; 5:20; 17:24). As believers, we need to be known for "love, which is the perfect bond of unity" (Col. 3:14). It's our ultimate apologetic to the unbelieving world (John 13:34–35).

ASK YOURSELF

Name one aspect of your life—whether at home with your family, or among your close relatives, perhaps in a work or community setting—where your decision to love could possibly make a change in the whole dynamic. How could you better love the people within the closest proximity to you? How would God be glorified by it?

THE RESULT OF TRUE UNITY

*"So that the world may believe [and] know that You sent Me, . . .
and loved them, even as You have loved Me."* —JOHN 17:21–23

Jesus' prayer for the visible unity of His church is focused on His mission of redemption. When the world observes the unity of the church, they see the results of the Father/Son mission to redeem the lost (Luke 19:10). The church united in its motive (to glorify God), its mission (to save the lost), and its message (the revealed truth of the gospel), united in holiness and love, is successful in showing the world that Christ is the Savior who redeems and transforms lives (cf. John 13:35).

The church's unity also provides evidence of the Father's love for believers. Paul wrote, "Therefore I, the prisoner of the Lord, implore you to walk in a manner worthy of the calling with which you have been called, with all humility and gentleness, with patience, showing tolerance for one another in love, being diligent to preserve the unity of the Spirit in the bond of peace" (Eph. 4:1–3).

That kind of unity is not of this world; it simply doesn't exist among unbelievers. When divine unity and love are reflected in the church, people see the distinguishing mark of the Father's love.

ASK YOURSELF

How desperate are you for others to see and recognize the love God has for them? How much of your praying and activity is taken up with concern for the eternal welfare of the people you know and meet? Why is it so easy for this focus to drop so low on our priority lists, almost forgotten? What could you do to restore a true heart for the hurting, needy, and spiritually starved of your world?

THE FULFILLMENT OF FUTURE GLORY

*"Father, I desire that they also, whom You have
given Me, be with Me where I am."* —JOHN 17:24a

The beauty of this final petition in Jesus' High Priestly Prayer is that the Lord wants to spend eternity with us, His chosen people. Humanly speaking, there is nothing to warrant such a staggering, overwhelming privilege. As Christians, each one of us had an inglorious beginning. We were God's enemies (Rom. 5:10), dead in our trespasses and sins (Eph. 2:1), separate from Christ (v. 12), and far from the glory of God (Rom. 3:23).

"But God, being rich in mercy," made us alive in Christ (Eph. 2:4–5). He forgave our sins by Christ's perfect atonement on the cross (Col. 1:13–14) and gave us the gift of divine righteousness in Christ (Rom. 3:21–22). We've been justified, reconciled to God (Rom. 5:9–10), "raised . . . up with [Christ], and seated . . . with Him in the heavenly places" (Eph. 2:6).

All that remains of our salvation is the redemption of our bodies (Rom. 8:23) when "we will be like Him, because we will see Him just as He is" (1 John 3:2). Then the consummation of our hope will fulfill this petition in Jesus' prayer, which is today's text—"I desire that they also, whom You have given Me, be with Me where I am" (John 17:24).

ASK YOURSELF

Stop for a moment to realize the gravity of this knowledge: the God of glory knows you, loves you, and desires to have a relationship with you. What could we possibly allow to interfere with so great and indescribable an invitation? What are you doing today to make the most of this astounding opportunity?

THE UNVEILING OF FUTURE GLORY

". . . so that they may see My glory which You have given Me." —JOHN 17:24*b*

The apostles beheld God's glory in Jesus Christ, glory as of the only Son from the Father, when they witnessed the incarnation (John 1:14). But here Jesus asks that the outward appearance conform with the inward reality. He longs for the permanent unveiling of His divine glory in the presence of all His disciples.

In conjunction with this glorious revelation, all believers will share Christ's glory. Paul told the Philippians, "For our citizenship is in heaven, from which also we eagerly wait for a Savior, the Lord Jesus Christ; who will transform the body of our humble state into conformity with the body of His glory, by the exertion of the power that He has even to subject all things to Himself" (Phil. 3:20–21; cf. Rom. 8:29; 1 Cor. 15:49).

One day every believer will enjoy the high and holy privilege of seeing Jesus just as He is (1 John 3:2; cf. 1 Cor. 13:12; Phil. 2:9–11). Then the heavens will resound with the song of the redeemed for all eternity: "Worthy is the Lamb that was slain to receive power and riches and wisdom and might and honor and glory and blessing" (Rev. 5:12–13).

ASK YOURSELF

What is able to veil the depths of Christ's reality from your heart? What do you allow to come between yourself and a daily, ongoing awareness of the greatness, glory, and exalted nature of God? How could this begin to be a more cognizant, tangible reality to you? How could you slice through the fog of doubt and complacency to seek the face of God in more deliberate, more earnest ways?

THE FORETASTE OF FUTURE GLORY

*"O righteous Father . . . I have made Your name known to them, and will make it known, so that the love with which You loved Me may be in them, and I in them." —*JOHN 17:25–26

Jesus had known the Father perfectly from all eternity (Matt. 11:27; John 1:1, 18; 7:29; 8:55; 10:15), and He had made the Father known to His disciples as well. They demonstrated their knowledge of the Father when they confessed Jesus' true identity and origin (v. 6; Matt. 16:15–17; John 1:18; cf. Matt. 11:27).

The Lord came to lead lost sinners into a personal relationship with God (Luke 19:10), which comes only through the knowledge of the Son (John 17:3, cf. 14:6; Acts 4:12). The knowledge of the Father comes initially at the moment of salvation, continues to grow and develop through the process of sanctification, and bursts forth in resplendent glory in the presence of the Father in glorification.

Proof positive that someone who *professes* the knowledge of God actually *possesses* the knowledge of God is the abiding quality of love. Love is the eternal badge of every true Christian, and love will permeate every facet of heavenly reality (John 13:34–35; 1 Cor. 13:8, 13). Love is also a present reality we practice here and now—the foretaste of future glory (Rom. 5:5).

ASK YOURSELF

What are your greatest challenges to loving others? What does any failure to love tell you about yourself, even when it is hard to express or it goes unrewarded? If your love for your spouse, your children, your parents, and others were truly unconditional, what would it look like? How would it be different from the kind of love you have been giving (or withholding) lately?

THE PREPARATION OF SOVEREIGN GRACE, PART 1

"You know that after two days the Passover is coming, and the Son of Man is to be handed over for crucifixion." —MATT. 26:2

Unbelieving skeptics have long tried to explain away Jesus' death as the unintended end of a well-meaning revolution, or perhaps the sad end to the delusions of a madman. Others picture Jesus as a forward-thinking visionary, or even an outspoken prophet who brought down the wrath of the religious establishment. Not only do these opinions fail to square with Scripture, they are downright blasphemous.

The truth is that Jesus predicted His death and resurrection several times. He was on a divine timetable, and no human plans or power could cause that timetable to vary in a single detail. "No one has taken [My life] away from Me," He declared, "but I lay it down on My own initiative" (John 10:18; cf. 19:10–11).

The many attempts on Jesus' life (Luke 4:16–30; John 5:18; 7:44–46) failed because none of them represented God's time or God's way for the Son to die. Jesus' death on the cross was the result of the preparation of sovereign grace. No human power could have accomplished it apart from God's will, and no human power could have prevented it, because it was God's predetermined plan (Luke 22:22; Acts 2:23).

ASK YOURSELF

What great determination Jesus showed in carrying out the Father's commission on His life. It is the same determination with which He administers both grace and discipline to us, never wavering in fulfilling His purposes. So rather than seeing His involvement in your life as an intrusion, how could you begin inviting His will to be done in you at whatever cost, through whatever means?

THE PREPARATION OF SOVEREIGN GRACE, PART 2

*"You know that after two days the Passover is coming, and the
Son of Man is to be handed over for crucifixion."* —MATT. 26:2

Jesus knew it was the Father's time for Him to die. After all, it was the beginning of the Passover, the divinely appointed time for Passover lambs to die; so it was Jesus' time to die.

Passover reminded Israel how God used the blood of a lamb to redeem them from Egypt. But the annual sacrifice of those lambs also looked ahead, anticipating the most significant redemption:"the Lamb of God who takes away the sin of the world!" (John 1:29). The sacrifices of all the other lambs were but faint symbols of what the true Lamb would accomplish for eternity.

Jesus was the Lamb who was led to slaughter but did not open His mouth (Acts 8:32–34); He is "Christ our Passover [who] also has been sacrificed" (1 Cor. 5:7); He is the unblemished Lamb "foreknown before the foundation of the world, but [who] has appeared in these last times for the sake of you" (1 Peter 1:19–20). And having accomplished eternal redemption for us, Jesus is forever worthy "to receive power and riches and wisdom and might and honor and glory and blessing" (Rev. 5:12).

ASK YOURSELF

Do you recognize any signs today that indicate God is calling you to a specific task—leading you to make a certain decision, directing you to repair a damaged relationship, guiding you to undertake an act of service or ministry? Will you be faithful, as Jesus was, to go where the Father is showing you? Will you submit to the draw of the Spirit to be obedient, to be brave, to be surrendered?

THE PREVAILING PLAN OF GOD

*Then the chief priests and the elders of the people were gathered together
in the court of the high priest, named Caiaphas; and they plotted together
to seize Jesus by stealth, and kill Him. But they were saying, "Not during
the festival, otherwise a riot might occur among the people."* —MATT. 26:3–5

While Jesus spoke to His disciples on the Mount of Olives, there was
another, more sinister conversation taking place. The Sanhedrin had
gathered in the court of Caiaphas, the high priest. As a shrewd politician,
Caiaphas valued compromise and pragmatic expediency (John 11:50). As
a wicked high priest, Caiaphas perpetuated the decadent religious system
that dominated Israel, skimming the profits of the money changers and
sellers of sacrificial animals (Matt. 21:12–13; John 2:14–16).

That night, Caiaphas and the Sanhedrin met for one purpose: to plot
the arrest and execution of Jesus. Their power and influence should have
guaranteed a stealthy arrest and private killing *after* the Passover. But the
Sanhedrin failed to factor the sovereignty of God into the planning.
Passover was the time God had chosen. All their authority and cunning
couldn't prevent what God had ordained, or *when* God ordained it; they
couldn't make a dent in the timetable. According to God's will, the Jewish leaders put Jesus to death at the very time they most wanted to avoid.

ASK YOURSELF

What opposition are you facing today in seeking to be faithful to God,
in trying to follow through on what His Word commands of you? How
does the divine timing of the Father's plan in Christ Jesus encourage
your heart today, reminding you that no threat or obstacle is powerful
enough to stop what He has determined to do in and through you?

A MEMORIAL OF WORSHIP

"Truly I say to you, wherever this gospel is preached in the whole world, what this woman has done will also be spoken of in memory of her." —MATT. 26:13

While visiting the home of Simon the leper in Bethany, Mary (sister of Martha and Lazarus, cf. John 12:3) anointed Jesus with a very costly perfume "to prepare [Him] for burial" (Matt. 26:12). It was a costly act; the vial was worth a year's wages for a common laborer or soldier (cf. Mark 14:5).

Mary had a special sensitivity to the Lord's teaching (cf. Luke 10:39), and she seems to have understood that her redemption was connected to Jesus' impending death. She had just witnessed His resurrection power in the raising of her brother, Lazarus. Didn't Jesus *have* to die in order to be raised again?

So, anticipating His death, Mary anointed Jesus' head and feet (Matt. 26:7; John 12:3). She lost all sense of restraint and economy, and poured out the expensive perfume to paint a perpetual picture of loving, Christ-centered worship.

Accounts of this story appear in three of the Gospels; the Holy Spirit's memorial of Mary's love and generous worship have fulfilled the Lord's prediction. Two thousand years later, we still read and talk about Mary's sacrificial act of love. She's a lasting example of unselfish, sacrificial adoration.

ASK YOURSELF

How have you been resistant to offer God the best of your worship, not wanting to pour yourself out completely, wanting to hold a few things back to enjoy and rely on? What might others see of the Lord Jesus in you if you were to stop being afraid of declaring yourself totally His, if you were to devote your all to following and worshiping Him?

THE BETRAYAL OF JUDAS

Then one of the twelve, named Judas Iscariot, went to the chief priests and said,
"What are you willing to give me to betray Him to you?". . . from then on he
began looking for a good opportunity to betray Jesus. —MATT. 26:14–16

Judas Iscariot proved to be the polar opposite of Mary. He went to the chief priests, probably while they were still assembled with the Sanhedrin at Caiaphas's house, and asked, "What are you willing to give me to deliver Him up to you?" The Jewish leaders must have been thrilled and amazed that one of Jesus' own disciples would be the means of their destroying Him. They eagerly weighed out to Judas thirty pieces of silver. For the price of a slave (cf. Ex. 21:32), Judas not only sold out his teacher, leader, and friend; he betrayed the very Son of God, his only Savior.

Irreversibly committed to the treachery, Judas began looking for a good opportunity to betray the Lord. He found it when Jesus was "apart from the multitude" (Luke 22:6) in the garden of Gethsemane. In the greatest example of forsaken opportunity the world has ever known, Judas forever turned his back on the Lord and on his own salvation. And the Lord forever turned His back on Judas.

ASK YOURSELF

Through the years, as you have read and thought about this painful part of Jesus' life, what have been some of your most compelling insights and lessons learned? How has Judas's betrayal of his Master spoken to you about your own heart? Has God brought it to mind at times when you might have contemplated turning your back on Him? How deeply does it make you want to follow Christ at all expense?

Setting Up the Final Passover

Now on the first day of Unleavened Bread the disciples came to Jesus,
saying, "Where do You want us to prepare for You to eat the Passover?"
—MATT. 26:17

It's clear that Jesus had made previous arrangements with the owner of the house to eat the Passover in his large upper room. As this account makes clear, He did it secretly, without informing His disciples.

The clandestine approach was necessary to prevent Jesus' premature betrayal. Had the Lord announced the place earlier, Judas would surely have told the chief priests and elders where to find Him (cf. Matt. 26:14–16). Even when He gave instructions to Peter and John, Judas had no way of knowing the location; he and the others wouldn't find out until they arrived that evening. By keeping the meeting place covert, Judas's plans were delayed.

The delay gave Jesus the undistracted time He needed to share an intimate Passover meal with His disciples, during which He would impart vital instruction (John 13–16). More than that, this evening turned out to be the monumental occasion when Jesus transformed the Passover supper of the old covenant into the Lord's Supper of the new covenant. The former was marked by the shedding of lambs' blood; the latter would be marked by the shedding of His own blood (Luke 22:20).

ASK YOURSELF

Think back to some of the most significant experiences you have had with Christ, those moments when His presence seemed so near. What have you taken from those times? How have they marked and changed you? How open do you remain to the possibility that He may choose to interact with you again in a close, meaningful way?

NEEDING TO KEEP THE FINAL PASSOVER

*The Teacher says, "My time is near; I am to keep the
Passover at your house with My disciples."* —MATT. 26:18

"Time" does not translate *chronos*, which refers to succession of time
but rather to *kairos*, a specific and often predetermined period or moment
of time. Jesus' time was also, of course, the Father's time, the divinely appointed time when the Son would offer Himself as the sacrifice for sins.
Until now, that monumental time had not come and could not have come
(cf. John 7:6), but at this particular Passover it could not fail to come, because it was divinely ordained and fixed. That last Passover supper
would set in motion the final, irreversible countdown, as it were, for the
crucifixion.

"I am to keep the Passover" is an indication of Jesus' mind-set. He
was on a divine mission set in a divine timetable, both of which were un-
alterable. Jesus was determined to keep the Passover for the same reason
He had been baptized: "to fulfill all righteousness" (Matt. 3:15). He *perfectly* obeyed every divine commandment of the Old Testament law. "Do
not think that I came to abolish the Law or the Prophets," He declared at
the beginning of His ministry. "I did not come to abolish, but to fulfill"
(Matt. 5:17).

ASK YOURSELF

Is there anything you feel you have left undone in your life so
far, a calling of God that you have either resisted or neglected or
lost amid the shuffle of your busy schedule? How might you begin
praying that God would restore to you the opportunity to follow
through on what you know you should do? What might it cost
you to be wholly faithful to the Spirit's prompting?

LEARNING HUMILITY AT THE FINAL PASSOVER

*Now when evening came, Jesus was reclining at
the table with the twelve disciples.* —MATT. 26:20

Although the original Passover meal in Egypt was eaten in haste while standing, with loins girded, sandals on the feet, and staff in hand (Ex. 12:11), the ceremony had relaxed through the years to become more leisurely. Just before the meal, as the twelve disciples began to take their places around the table, Jesus found an occasion to teach.

"A dispute [arose] among [the disciples] as to which one of them was regarded to be greatest" (Luke 22:24). Failing to sense the gravity of the hour, they manifested hearts of pride and ambition. In response, Jesus "rose from supper, and laid aside His garments; and taking a towel . . . began to wash the disciples' feet" (John 13:4–5).

The Lord took the part of a slave, washing their feet "as an example that you also should do as I did to you" (v. 15). Jesus' humble, selfless ministry was a stinging rebuke of the disciples' pride and a profound lesson in condescending love. To make sure they didn't miss the point, Jesus said, "The kings of the Gentiles lord it over them . . . Not so with you, but let him who is the greatest among you become as the youngest, and the leader as the servant" (Luke 22:25–26).

ASK YOURSELF

Where have pride and self-importance sneaked into your life, even in almost imperceptible ways, even in culturally acceptable ways? What kinds of damage does pride always have the likelihood of doing to your heart, to your relationships with others, to the purity and openness of your relationship with God? How have you suffered from its side effects in days past?

IDENTIFYING THE TRAITOR, PART 1

He said, "Truly I say to you that one of you will betray Me."
—MATT. 26:21

The disciples were well aware of Jesus' many enemies, so it hardly surprised them that He would be betrayed. It did shock them to learn that the betrayer would be one of their own group. Understandably, they were deeply grieved and "at a loss to know of which one He was speaking" (John 13:22).

Judas was perhaps among the least suspected (as the treasurer, his integrity was thought to be beyond reproach), but the others began to say, "Surely not I, Lord?" Jesus said nothing to alleviate their anxiety. Instead, He intensified it with a cryptic saying: "He who dipped his hand with Me in the bowl is the one who will betray Me" (cf. Ps. 41:9). The betrayer was still among them.

Jesus wasn't as concerned with revealing His betrayer as He was with giving His disciples the right perspective about His betrayal. They needed to understand that the heinous act they would soon witness was part of God's sovereign plan: "The Son of Man is to go, just as it is written of Him." Peter's sermon at Pentecost shows that they *did* come to understand. "This Jesus [was] delivered up by the predetermined plan and foreknowledge of God" (Acts 2:23).

ASK YOURSELF

Have you ever been let down by a friend, someone you trusted and in whom you never saw signs of unfaithfulness? Have you ever been the one doing the betraying? Have you ever disappointed someone who truly cared about you? Why should we not be surprised at the fickleness of the human heart? How can you guard your own heart from being led astray into doing once unthinkable things?

IDENTIFYING THE TRAITOR, PART 2

And Judas, who was betraying Him, said, "Surely it is not I, Rabbi?"
*Jesus said to him, "You have said it yourself." —*MATT. 26:25

Judas imitated the astonished disbelief expressed by the rest of the disciples; he parroted their anxious queries and even feigned loyalty, calling Jesus *Rabbi.* Jesus didn't respond with a direct accusation; He simply said, "You have said it yourself." Judas had condemned himself.

The other disciples didn't overhear this brief exchange, so Peter privately prompted John to find out the betrayer's identity. Jesus responded: "[He] is the one for whom I shall dip the morsel and give it to him" (John 13:26; cf. Ps. 41:9). He then turned and handed the accusing morsel to Judas.

When Judas took the morsel, he sealed his destiny for all eternity— "Satan then entered into him" (John 13:27). God's supreme adversary, the ruler of darkness, became Judas' inner companion until the deed was done. By betraying the Son of God, Judas became the arch sinner of all human history.

Now that the betrayer was identified, there was no reason he should remain among them, so Jesus set him loose. "What you do, do quickly" (v. 27*b*). With Satan and his slave out of their midst, Jesus was free to spend His last precious moments with His *true* disciples.

ASK YOURSELF

The harboring of sin and deception always leads us to run from the presence of God, unable to withstand the conviction of His nearness. Are you avoiding His presence in any way? Have you routinely found yourself turning to all kinds of substitutes for spending time with Him? What do you think is the root cause of your desire to avoid His gaze?

A NEW MEMORIAL

Jesus took some bread . . . broke it and gave it to the disciples . . . and when He had taken a cup and given thanks, He gave it to them. —MATT. 26:26–27

Eating the bread and drinking the wine were normal features of the Passover. Unleavened bread and wine were featured at several points during the meal, but this was probably the third cup, called the cup of blessing. What happened next, though it came about in quiet, unadorned simplicity, forever shifted the focus from Passover lambs to the perfect, final Lamb of God.

First, Jesus took some bread and offered a blessing of thanks to His heavenly Father, as He always did before eating (e.g., Matt. 14:19; 15:36). The unleavened bread was baked in large, flat, crisp loaves, which Jesus broke into pieces before He gave it to the disciples: "Take, eat; this is my body" (cf. John 6:48–58). Shortly after that, when He had taken a cup and given thanks again, He gave it to them, saying, "Drink from it, all of you (Matt. 26:27*b*)."

Jews continue to celebrate Passover, remembering the day when God redeemed Israel from Egypt. But we Christians celebrate the fulfilled Passover in the Lord's Supper, a perpetual memorial of our spiritual redemption, secured by the perfect atonement of Jesus Christ on the cross.

ASK YOURSELF

What does your participation in the Lord's Supper mean to you? How does He bring refreshment to your soul as you partake, inspiring you to worship in newer, deeper ways? Why is it so important to regularly join with your church fellowship in this shared meal of repentance and celebration? What would you say to someone who belittled its value as a means of spiritual refreshment to His people?

THIS IS MY BODY

"Take, eat; this is My body." —MATT. 26:26

When Jesus said, "This is My body," He was obviously not speaking literally. Some of the Pharisees, misconstruing His meaning, ridiculed Him, and many superficial disciples deserted Him (cf. John 6:48–66). The same misunderstanding is reflected in the Roman Catholic doctrine of transubstantiation, severely misinterpreting Jesus, making Him sound absurd. Jesus' statement about eating His body was no more literal than His saying He is the Vine and His followers are the branches (John 15:5), or than John the Baptist's calling Him the Lamb of God (John 1:29).

What Jesus did when He said "This is My body" was to invest the traditional Passover ceremony with new meaning. The original unleavened bread symbolized severance from the old life in Egypt. The children of Israel were to carry nothing of its pagan and oppressive "leaven" into the Promised Land. That bread represented a separation from worldliness and sin and the beginning of a new life of holiness and godliness.

By His divine authority, Jesus transformed this symbolism into another. From that point forward, the bread would represent Christ's own body, sacrificed for the salvation of men. Luke records additional words from Jesus: "given for you; do this in remembrance of Me" (22:19). Jesus had instituted a profound memorial of His sacrificial death, which the church has observed now for centuries.

ASK YOURSELF

There is perhaps a point where focusing on the physical suffering of Jesus on the cross can border on idolatry, thinking only of the blood and drama, not of the deeper spiritual meanings. But how does reflecting on His grief and pain assist you in worshiping Him? How does His suffering motivate you to suffer all things for Christ?

THIS IS MY BLOOD

"Drink . . . for this is My blood of the covenant, which is poured out for many for forgiveness of sins." —MATT. 26:27–28

When God made covenants with Noah, Abraham, and Moses, He ratified the covenants with blood (Gen. 8:20; 15:9–10; Ex. 24:8). Reconciliation with God always comes at a cost, the price of blood, because "without shedding of blood there is no forgiveness" (Heb. 9:22; cf. 1 Peter 1:2).

Although Jesus did not bleed to death, He did bleed both before He died and as He died; blood poured from the wounds of the crown of thorns, the lacerations of the scourging, and the nail holes in His hands and feet. Even after He was dead, a great volume of His blood poured out from the spear thrust into His side. Christians are truly redeemed with precious blood (1 Peter 1:19).

But it's not the chemistry of Christ's blood that saves; it's the sacrificial death that secured the forgiveness of sins (blood is being used as a figure of speech called *metonymy*, in which blood stands for the concept of death). Jesus gave His unblemished, pure, and wholly righteous life for the corrupt, depraved, and wholly sinful lives of unregenerate men. In an unrepeatable act of mercy and sacrifice, He made complete atonement for the sins of all who place their trust in the Lord Jesus Christ.

ASK YOURSELF

Celebrate today what Christ has won for you through His sinless life, His perfect sacrifice, and His complete devotion to the plans of the Father on your behalf. What more could He have done to secure your life in His faithful hands? What more could you do to express gratitude for the lengths He went to save you?

A LASTING MEMORIAL

"I will not drink of this fruit of the vine from now on until that day when I drink it new with you in My Father's kingdom." —MATT. 26:29

Jesus instructed His disciples to remember Him in the eating of the unleavened bread, which represents His sacrificed body, and in the drinking of the cup, which represents His shed blood as a sacrifice for sin. "Do this," He said, "as often as you drink it, in remembrance of Me" (1 Cor. 11:25). It's a memorial that will continue until "that day" in His Father's kingdom.

The Lord's promise to drink with the disciples in that future kingdom was another assurance to them of His return. This assurance took on an intensified meaning after His death, resurrection, and ascension. "When I return to establish My kingdom," He promised them, "you will all be there and you will all drink the cup new with Me." In other words, the Lord's Supper is not just a reminder of our Lord's sacrifice for our sins; it's also a reminder of His promise to return and share His kingdom blessings with us.

ASK YOURSELF

Why is it so difficult to maintain a steady focus on the assurance of your future with Christ? How many of your dreads and anxieties are largely the result of being too tightly focused on the present, uncomforted by the living fact that your destiny (if you have surrendered your heart to the Lord Jesus) has already been prepared for you? How could you begin embracing this mind-set on a regular basis? What reminders would help you keep everything else in better prespective?

IGNOMINY AND GLORY

Then Jesus said to them, "You will all fall away because of Me this night . . . But after I have been raised, I will go before you to Galilee."
—MATT. 26:31–32

Being God, Jesus was able to see all things clearly—past, present, and future. He possessed the perfect interpretation of all history and could give the most accurate foretelling of everything future. When Jesus spoke from divine omniscience, it often proved uncanny and unsettling for His disciples.

On this occasion, Jesus predicted the falling away and restoration of His disciples. Their falling away was necessary to fulfill Zechariah 13:7: "I will strike down the shepherd, and the sheep of the flock shall be scattered." This seems to be all the disciples heard. Speaking for the rest of the disciples, Peter said, "I will never fall away . . . I will not deny You" (Matt. 26:33, 35); and "all the disciples said the same thing too" (v. 35).

Jesus' disciples were fixated on imminent defeat (cf. vv. 33–35)—and who could blame them? But what they failed to hear in Jesus' words was the promise of resurrection and restoration: "But after I have been raised, I will go before you to Galilee" (v. 32). Glory would outshine ignominy when the supposed victim was revealed as the foreordained Victor. Even in the looming darkness, God was still on the throne.

ASK YOURSELF

Are you experiencing anything in your life right now in which all you can see is the loss, the pain, the sacrifice? What are some of the positives that God may be working in the midst of this difficult season or circumstance? What would be different if your despondency could turn to expectation of what He might do?

PRIDE, IGNORANCE, AND FORGIVENESS

*Peter said . . . , "I will never fall away.". . . Jesus said . . . , "you
will deny Me three times." Peter said, ". . . I will not deny You." All
the disciples said the same thing too.* —MATT. 26:33, 34, 35

Though he'd previously confessed Jesus' messiahship and deity (Matt.
16:16), Peter wouldn't accept the Lord's prediction. Why? His pride
wouldn't let him. He contradicted the Lord (cf. 16:22); he considered himself better than his fellow disciples (26:33); and he foolishly trusted his own
strength. "Even if I have to die with You, I will not deny You" (v. 35).

The disciples were obviously ignorant of many things—their weakness and Satan's strength; the great power that fear would soon have over
them; and the necessity that prophecy be fulfilled (cf. v. 31). In fact, they
were *willfully* ignorant, elevating their own understanding above the
Lord's. We believers can be like that, claiming to be wise, courageous,
and self-sufficient. And sometimes, as with the disciples, the Lord allows
us to learn the hard way that we are really foolish, cowardly, and weak.

But that's why Jesus went to the cross: to shed His blood for proud,
foolish, and sinful disciples. In spite of pride, weakness, desertion, and
denials, Jesus draws His own to Himself again in perfect love, restoring
them in grace, mercy, and forgiveness. We confess our sins, and He's
faithful to forgive us (1 John 1:9).

ASK YOURSELF

Take this opportunity today to reflect on your own inadequacies
in following through on what you have promised to the Lord,
discovering as His Word says, that Christ's power dwells in those
who boast in their weaknesses (see 2 Cor. 12:9). How different does
spiritual success feel when you know it is all His doing, not your own?

SORROW IN GETHSEMANE

"My soul is deeply grieved, to the point of death." —MATT. 26:38

The agony of this temptation was unequaled; it was Jesus' most intense struggle with Satan. His subcutaneous capillaries dilated and burst under the pressure of deep distress. Blood leaked through the pores of His skin, mingled with His sweat and "falling down upon the ground" (Luke 22:44). In such deep sorrow Jesus knew His only solace was with His heavenly Father, so He retreated to a place of seclusion some distance away (cf. vv. 36, 39, 42).

Jesus was not grieved because of fear, as if He would succumb to Satan's temptations. Nor was He grieved over possible failure, not conquering sin or surviving death. Jesus was deeply grieved because of the role He was about to take on—becoming the sin-bearer (cf. 2 Cor. 5:21). In perfect holiness, He was repulsed by sin (cf. Hab. 1:13) and would soon face the rejection of the Father (Matt. 27:46).

But His extreme distress over the cross, bearing sin and experiencing divine rejection, would give way to profound joy (Isa. 53:10–12; Heb. 12:2). His sacrifice secured eternal salvation for His people (cf. Isa. 53:4–6). What started with intense sorrow would end in songs of praise (cf. Heb. 2:10–13).

ASK YOURSELF

We know what the weight of our own personal sin feels like when it bears down hard on our spirits. Try imagining the sins of all His people, weighing on His heart all at one time. How does it clarify your view of the cross by seeing the primary cause of His suffering to be the burden of human sin rather than the physical pain He allowed Himself to receive? How does this deepen your worship?

SUPPLICATION IN GETHSEMANE

"My Father, if it is possible, let this cup pass from Me;
yet not as I will, but as You will." —MATT. 26:39

By saying "if it be possible," Jesus wasn't trying to escape the Father's will; rather, He was asking if avoiding the cross were possible within the Father's redemptive plan and purpose. It's the cry of a uniquely perfect man, the sinless Son of God for whom the sentence of death should not apply (cf. 1 Peter 1:22–23). So He looked longingly to His Father for another option.

But there was no other option. God's wrath and judgment, often pictured in the Old Testament as a cup to be drunk (e.g., Ps. 75:8; Isa. 51:17; Jer. 49:12), were to be poured into Jesus' cup. The Son would drink the full measure of His Father's wrath against the sins of His people. In full submission, resting completely in the perfect will of His Father, Jesus accepted what was to come: "yet not as I will, but as You will," cf. Matt. 26:42, 44).

This account shows how Jesus was "tempted in all things as we are, yet without sin" (Heb. 4:15). The more Satan tried to divert Jesus from His Father's will and purpose, the more closely He drew into His Father's presence, leaving us a pattern to follow in His steps.

ASK YOURSELF

To what do you typically turn when your emotions unravel, when your pain intensifies, when your stress reaches a high degree? Instead of pressing harder into relationship with God, what do you often choose as a substitute? Why do we tend to look for strength and relief from other quarters rather than drawing it up from the boundless well of His compassion and power?

Sleeping in Gethsemane

He came to the disciples and found them sleeping, and said to Peter,
*"So, you men could not watch with Me for one hour?" —*MATT. 26:40

Finding His disciples asleep must have added greatly to Jesus' grief and distress. How could they sleep on the eve of His crucifixion, in the last hours of His life?

In one sense, their sleepiness was understandable. It was probably after midnight, a normal time for sleep, and they had endured a long, eventful day—a large meal, followed by intense teaching and a mile walk from the upper room to the Mount of Olives. Furthermore, they were distressed by the ominous words Jesus had spoken about His departure. Sleep for them may have been a means of escape from the weariness of sorrow, frustration, confusion, and depression (cf. Luke 22:45).

Still, they were oblivious to the agony of the Lord and the need of the hour. Despite His warnings of their abandonment and of Peter's denial, they weren't mindful of the need to be alert, much less to seek God's strength and protection. In truth, their lack of vigilance was inexcusable. Had they accepted Jesus' word at face value, their minds and emotions would have been far too exercised to allow sleep. They should have watched with Him, praying that they would not fall into temptation (cf. Matt. 26:41).

ASK YOURSELF

When was the last time a matter of significant life importance demanded your full alertness and attention, but you sought to drown it in escape? What did you miss by not being spiritually equipped to handle what would be needed of you, not ready to discern the wise, prayerful decisions you would be called upon to make? What will you do differently when such an event arises again?

WATCH AND PRAY

"Watch and pray that you may not enter into temptation." —MATT. 26:41a

Considering the circumstances, Jesus' rebuke was especially mild. He didn't intend to shame His disciples but rather to strengthen them, teaching them their need for divine help.

"Watch" and "pray" are present tense verbs, commanding continuous action, because the need for spiritual vigilance is not occasional but constant. The only way to keep from being engulfed in temptation is to anticipate Satan's craftiness in prayer. Overcoming temptation isn't possible in the flesh, and spiritual tragedy awaits anyone who thinks they can find victory by their own power.

When a military observer spots the enemy, he doesn't single-handedly engage; he reports what he saw to his commanding officer who has the resources to deal with the threat. Likewise, we dare not attempt to fight temptation on our own. We look to the Lord, who is ever ready to deliver us from temptation and evil (cf. Matt. 6:13).

Peter seems to have learned the lesson Jesus taught that night in the garden. As an older, wiser Christian, he taught, "Be of sober spirit, be on the alert. Your adversary, the devil, prowls about like a roaring lion, seeking someone to devour" (1 Peter 5:8); for "the Lord knows how to rescue the godly from temptation" (2 Peter 2:9).

ASK YOURSELF

Have you been struggling recently against a particularly knotty sin habit or rebellious tendency? What have you learned anew from this latest battle? What have been the most damaging decisions you've made in navigating your way through the temptations and deceptions? How have you failed at times to tap into the power of Christ at work in you? When have you experienced real victory?

HOW TO AVOID SPIRITUAL DEFEAT

"The spirit indeed is willing, but the flesh is weak." —MATT. 26:41*b*

Matthew 26:36–46 gives the pattern and sequence of spiritual defeat for the believer: confidence, sleep, temptation, sin, and disaster.

Just like the disciples who thought they'd never forsake the Lord, a false sense of *confidence* in your own power will eventually lead to sin (cf. Matt. 26:35). Self-confidence leads to *sleep*—indifference to evil and a lack of moral and spiritual vigilance (Rom. 13:11; 1 Thess. 5:6). The sleeping believer is completely vulnerable to *temptation*, Satan's enticements for the unwatchful Christian.

Spiritual self-confidence and a sleepy indifference to sin leaves you wide-open to temptation and inevitable *sin*. No person, not even the strongest Christian, has the capacity within himself to withstand Satan and avoid sin. If sin doesn't awaken you to your desperate condition, you'll spiral into spiritual *disaster*. Unacknowledged, unconfessed sin leads to spiritual tragedy.

That's the pattern the disciples followed that last night of Jesus' earthly life, and it's been the same for every believer since. But this passage also contains the key to spiritual victory: the example of Jesus. His confidence was in God, not self; He was morally and spiritually vigilant, not indifferent; He resisted temptation in God's power, not His own; and He held fast to obedience rather than caving in to sin.

ASK YOURSELF

Which of these elements in sin's downward cycle are you most susceptible to? As you seek to follow Christ's example more faithfully and completely, what do you expect to change? How deeply would freedom from chronic sin affect absolutely everything about the way you relate to others and live each day?

SETTING THE TIME AND PLACE

[Jesus] went forth with His disciples over the ravine of the Kidron, where there was a garden, in which He entered with His disciples. —JOHN 18:1

Jesus had a strategic reason for entering the garden of Gethsemane that night; He knew His betrayer would look for Him there. Though Jesus had eluded capture previously (His hour had not yet come, cf. John 2:4; 7:30; 8:20), the time had come for Him to offer His life (cf. Luke 22:53). So the Lord chose the time and place of His betrayal.

Jesus had another reason for allowing His enemies to seize Him in Gethsemane. Throngs of pilgrims visiting Jerusalem had fervently hailed Him as the Messiah just a few days earlier. A public arrest would have sparked an insurrection by the passionately nationalistic crowds, which is what the Jewish leaders feared (cf. Matt. 26:4–5). Jesus didn't want a popular revolt either. He didn't come as a military conqueror seeking to overthrow the Romans (cf. John 6:15); He came to die as a sacrifice for sin (Matt. 1:21; John 1:29).

The plans Judas set in motion with the Jewish authorities a few days earlier were about to come to fruition. Having received the Roman co-hort and officers from the chief priests and the Pharisees, Judas led this "large crowd" (Matt. 26:47) to Gethsemane, where he knew Jesus would be waiting.

ASK YOURSELF

How does the humilty and self-restraint of Christ inspire you today? What are some of the situations in your life in which you struggle to stay deliberate and faithful to hold strong to your convictions? What might you intend to change about this in the days ahead? What are the greatest obstacles to overcome?

CHRIST'S SUPREME COURAGE

Judas then, having received the Roman cohort and officers from the chief priests and the Pharisees, came there with lanterns and torches and weapons. So Jesus, knowing all the things that were coming upon Him, went forth. —JOHN 18:3–4a

The large procession, with Judas in the lead (Luke 22:47), "came there with lanterns and torches and weapons" to seize Jesus. The lanterns and torches would not have been necessary to light the way to Gethsemane; since it was Passover, which was celebrated when there was a full moon, there would have been ample light. Evidently, they anticipated that Jesus would attempt to flee, and that they would have to search for Him on the mountainside.

But the Lord had no intention of hiding or fleeing. Instead, with majestic calmness, absolute self-control, and supreme courage, "Jesus, knowing all the things that were coming upon Him, went forth" out of the garden and met those who came to arrest Him. John's note that Jesus knew all the things that were coming upon Him emphasizes both His omniscience and His complete mastery of the situation. The Lord's voluntary surrender stresses again that He willingly laid down His life (John 10:17–18).

ASK YOURSELF

Where are you lacking in courage today? What challenge or confrontation are you avoiding simply because the thought of it makes you draw back in fear? What calling of God are you shrinking away from, unsure that you are capable of following Him where He has asked you to go? Who is depending on you for something that can be accomplished only by stepping out in bold reliance on God? How will it feel to look back and know that you were afraid to act?

CHRIST'S SUPREME POWER

So when He said to them, "I am He," they drew back and fell to the ground.
—JOHN 18:6

When Jesus asked the officers of the Roman cohort "Whom do you seek?" (John 18:4), He forced them to articulate their arrest orders. They gave the appropriate, official response: "Jesus the Nazarene" (v. 5). What happened next demonstrated His divine dominance in a stunning manner. Jesus, the intended victim, took charge of the situation.

Jesus replied, "I am He," and the entire crowd drew back and fell to the ground. Some unbelievers foolishly deny this display of supernatural power, saying Jesus actually startled the column of soldiers. By lurching backward, soldiers in front knocked down those who followed, and the whole cohort supposedly fell down like dominoes. That might work for the Keystone Kops, but it's far from reality. Hundreds of experienced officers and trained soldiers were ready for a fight should Jesus' disciples try to attack.

All Jesus had to do was speak His name and His enemies were rendered helpless. This amazing demonstration of His power clearly reveals that they did not seize Jesus. He went with them willingly, carrying out the divine plan of redemption that called for His sacrificial death. John's account highlights Christ's divine power; at His word His enemies were thrown backward to the ground.

ASK YOURSELF

What enemies in your life need to be thrown back by the power of God? Any sins that have done far too much damage already? Any regrets that are keeping you from feeling free to move ahead with God? Any guilt you are carrying for transgressions that have long been forgiven? Any destructive memories that eat away at your spiritual confidence? Bring them to God today, and invite Him to claim victory.

Under Christ's Protection

to fulfill the word which He spoke, "Of those whom
You have given Me I lost not one." —John 18:9

After His stunning display of divine power, Jesus again asked His dazed, would-be captors, "Whom do you seek?" (John 18:7) Picking themselves up off the ground, they repeated their orders and replied, "Jesus the Nazarene (v. 7*b*)." "I told you that I am He," Jesus reminded them, and then commanded them, "if you seek Me, let these go their way" (v. 8).

By making His captors state their orders twice, the Lord forced them to acknowledge the scope of their authority; they were allowed to arrest Him only, having no authority to arrest His disciples. His awesome power display provided further motivation to stay within the boundaries of their orders.

Why did Jesus shield the disciples from arrest? He's the Good Shepherd who protects His sheep. He's no hired hand who flees when the wolf approaches (John 10:12–13). Jesus prevented the disciples' arrest to fulfill His own word: "Of those whom You have given Me I lost not one" (cf. 6:39, 40, 44; 10:28; 17:12). Every one of Jesus' disciples is a gift from His Father, and He'll never let them go (cf. 6:37–40).

ASK YOURSELF

Does Jesus' loyalty to His followers bring to mind a situation in which you had a choice to express loyalty to your spouse, a child, a friend, a church member, a work associate? What happens in these relationships when the other person knows you will stay devoted to and protective of him or her no matter what the cost to you? As you face another chance in the future to commit your allegiance to someone special, what do you intend to do?

CHRIST'S SUPREME POWER

Jesus said to Peter, "Put the sword into the sheath; the cup which the Father has given Me, shall I not drink it?" —JOHN 18:11

Sensing what was about to happen, Peter impulsively (and needlessly) charged to the Lord's defense. He drew his sword, intending to hack his way through the entire detachment. Peter's first victim was Malchus, the high priest's slave. He aimed for his head, but missed (or Malchus managed to duck) and cut off his right ear. It was a futile, reckless act that could have ended with the death or arrest of all the disciples—exactly what Jesus was trying to prevent.

The Lord quickly defused the situation. He sharply rebuked Peter ("Stop! No more of this," Luke 22:51; cf. Matt. 26:52). With angelic resources at His disposal (Matt. 26:53), He didn't need His human disciples to fight to protect Him (John 18:36). Then the Lord "touched [Malchus's] ear and healed him" (Luke 22:51). The troops should have fallen at His feet in worship at this gracious display of divine power, but they didn't; they arrested Jesus instead.

Peter's brave but impetuous act revealed his continued failure to understand the necessity of Jesus' death. The hour had arrived, not for a physical battle with swords and spears but for a spiritual battle for the souls of men, from which Christ would emerge the Victor.

ASK YOURSELF

How often do you feel the need to defend yourself against attacks on your reputation or against unfair appraisals of your intentions? How in practical terms could you allow the Lord to be your defender, even returning a blessing to those who are working to misrepresent you? What might be the result if you did?

JESUS' TRIAL: ACT ONE

So [they] arrested Jesus and bound Him, and led Him to Annas first;
for he was father-in-law of Caiaphas, who was high priest that year.
Now Caiaphas was the one who had advised the Jews that it was expedient
for one man to die on behalf of the people. —JOHN 18:12–14

Annas was a proud, ambitious, and notoriously greedy man. A significant source of his income came from the concessions in the temple, a share of the proceeds from the sale of "approved" sacrificial animals. Temple inspectors would reject sacrifices brought by the people so they could promote the sale (for exorbitant prices) of sacrifices approved by the high priest.

Annas also profited from the fees the money changers charged to exchange foreign currency into the Jewish money that alone could be used to pay the temple tax (cf. 2:14). So infamous was his greed that the outer courts of the temple, where those transactions took place, became known as the Bazaar of Annas.

Annas had a special hatred for Jesus; He had twice disrupted his business operations by cleansing the temple (Matt. 21:12–13; John 2:13–16). But his triumph over Jesus only served the purposes of God, as spoken by his son-in-law Caiaphas, that one man should die on behalf of the people (cf. John 11:49–52).

ASK YOURSELF

How interesting do you find it that Jesus, the epitome of holy perfection, was brought for judgment before a corrupt leader of the people? Why should we never be surprised by the disdain others feel and communicate toward Christ, nor by the demeaning opinions they may have toward us as His followers?

PETER'S DENIAL

Peter then denied it again; and immediately a rooster crowed. —JOHN 18:27

Peter had managed to regain his composure after Jesus' arrest, and he followed Jesus and the arresting party into the courtyard of the high priest (John 18:15–18). As he did, the slave girl who kept the door jolted Peter with an unexpected question: "You are not also one of this Man's disciples, are you?" Caught off guard, Peter lost his nerve and tersely blurted out, "I am not."

Desperate to avoid further questions, Peter hurried across the courtyard to warm himself where others were standing beside a charcoal fire. Someone asked the suspicious newcomer, "You are not also one of His disciples, are you?" Again, failing to be courageously honest, he denied it: "I am not."

These questions aroused the suspicions of Malchus's relative (of the Malchus whose ear Peter cut off earlier); he challenged Peter with the most specific accusation of all: "Did I not see you in the garden with Him?" Panic-stricken, Peter emphatically denied for the third time any knowledge of Jesus.

Immediately after Peter's third denial, a rooster crowed. At that very moment, "the Lord turned and looked at Peter. And Peter remembered the word of the Lord" (Luke 22:61). Overwhelmed with shame, guilt, and grief at his sins of denial, Peter "went out and wept bitterly" (v. 62).

ASK YOURSELF

Having read this account so many times, what have you chiefly taken away from Peter's denial? How has it served as a signpost on the road of your life, reminding you of the courage required to be a sincere follower of Christ? When have you had an experience similar to Peter's gaze meeting the eyes of his Master, and how has it marked your desire to stay devoted to Him?

JESUS' TRIAL: ACT TWO

The high priest then questioned Jesus about His disciples, and about His teaching.
—JOHN 18:19

Jesus' trial before the Jewish authorities was a sham. They'd already planned to murder Him (John 11:47–48, 53), so they weren't concerned about true guilt or innocence. They simply hoped to cover the murder with a veneer of legality.

Since Annas had no charges or evidence against Him, he tried to get Jesus to incriminate Himself. Jesus answered Annas's questions about His disciples and teaching: "Question those who have heard what I spoke to them; they know what I said." It wasn't an act of defiance. Jewish law protected the accused from self-incrimination, so He asked that they uphold the requirements of Jewish jurisprudence.

This unmasked Annas's hypocrisy, causing him to lose face; so one of the officers standing nearby struck Jesus, saying, "Is that the way You answer the high priest?" Jesus, however, maintained a majestic calm (cf. 1 Peter 2:23), and answered the one who struck Him, "If I have spoken wrongly, testify of the wrong; but if rightly, why do you strike Me?"

Once again Jesus demanded a fair trial, exposing the nefarious intentions of His accusers. Annas was getting nowhere with his questioning, so he sent Jesus bound to Caiaphas. Only Caiaphas, the reigning high priest, could bring legal charges against Jesus before Pilate.

ASK YOURSELF

Do you struggle to stay calm and keep a clear head in high-pressure situations? Do you often think back to things you wish you had said (or hadn't said) when you were in the heat of a quick-thinking moment? How can you appropriate the Lord's wisdom on a more consistent, more confident basis?

ACCUSATION AND PROVIDENCE

*Pilate went out to them and said, "What accusation
do you bring against this Man?"* —JOHN 18:29

Pilate's question "What accusation do you bring against this Man?"
formally opened the legal proceedings. The Jewish leaders had undoubtedly already communicated with him about this case, since Roman troops
took part in Jesus' arrest. They evidently expected him to rubber-stamp
their judgment and sentence Jesus to death. Instead, exercising his prerogative as governor, he ordered a fresh hearing over which he would
preside.

But the last thing the Jewish leaders wanted was a trial. They wanted
a death sentence; they wanted Pilate to be an executioner, not a judge.
They knew that their charge against Jesus, that He was guilty of blasphemy because He claimed to be God incarnate, would not stand up in a
Roman court. Their reply skirted the issue.

Though Pilate initially stood his ground, exposing the Jews' unrighteous intentions, he eventually caved in to their demands. But the unsettling partnership between Pilate and the Jews had a much deeper
significance. Pilate's involvement fulfilled Jesus' prediction that the
Gentiles would take part in His death (cf. Mark 10:33–34). Further, it
guaranteed the form of His execution—Roman crucifixion rather than
Jewish execution by stoning (3:14; 8:28; 12:32). God providentially controlled the events of Jesus' trial to ensure His prophetic words would
come to pass.

ASK YOURSELF

How does seeing God's sovereign plan at work in Christ's life
uplift your spirit, knowing He is working His will in your life as
well? Pray that your trust in Him will grow as you come to realize
that He is involved in even the smallest detail, orchestrating behind
the scenes, performing grander purposes through your life than
you can typically observe in the moment.

NOT OF THIS WORLD

Jesus answered, "My kingdom is not of this world." —JOHN 18:36

The Jews tried to portray Jesus as an insurrectionist, bent on over-throwing Roman rule and establishing His own. Pilate needed to investigate potential threats to Roman power, so he asked, "Are You the King of the Jews?" (John 18:33). Was Jesus pleading guilty or not guilty to the charge of
insurrection?

Jesus answered Pilate: "My kingdom is not of this world." Its source was not the world system, nor did Jesus derive His authority from any human source. If His kingdom were of this world, His servants would be fighting to prevent His being delivered over to the Jews. No earthly king would have allowed himself to be captured so easily.

Christ's kingdom has nothing to do with human effort; its power is manifest in the Son of Man's victory over sin in the lives of His subjects. His kingdom is spiritually active in the world today, and one day He will return to physically reign on the earth in millennial glory (Rev. 11:15; 20:6). Until then, His kingdom exists in the hearts of believers, where He is the undisputed King and sovereign Lord. Standing before Pilate, He posed absolutely no threat to the national identity of Israel, or to the political and military identity of Rome.

ASK YOURSELF

How would you describe the evidence of God's kingdom on display in the activities you see around you today, in your church or your city or your neighborhood? How does it energize you to know that you are personally involved in the eternal plans of God, and that you are always in a sure place when you yield to Him as King over all?

A MISSION OF TRUTH

*"For this I have been born, and for this I have come
into the world, to testify to the truth."* —JOHN 18:37

Jesus' mission was not political but spiritual: to testify to the truth by "proclaiming the gospel of the kingdom" (Matt. 4:23). Christ proclaimed the truth about God, men, sin, judgment, holiness, love, eternal life— "everything pertaining to life and godliness" (2 Peter 1:3). What people do with the truth Jesus proclaimed determines their eternal destiny.

Jesus' words, an implied invitation to Pilate to hear and obey the truth about Him, were completely lost on the governor. Pilate abruptly ended his interrogation of Christ with the cynical, pessimistic remark, "What is truth?" Like skeptics of all ages, including contemporary postmodernists, Pilate despaired of finding universal truth.

That's the tragedy of fallen man's rejection of God. Without God, there can be no absolutes; without absolutes, there can be no objective, universal, normative truths. Truth becomes subjective, relative, pragmatic; objectivity gives way to subjectivity; timeless universal principles become mere personal or cultural preferences. Fallen mankind has forsaken God, "the fountain of living waters, to hew for themselves cisterns, broken cisterns that can hold no water" (Jer. 2:13). Pilate's flippant retort proved his condition; since he didn't belong to Christ, he couldn't hear and obey the truth.

ASK YOURSELF

What are some of today's biggest misunderstandings about Christian faith and doctrine? If called upon to defend your biblical viewpoints on some of these, do you feel as though you could explain your position well? What value do you place on being able to discuss such meaningful, substantive issues?

OUT OF OPTIONS

"Take Him yourselves and crucify Him, for I find no guilt in Him."
—JOHN 19:6*b*

Pilate tried repeatedly, but unsuccessfully, to rid himself of this explosive case. He tried to push it back to Jewish jurisdiction (cf. 18:31), but it was the Romans who adjudicated capital cases. He tried to transfer the case to Herod Antipas in Jesus' home region of Galilee (Luke 23:7); Herod merely mocked Jesus and sent Him back to Pilate (v. 11). Pilate finally tried to release Jesus as a goodwill gesture at Passover (a custom of Roman occupation), but the Jews preferred Barabbas, a notorious, murderous insurrectionist.

Pilate was caught on the horns of a dilemma. He had formally pronounced Jesus' innocence (18:38; cf. 19:4, 6) and should have released Him. But that would have infuriated the Jews, possibly causing a riot that could have cost his governorship. In the end, Pilate succumbed and had Jesus scourged. He brutally punished a man he had already declared innocent, completely cementing his miscarriage of justice.

Disgusted with the Jews' callous attitude and wanting simply to be rid of Jesus, Pilate said to them, "Take Him yourselves and crucify Him, for I find no guilt in Him." The statement is a non sequitur: "Take this man and crucify Him, because I find Him not guilty." It was a clear sign Pilate had lost control.

ASK YOURSELF

Have you ever made a choice you knew was probably wrong, but you were under pressure to do something, and this seemed like the most expedient thing to do at the moment? How does Pilate show in tragic, extreme detail the disaster that can befall from letting fear and lack of conviction play into your decision making?

PILATE'S FATAL PANIC, PART 1

Pilate . . . was even more afraid . . . and said to Jesus, "Where are You from?"
—JOHN 19:8– 9

When Pilate heard Jesus claimed to be the Son of God (John 19:7), he became "even more afraid." He may have been cynical (cf. 18:38), but he was also a typical Roman—very superstitious. The possibility that Jesus might be a man with divine powers, a god, or son of a god in human form (cf. Acts 14:11) frightened him. Having just ordered Jesus' scourging, he now faced the possibility of supernatural revenge.

Pilate returned to the Praetorium to ask Jesus, "Where are You from?"—from earth or from the realm of the gods? But Jesus gave him no answer, which only increased his anxiety. Pilate asked, "Do You not know that I have authority to release You, and I have authority to crucify You?" (John 19:10). He may have had the right, but he didn't have the courage to do either one.

Breaking His silence, Jesus answered, "You would have no authority over Me, unless it had been given you from above [i.e., from God]" (v. 11*a*). Although Pilate was a responsible moral agent, accountable for his actions, he didn't have ultimate control. Nothing that happens, even the death of Jesus Christ, is outside the sovereignty of God. The Father's sovereign control of events was Jesus' comfort in His darkest hour (cf. 6:43–44, 65).

ASK YOURSELF

How much more trouble do you generally invite upon yourself by saying too much rather than saying too little? In what situations or dynamics are you typically better off by remaining silent? What would have been different if you had chosen this alternative in a recent altercation at home, at work, or within your extended family?

PILATE'S FATAL PANIC, PART 2

"If you release this Man, you are no friend of Caesar; everyone who makes himself out to be a king opposes Caesar." —JOHN 19:12

To the very end, the governor remained unconvinced that Jesus was guilty of anything worthy of death. Therefore Pilate made efforts to release Him, either by further attempts at reasoning with the crowd, or by preparing to pronounce Him innocent. But his attempts were brought to an abrupt halt.

The Jews had failed to convince Pilate of Jesus' guilt, and being afraid the governor would set Him free, they cried out, "If you release this Man, you are no friend of Caesar; everyone who makes himself out to be a king opposes Caesar." This is yet another corrupt, hypocritical irony—the Jews' hated Roman rule and could hardly be considered friends of Caesar.

This was the last straw for Pilate. He couldn't risk a bad report to Caesar, that he failed to deal with a rival to Caesar's throne. The current emperor, Tiberius, was noted for his suspicious nature and willingness to exact ruthless punishment on his subordinates. Pilate feared for his position, his possessions, even for his life. He felt that he had no choice now but to give in to the Jews' wishes. He gave the people what they wanted.

ASK YOURSELF

None of us can claim perfection, of course, and we all could confess to certain struggles over not being totally honest with ourselves, being blind to faults we don't want to see. But how appalled are you at the hypocrisy of these religious leaders? How appalled are you at any hypocrisy you may still observe in your own life? What could you begin doing to eliminate it, to make personal dishonesty unwelcome in your heart?

PILATE'S FINAL PRONOUNCEMENT

"Behold, your King!" . . . *"Shall I crucify your King?"* —JOHN 19:14–15*b*

Thoroughly frustrated, Pilate taunted the Jews one last time, saying, "Behold, your King!" This beaten, bloody, helpless Man was all the King they deserved. Enraged, they cried out, "Away with Him, away with Him, crucify Him!" (John 19:15*a*). Either in continued mockery, or perhaps seeking one final time to escape his dilemma, Pilate said to them, "Shall I crucify your King?" In a chilling act of appalling hypocrisy, the chief priests answered, "We have no king but Caesar" (v. 15*c*).

Though said with blatant duplicity, there was ironic truth in their statement. Having rejected their messianic King, they were left with only Caesar. Those who falsely accused Jesus of blasphemy committed the ultimate blasphemy, since God alone was Israel's true King (cf. Judg. 8:23; 1 Sam. 8:7; Ps. 149:2; Isa. 33:22).

Pilate's question, "What shall I do with Jesus who is called Christ?" (Matt. 27:22), is the same one facing every person. There are only two alternatives: stand with His rejecters and crucifiers to face eternal damnation (Heb. 6:6), or acknowledge Him as Lord and Savior (Rom. 10:9) and be saved. Pilate's futile attempts to evade the issue reveal clearly that there is no middle ground for, as Jesus declared, "He who is not with Me is against Me; and he who does not gather with Me scatters" (Matt. 12:30).

ASK YOURSELF

With lies, weakness, unbelief, and bitter hatred flying around Him in all directions, Jesus remained unmoved, resolved to continue His reliance upon and yieldedness toward the Father—even though He had the power to call everyone to account for their shameful behavior. What do you learn from His example? How does this cause you to be in awe of Him even more?

PROPHETIC FULFILLMENT IN THE CRUCIFIXION, PART 1

. . . and He went out, bearing His own cross . . . —JOHN 19:17*a*

In keeping with Old Testament law (Num. 15:36) and Roman practice, executions took place outside the city. Likewise, according to Mosaic law, the sin offerings were to be taken outside the camp of Israel. Exodus 29:14 reads, "But the flesh of the bull and its hide and its refuse, you shall burn with fire outside the camp; it is a sin offering" (cf. Lev. 4:12; 16:27). Therefore, Jesus' crucifixion had to happen outside of Jerusalem, where He would become the sin-bearer, fulfilling Old Testament typology.

The author of Hebrews highlights the theological significance of Jesus, the final sin offering, being executed outside the city. He wrote, "For the bodies of those animals whose blood is brought into the holy place by the high priest as an offering for sin, are burned outside the camp. Therefore Jesus also, that He might sanctify the people through His own blood, suffered outside the gate" (Heb. 13:11–12).

Jesus bore our reproach outside the camp when He suffered and died on the cross, and that becomes a compelling reason for our identifying with Him outside the camp. The author of Hebrews says, therefore, "let us go out to Him outside the camp, bearing His reproach" (Heb. 13:13).

ASK YOURSELF

How much are you willing to suffer or be misunderstood or be pitied by those who feel sorry for the things you must give up to stay devoted to Christ? Nothing is easy about bearing any shame or reproach for wearing His name, but what have you learned about the alternative? What is always the result of compromising your loyalty, being unwilling to live without others' acceptance?

PROPHETIC FULFILLMENT
IN THE CRUCIFIXION, PART 2

They took Jesus . . . to the place called the Place of a Skull . . .
There they crucified Him . . . —JOHN 19:17–18a

When the Israelites complained against Moses in the wilderness, "the Lord sent fiery serpents among the people and they bit the people, so that many people of Israel died" (Num. 21:6). The fiery serpents stimulated some hasty self-examination; the people acknowledged their sin to Moses, pleading with him to intercede before the Lord.

Moses did intercede (v. 7), and the Lord responded, saying, "'Make a fiery serpent, and set it on a standard; and it shall come about, that everyone who is bitten, when he looks at it, he will live.' And Moses made a bronze serpent and set it on the standard; and it came about, that if a serpent bit any man, when he looked to the bronze serpent, he lived" (vv. 8–9).

In John 3:14 Jesus referred to that incident as a typological prediction of His own death: "As Moses lifted up the serpent in the wilderness, even so must the Son of Man be lifted up" (cf. 8:28; 12:32–33). Thus the crucifixion of Jesus Christ by the Romans specifically fulfilled both the picture of Numbers 21 and the predictions of the Lord Himself.

ASK YOURSELF

Satan works hard to keep you from sensing the "fiery serpent" bite of sin until you're drawn in and entangled, until you feel too at home or discouraged to pull away. May this be a day when you ask the Lord to show you just how dangerous and damaging your sin is, how deadening it is to your spirit. May you run to Jesus as your Savior, not only as your eternal Redeemer but also as your constant, daily Deliverer from Satan's deception.

PROPHETIC FULFILLMENT
IN THE CRUCIFIXION, PART 3

This was to fulfill the Scripture: "They divided My outer garments among them, and for My clothing they cast lots." Therefore the soldiers did these things.
—JOHN 19:24*b*

Penned by David centuries before it happened, Psalm 22 may be the most graphic picture of Christ's crucifixion. Jesus' cry of profound sorrow is the first line of the psalm (cf. Matt. 27:46); and Jesus experienced all the derision depicted by the psalmist (compare Ps. 22:6–8 with Matt. 27:39–43).

David was also explicit about Jesus' physical torment: exhaustion (v. 14); His unnatural bodily position that caused His bones to be out of joint (v. 14) and put stress on His heart (v. 14); failing strength and raging thirst (v. 15); nails through His hands and feet (v. 16); and His taut, emaciated body (v. 17).

The independent actions of the soldiers, after they had crucified Jesus, fulfilled the words of Psalm 22:18. As the four soldiers on the execution squad sat down to divide His clothing, they parceled out His outer garments (head covering, belt, sandals, outer robe) equally among them. But Jesus' tunic was seamless, woven in one piece. They "said to one another, 'Let us not tear it, but cast lots for it, to decide whose it shall be'" (John 19:24*a*). They unwittingly fulfilled David's prophetic psalm, furthering the sovereign plan of God and validating biblical accuracy.

ASK YOURSELF

When you see Scripture folding together in such intricate harmony, forming a unity of theme and message that could be achieved only by the hand of God, how does it lay aside any insecurities about your salvation? How does He encourage your heart in very personal, specific ways by speaking to you through His Word, by confirming His control and capabilities?

THE SUPERSCRIPTION

"What I have written I have written." —JOHN 19:22

Pilate instructed that an inscription be affixed above Jesus' head on the cross. The placard normally listed the crimes of the sentenced criminal, but since Jesus had committed no crime (1 Peter 2:22), Pilate wrote, "JESUS THE NAZARENE, THE KING OF THE JEWS" in Hebrew, Latin, and Greek (see John 19:19*b*).

This infuriated the Jews. The idea that a man from a despised town like Nazareth, dying a criminal's death on a cross, could be their king was ludicrous. It was a direct affront both to the leaders and the nation. Pilate was expressing his contempt for the Jewish people, implying that such an individual was the only kind of king they deserved.

Here again is an example of God using sinful men to accomplish His sovereign purposes. Neither Pilate nor the Jewish leaders believed that Jesus was the king of Israel. Yet the animosity between them ensured that the governor would write an inscription proclaiming that Jesus was Israel's King, as in fact He is. He is the "King of kings, and Lord of lords" (Rev. 19:16), and "at the name of Jesus every knee will bow, of those who are in heaven and on earth and under the earth, and . . . every tongue will confess that Jesus Christ is Lord, to the glory of God the Father" (Phil. 2:10–11).

ASK YOURSELF

If you have surrendered your life to Christ, you are protected by One who will never change, no matter what others say about Him or expect Him to be. How dearly do you wish to be that kind of person yourself, one who is faithful and constant, always dependable, unaffected by others' views and opinions?

PRACTICAL CONSIDERATIONS OF SELFLESS LOVE

He said to His mother, "Woman, behold, your son!" Then He
said to the disciple, "Behold, your mother!" —JOHN 19:26b–27a

The only man among the group of faithful women who gathered at the foot of the cross was John, the disciple whom Jesus loved. John's presence led the Lord to establish a very important relationship, a practical consideration of selfless love. Jesus was suffering, dying on the cross, bearing man's sin and God's wrath in His body. And yet He looked beyond the suffering to care for those He loved (cf. John 13:1, 34; 15:9, 13).

Evidently Jesus' earthly father, Joseph, was already dead. The Lord could not commit Mary into the care of His half brothers, the children of Mary and Joseph, since they were not yet believers (7:5). They did not become believers in Jesus until after His resurrection (Acts 1:14; cf. 1 Cor. 15:7). Therefore Jesus entrusted the care of His mother to John; he became as a son to her in Jesus' place, and from that hour he took her into his own household.

This may seem a very mundane thing to be concerned about in the hour of His greatest sacrifice, but the beauty of the Savior's love and compassion for His widowed mother, in the midst of His own excruciating pain, reflects His love for His own (cf. John 13:1).

ASK YOURSELF

Jesus continually showed His character by fulfilling the prophecies of Scripture and being devoted to building and maintaining relationships. How well does your life mirror these aims: staying true to the Word of God and caring for the needs of others? What if anything has taken the place of these priorities in your heart?

PROPHETIC THIRST

*Jesus, knowing that all things had already been accomplished,
to fulfill the Scripture, said, "I am thirsty."* —JOHN 19:28

After Jesus knew everything had already been accomplished to fulfill
the Scripture, He said, "I am thirsty." From a jarful of sour wine that was
standing nearby, one of the bystanders put a sponge full of the sour liquid
on a branch of hyssop (cf. Ex. 12:22) and brought it up to His mouth.

This was the cheap wine that the soldiers commonly consumed. It
was not the same beverage that the Lord had earlier refused (Matt.
27:34). That beverage, which contained gall, was intended to help deaden
His pain so He would not struggle as much while being nailed to His
cross. Jesus had refused it, because He wanted to drink the cup of the Father's wrath against sin in the fullest way His senses could experience it.

Jesus requested the drink because He knew there was only one remaining prophecy to be fulfilled. In Psalm 69:21 David wrote, "They
also gave me gall for my food and for my thirst they gave me vinegar to
drink." Jesus knew that by saying "I am thirsty" He would prompt the
soldiers to give Him a drink. They were all too happy to increase the
Lord's torment by prolonging His life.

ASK YOURSELF

Have you made a new commitment or promise to the Lord lately,
yet the ensuing days have seen you fall back into familiar patterns,
fatigued at the cost of constant faithfulness? We can never fulfill our
desires for wholehearted obedience without relying on His
empowerment, but how does seeing Him pay the full price for our
sin—undiluted—inspire you to surrender your will to Him afresh?

IT IS FINISHED!

He said, "It is finished!" And He bowed His head and gave up His spirit.
—JOHN 19:30

Jesus shouted, "It is finished!" with a loud cry (Matt. 27:50; Mark 15:37). It was a shout of triumph, the proclamation of a victor. The work of redemption that the Father had given Him was accomplished: He atoned for sin (Heb. 9:12; 10:12;) and defeated Satan, rendering him powerless (Heb. 2:14; cf. 1 Peter 1:18–20; 1 John 3:8). He satisfied every requirement of God's righteous law; He appeased God's holy wrath against sin (Rom. 3:25; Heb. 2:17; 1 John 2:2; 4:10); He fulfilled every prophecy.

The completed work of Christ's redemption means that nothing needs to be, *nor can be* added to it. Salvation is not a joint effort of God and man; it is entirely a work of God's grace, appropriated solely by faith (Eph. 2:8–9).

His mission accomplished, He bowed His head and gave up His spirit. Jesus surrendered His life by a conscious act of His own sovereign will (John 10:18). He still had the strength to shout loudly, which means He wasn't physically at the point of death; Jesus actually died sooner than normal crucifixion victims (Mark 15:43–45), indicating again that He gave up His life of His own will.

ASK YOURSELF

Celebrate anew the finished work of Christ on your behalf. Whether you are just beginning your day, or preparing for bed, or perhaps somewhere right in the middle of it, lift up your face to the heavens and praise Him for doing everything required to win the salvation of all His own. How has His cross truly changed you? What makes it more than just a familiar story? How can you thank Him even more specifically for His sacrifice?

SOVEREIGN IN HIS DEATH

. . . coming to Jesus, when they saw that He was already dead . . . —JOHN 19:33

One of the most unsettling aspects of death is the element of surprise. Death frequently comes suddenly and unexpectedly, leaving words unsaid, plans unfinished, dreams unrealized, and hopes unfulfilled. That was not the case with Jesus, however. Death could not surprise Him because He controlled it.

The death of Christ was not the death of a victim; it was the death of a victor. In fact, He died much sooner than was normal for victims of crucifixion. Most victims lingered for two or three days, but Jesus was on the cross for only six hours. For example, both robbers crucified alongside Jesus were still alive after He died (19:32). And when Joseph of Arimathea asked Pilate for Jesus' body, the governor couldn't believe it; he had to question the commander of the execution squad to see "whether He was already dead" (Mark 15:44).

Jesus had said, "I lay down My life so that I may take it again. No one has taken it away from Me, but I lay it down on My own initiative. I have authority to lay it down, and I have authority to take it up again" (John 10:17–18). Jesus proved this claim when He voluntarily gave up His life, just as He had said He would (19:30). He was sovereign, even in His death; He died when He willed to do so.

ASK YOURSELF

How does this perspective on Christ's death only add to the power of His love and sacrifice for you? What does this kind of control under pressure inspire in you as one who bears His Spirit within you by faith, able to apply His overcoming nature to any situation you face?

FULFILLING PROPHECY IN HIS DEATH

For these things came to pass to fulfill the Scripture . . . —JOHN 19:36

The Jews secured Pilate's permission to have the bodies removed from the crosses before the Sabbath (19:31). While crucifying their Messiah, they hoped to avoid violating the law of Moses: "if a man . . . is put to death, and you hang him on a tree, his corpse shall not hang all night on the tree, but you shall surely bury him on the same day" (Deut. 21:22–23). How ironic.

To hasten death, Roman soldiers would smash the victim's legs with an iron mallet; if the shock and additional blood loss didn't kill them, the resulting asphyxiation would. The soldiers broke the legs of the two robbers, and "coming to Jesus, when they saw that He was already dead, they did not break His legs" (John 19:33). To make certain, "one of the soldiers pierced His side with a spear, and immediately blood and water came out" (v. 34). That was proof positive; Jesus was dead (Mark 15:44–45).

Like the Passover lamb (Ex. 12:46; Num. 9:12), God ensured the bones of the true Lamb of God would remain unbroken ("He keeps all his bones, not one of them is broken," Ps. 34:20). And His early death led to the piercing of His side, so that one day Israel could "look on [Him] whom they [had] pierced," and repent (Zech. 12:10). Even in death, Jesus fulfilled prophecy as the Messiah of God.

ASK YOURSELF

In what current situation do you need to be reminded that your Father in heaven pays strict attention to detail, not letting even one experience go wasted, using every single moment of every single day to accomplish His desires in your life?

FULFILLING PROPHECY IN HIS BURIAL

*Now . . . in the garden [there was] a new tomb in which no
one had yet been laid. . . . they laid Jesus there.* —JOHN 19:41–42

Isaiah 53:9 foretold that though Messiah's "grave was assigned with
wicked men, yet He was with a rich man in His death." Humanly speaking, that was not likely. The Romans normally refused burial for crucifixion victims, and the Jews buried criminals outside of Jerusalem.

And yet, Jesus, "having been put to death in the flesh, but made alive
in the spirit" (1 Peter 3:18), moved the heart of Joseph of Arimathea.
Joseph, a wealthy, prominent member of the Sanhedrin (Mark 15:43),
had disagreed with its decision to condemn Jesus (Luke 23:51). But the
Lord strengthened Joseph to approach Pilate about Jesus' body (he'd
formerly been a secret disciple, fearing the Jews; John 19:38). According
to God's sovereign plan, Pilate released the body to Joseph.

Assisted by Nicodemus (another formerly secret disciple), Joseph
prepared Christ's body for burial (an expensive and involved process)
and "laid it in his own new tomb" (Matt. 27:60). Not only did that action
fulfill Isaiah 53:9, the timing of the burial guaranteed Jesus' words "the
Son of Man [will] be three days and three nights in the heart of the earth"
(Matt. 12:40). In His burial, as well as His death, Jesus orchestrated all
the details to accomplish God's already revealed purpose.

ASK YOURSELF

What would represent a daring act of faith on your part—a task
of similar boldness to the ones initiated by Joseph and Nicodemus?
How has God perhaps been speaking to your heart about following
His lead on a matter that has long intimidated you? What
keeps you from exercising spiritual bravery?

THE RESURRECTION

. . . and he saw the linen wrappings lying there, and the face-cloth which had been
on His head, not lying with the linen wrappings, but rolled up in a place by itself.
—JOHN 20:6b–7

Though they were initially skeptical of Mary's and the other women's reports of the empty tomb (Luke 24:11), Peter and John eventually went to the tomb. What they saw was startling. Jesus' body was nowhere to be seen. All that was left were the linen wrappings in which He had been buried.

Unlike Lazarus, who needed help getting out of his grave clothes after his resurrection (John 11:44), Jesus' glorified resurrection body simply passed through the linen wrappings (less difficult than entering a locked room through the walls; 20:19, 26). Even the face-cloth, which had been wrapped around His head, wasn't lying with the linen wrappings; it was rolled up in a place by itself. This seemingly minor detail shows how Jesus left the tomb in a neat, orderly condition. Grave robbers wouldn't have taken time to remove the grave clothes; they would've transported the body still bound, unwrapping it later only to obtain the expensive spices.

Folded grave clothes and a rolled up face-cloth point to resurrection, not grave robbery (cf. Matt. 28:11–15). John believed when he saw it (John 20:8), as do all who have eyes to see and ears to hear.

ASK YOURSELF

What have you seen of Christ, whether in His dealings with you personally or His obvious transformation of people you know and care about, to prove beyond any doubt in your mind that He is absolutely who He says He is? How could you make these events easier to recall when you're tempted to believe He's quit caring or has become incapable of providing for you?

GRIEF TURNED TO JOY

Jesus said to her, "Mary!" She turned and said to Him in Hebrew, "Rabboni!"
—JOHN 20:16

As Mary stood outside Jesus' tomb, weeping and grief-stricken, two angels interrupted her sorrow with a simple question: "Woman, why are you weeping?" (John 20:13). Mary failed to perceive the identity of the angels, and she didn't immediately recognize the Lord either. Perhaps she was blinded by grief, or perhaps Jesus' resurrected body looked significantly different from the battered and bloodied corpse she'd seen on the cross. In any case, Mary was prevented from recognizing Him until He chose to reveal Himself to her (cf. 21:4; Luke 24:16).

Jesus repeated the question, "Woman, why are you weeping?" and then probed further: "*Whom* are you seeking?" (John 20:15, emphasis added). Supposing Him to be the gardener, she solicited His help in locating the missing corpse. Her narrow expectations kept her focused on finding His dead body. With a single word, Jesus opened Mary's eyes. He spoke her name: "Mary!" In a flash, all her doubt, confusion, and sorrow vanished. Recognizing Jesus in that moment, she fell at His feet and clung to Him with affection and joy.

Mary wasn't a prominent figure in the Gospel accounts, yet the Lord chose to appear first to her, a woman. Jesus' appearance to Mary symbolizes His special love and faithfulness to all believers, no matter how insignificant they seem to be.

ASK YOURSELF

Can believers live with such low spiritual expectations that they are not moved in any significant way by even a powerful intervention of God in their circumstances? What keeps our emotions, interests, and excitement from being piqued by God's activity? Why do we tend to belittle His kingdom priorities?

THE MISSION OF MARY MAGDALENE

" . . . go to My brethren, and say to them, 'I ascend to My Father and your Father, and My God and your God.' " —JOHN 20:17

It's easy to forgive Mary for clinging to the Lord, not wanting to release Him, but He still had work to do, and so did she. Jesus had to ascend to His Father; Mary had to deliver a message.

The Lord sent Mary to the apostles to tell them of His impending ascension, and His announcement made a significant distinction. Jesus was going to *His* Father and *His* God, who is also *their* Father and *their* God. Jesus' relationship with the Father was different from theirs. God is not our Father in the same way He is the Father of Jesus Christ.

At the same time, Jesus referred to His disciples as "brethren." They had been slaves and friends (John 15:15), but His atonement had secured a new kind of intimacy. Christ's work of redemption on the cross brought about a new relationship between Jesus and those He redeemed. God adopts all believers into His family (Rom. 8:14–15; Gal. 3:26; Eph. 1:5), and as a result, Jesus "is not ashamed to call them brethren" (Heb. 2:11). He has become "the firstborn among many brethren" (Rom. 8:29).

ASK YOURSELF

Based on what Christ has accomplished in your life and what He has shown you in the midst of your relationship with Him, what might be the primary message He wants you to proclaim through your life? How might this translate into your work, your ministry commitments, your family interactions, even your casual conversations with others?

JESUS VISITS THE TEN

Jesus came and stood in their midst and said to them, "Peace be with you."
—JOHN 20:19*b*

The disciples (minus Thomas) had gathered together in an unspecified location; the doors were shut and locked tight. They were in hiding for fear of the Jews, expecting any minute the temple police to arrive and arrest them. Since the authorities had executed their Master, it wasn't unreasonable to think they might be next (cf. John 15:20).

Suddenly, something happened that was far more startling than the arrival of the temple police: Jesus came and stood in their midst. The locked doors were no deterrent to Him; His glorified resurrection body simply passed through the walls. Thinking they were seeing a ghost (Luke 24:37; cf. Matt. 14:26), the disciples were terrified. But Jesus spoke reassuringly to them, "Peace be with you" (John 20:19; cf. 14:27).

To convince the frightened disciples of His identity, Jesus showed them both His hands and His side (20:20). Luke records His words: "See My hands and My feet, that it is I Myself; touch Me and see, for a spirit does not have flesh and bones as you see that I have" (Luke 24:39). To persuade them that He wasn't an apparition but real flesh and blood, Jesus even ate a piece of broiled fish (Luke 24:41–43). That did it. Recognizing Him at last, the disciples then rejoiced when they saw the Lord.

ASK YOURSELF

How has Christ come to you in your fears and aroused you to confidence in His ability to sustain you? What are some of the most pressing doubts and fears in your life right now, and how does faith in Christ speak a different word than your emotions often communicate?

MISSION AND MEANS

"As the Father has sent Me, I also send you . . . Receive the Holy Spirit."
—JOHN 20:21–22

After convincing His disciples He had risen from the dead, Jesus gave them a preview of their marching orders and the means by which they would accomplish His mission. Jesus told them, "As the Father has sent Me, I also send you" (cf. John 17:18). While this wasn't the Great Commission, which came later in Galilee (Matt. 28:19–20), it was enough to help them understand that the Father's work for them didn't end with Jesus' death and resurrection. In fact, their role had only just begun.

What Christ would commission them to do would require the power of the Holy Spirit, whom He had promised to send them (cf. John 14:16–17, 25; 15:26; 16:7–14). Signifying this coming reality, Jesus breathed on them and said, "Receive the Holy Spirit." This was a purely symbolic and prophetic act, reminiscent of the vivid object lessons frequently employed by Old Testament prophets to illustrate their messages (cf. Jer. 13:1–9; 19:1–11; Ezek. 4:1–4). In other words, Christ did not through this puff of breath actually and literally impart the Spirit in His fullness to them; rather, He declared in a visible figure what would happen to them at Pentecost (Acts 2:1–4).

ASK YOURSELF

Whether by default if not by deliberate decision, have you ever let the completion you feel by virtue of salvation and forgiveness of sins become a hindrance to heeding God's present calling on your life? What can keep you from living with a sense of mission and purpose, not applying the transforming work God has accomplished in you onto other areas where He has placed you to serve?

DELEGATED AUTHORITY

"If you forgive the sins of any, they are forgiven them; if you retain the sins of any, they are retained." —JOHN 20:23

Jesus did not designate a group of men or an ecclesiastical body to act as a second mediator; "there is one God, and one mediator also between God and men, the man Christ Jesus" (1 Tim. 2:5). The New Testament never records an instance of the apostles (or anyone else) absolving people of their sins; God alone forgives sins (Mark 2:7; cf. Dan. 9:9). But making judgments about a person's spiritual condition would be a significant, necessary part of the Great Commission.

Jesus' statement was not new information to the disciples; the Lord had spoken very similar words long before in Caesarea Philippi. "I will give you the keys of the kingdom of heaven; and whatever you bind on earth shall have been bound in heaven, and whatever you loose on earth shall have been loosed in heaven" (Matt. 16:19).

Any Christian can declare that those who genuinely repent and believe the gospel will have their sins forgiven by God. On the other hand, they can warn that those who reject Jesus Christ will die in their sins (John 8:24; Heb. 10:26–27). That's the Christian's duty, based on authority delegated from Christ Himself.

ASK YOURSELF

We tend to overlook or downplay things that are easily taken for granted. But if asked to articulate some of the truths that have been revealed to you solely because of your relationship with Christ and His Word, what would be the first ones that come to mind? How does this underscore the fact that God speaks to us through His Word—and from it in ways we don't always realize?

"MY LORD AND MY GOD"

Thomas answered and said to Him, "My Lord and my God!" —JOHN 20:28

Thomas had missed Jesus' first appearance to the other ten disciples and doubted their exuberant reports: "We have seen the Lord!" (John 20:25*a*). He refused to get his hopes up only to have them dashed once more, so he announced skeptically, "Unless I see in His hands the imprint of the nails, and put my finger into the place of the nails, and put my hand into His side, I will not believe" (v. 25*b*).

Thomas would soon be taken up on his skeptical offer. As He had done eight days earlier, Jesus came in and stood in their midst. He immediately singled out Thomas. Ever the sympathetic High Priest (Heb. 4:15), the Lord met Thomas at the point of his weakness and doubt. "Reach here with your finger, and see My hands; and reach here your hand and put it into My side; and do not be unbelieving, but believing" (John 20:27).

That was enough for Thomas; his melancholy skepticism dissolved forever in light of the irrefutable evidence confronting him. Overwhelmed, he made perhaps the greatest confession of all: "My Lord and my God!" (v. 28). Significantly, Jesus did not correct him. Instead, He accepted Thomas's affirmation of His deity, received his worship, and praised Thomas's faith.

ASK YOURSELF

When caught in an act of inadequate faith, are you usually as quick as Thomas to admit your error? Why do we often delay our repentance, or perhaps consider ourselves on a sort of probation, awaiting a time when God will consider us trustworthy again? What can we learn from Thomas's willingness to rush back into relationship with Christ, accepting His forgiveness with humble joy?

LIFE IN HIS NAME

These have been written that you may believe that Jesus is the Christ, the
Son of God; and that believing you may have life in His name. —JOHN 20:31

Thomas's confession ("My Lord and my God!") gave the apostle John
the perfect segue to state the purpose of his written work. The gospel of
John is an evangelistic book. Those who will never have an eyewitness
perspective on Jesus' life, ministry, death, and resurrection will depend
on John's gospel to hear the word concerning Christ (Rom. 10:17). Only
then will they receive new birth from the Spirit, and the gift of faith.

Jesus did many miraculous signs beyond those recorded in John's
gospel, beyond those recorded in the other three Gospels as well (cf.
John 21:25). However, what has been written is sufficient: "These have
been written so that you may believe that Jesus is the Christ, the Son of
God; and that believing you may have life in His name."

Jesus Christ is God incarnate (1:1, 14), the Lamb of God who takes
away the sin of the world (1:29), and the resurrection and the life (11:25).
To believe in Him is to find forgiveness of sin and eternal life (3:16).

ASK YOURSELF

What helps you stay aware of opportunities, for example, to inject into
conversation an eternal context for a current news event, or to help
someone personalize their need for Christ rather than to speak always in
general terms? Instead of fishing for another common area of small talk,
what if we followed John's lead and looked for ways to make spiritual
connections into people's lives?

NO GOING BACK

They went out and got into the boat, and that
night they caught nothing. —JOHN 21:3

The disciples had a lot to learn about Christ's new direction for their lives. This lesson came in familiar territory, fishing on the Sea of Galilee. The disciples had joined Peter in his former profession. Perhaps they felt inadequate to carry on any spiritual ministry on behalf of the kingdom of God, but fishing was something they could do successfully.

As experienced fishermen, they knew the right time and place to catch fish, nighttime on the Sea of Galilee (cf. Luke 5:5). But that night they caught nothing. Heading back to shore after a long, frustrating night, a man called out to them from the shore: "Children, you do not have any fish, do you?" (John 21:5). Jesus planned to provide a miraculous catch of fish, but not before forcing them to face their inability, their total dependence on Him, and their new direction. It's as if He said, "Do anything else and I will see that you fail!"

There was nothing wrong with fishing; it was a respectable profession. But the Lord had not called them to fish; Jesus chose them to be fishers of men (Matt. 4:19). Having left their nets to follow Him (v. 20; cf. Luke 9:23), there was no going back.

ASK YOURSELF

To what activities do you tend to return when you're confused about your sense of direction or wishing to avoid a harder undertaking? How can you discern when you're merely enjoying a restful getaway, or you're using a familiar "known" to get out of an assignment, to put off responsibility, to get out of having to engage or think about anything else?

A Miraculous Breakfast, Part 1

"Cast the net on the right-hand side of the boat, and you will find a catch."
—John 21:6

The disciples were no doubt exhausted and frustrated after their failed fishing expedition, and yet there was something authoritative in the command from the shore that compelled them to obey. They cast their nets on the right-hand side of the boat. Just as He had rerouted all the fish away from their boat all through the night, Jesus now redirected a massive school into their nets. The catch was so large that all seven couldn't haul it in.

The disciple whom Jesus loved immediately recognized the stranger; only Jesus had such supernatural knowledge and power. So John said to Peter, "It is the Lord" (John 21:7). If John was quicker to perceive, Peter was quicker to act. He threw himself into the sea and waded to shore, so intense was Peter's desire to be with Jesus.

They arrived to find a charcoal fire cooking fish for breakfast. Once again, Jesus demonstrated compassion for His tired, hungry disciples. He had said to them earlier, "I am among you as the one who serves" (Luke 22:27), and He had washed their feet as an example of humble service (John 13:1–15). Now the risen Lord showed He would still serve His faithful disciples by meeting their needs.

ASK YOURSELF

How does the freedom and openness exhibited by Christ in this post-resurrection event relate to our position as forgiven believers? Why should we not be equally alert to opportunities for serving, eager to keep our relationships strong, watching for ways to interact joyfully with others, whether they are celebrating a success or exhibiting a need?

A MIRACULOUS BREAKFAST, PART 2

*Jesus said to them, "Come and have breakfast." —*JOHN 21:12

The Lord's invitation "Come and have breakfast," was a call to full fellowship. Perhaps the apostles felt guilty for trying to return to their former trade; they were uneasy, hesitant, and uncertain. Evidently the disciples were too overwhelmed to accept Jesus' invitation and start eating. Acting as a gracious host, Jesus came and took the bread and gave it to them, and the fish likewise, thus beginning the meal.

The Lord, as always, uses weak and sinful people to advance His kingdom; there are no other kinds of people (cf. Isa. 6:5–8; 1 Cor. 1:26–31; 2 Cor. 12:7–10; 1 Tim. 1:12–15). And just as their disobedience had resulted in failure, the disciples' obedience brought overwhelming success (obedience *always* brings blessing; cf. Ex. 19:5; Ps. 19:11; Isa. 1:19; John 13:17; James 1:25; Rev. 22:7).

Through this miraculous catch of fish on the Sea of Galilee, Jesus taught His disciples, in the most kind and gentle manner, to never return to their old ways. He wanted them to settle forever in their minds that they were called to serve the Lord Jesus Christ for the rest of their lives.

ASK YOURSELF

How easily do you allow others back into relationship with you, even after they've ignored your advice or acted disrespectfully toward you? Why do we often continue to hold people at arm's length, forcing them to jump through additional hoops before we consider them worthy of forgiveness? How much less complicated would your interactions be without the added burden of keeping long accounts? Who needs to know that you accept their apology and desire restoration?

The Mark of a Real Christian, Part 1

*Jesus said to Simon Peter, "Simon, son of John,
do you love Me more than these?" —John 21:15a*

The primary mark of the redeemed has always been love for God. The Shema, the great Old Testament confession of faith, declares, "You shall love the Lord your God with all your heart and with all your soul and with all your might" (Deut. 6:5). Later in Deuteronomy, Moses exhorted Israel to manifest that love by obeying God's commandments (10:12–13; 11:1). The theme of loving God was also on the heart of David, who wrote, "I love You, O Lord, my strength" (Ps. 18:1).

The New Testament also teaches that love is the mark of a true believer. When asked to name the greatest commandment of the law, Jesus replied, "You shall love the Lord your God with all your heart, and with all your soul, and with all your mind" (Matt. 22:37). In 1 Corinthians 8:3, Paul wrote, "If anyone loves God, he is known by Him." On the other hand the apostle warned, "If anyone does not love the Lord, he is to be accursed" (1 Cor. 16:22).

Peter wrote in his first epistle, "Though you have not seen Him [Christ], you love Him" (1 Peter 1:8). As he learned on the shore of Galilee, love is the driving, compelling force that motivates Christian service.

ASK YOURSELF

Knowing this truth as well as we do, why are we not always as loving toward others as we ought to be? To whom have you been withholding your love, either on purpose or by neglect? How much of a factor is your busy schedule in keeping you from being free and available to extend love to those around you?

THE MARK OF A REAL CHRISTIAN, PART 2

[Peter] said to Him, "Yes, Lord; You know that I love You." —JOHN 21:15*b*

Peter learned the hard way what it means to love Jesus Christ. He had vociferously declared his unfailing devotion to Him more than once. At the Last Supper, Peter told Jesus, "Lord . . . I will lay down my life for You" (John 13:37). A short while later he boldly proclaimed, "Even though all may fall away because of You, I will never fall away" (Matt. 26:33). It took only a mildly threatening situation to deflate Peter's vaunted courage; he openly denied three times that he even knew Jesus.

Peter's failure highlights the biblical truth that obedience is the essential evidence of genuine love. In John 14:15 Jesus puts it plainly: "If you love Me, you will keep My commandments." In verse 21 He adds, "He who has My commandments and keeps them is the one who loves Me" (cf. 15:10).

To play the crucial role in the early church that God had chosen for him, Peter needed to be restored. The Lord had already appeared to Peter privately (Luke 24:34; cf. 1 Cor. 15:5), but Scripture does not record any details of that meeting. Since his denials were public knowledge, his restoration needed to be public as well. To submit to his leadership, the other disciples needed to hear Peter's reaffirmation of his love for Christ and Christ's recommissioning of him.

ASK YOURSELF

How do we attempt to affirm our love for God or for others without consistently proving it by our actions? What kind of interference does this cause in your various relationships? Why is obedient devotion to God often the easiest to delay or devalue, even though we owe it to Him the most?

The Mark of a Real Christian, Part 3

*[Jesus] said to him, "Tend My lambs." —*John 21:15c

As soon as they had finished breakfast (cf. John 21:12–13), Jesus initiated the restoration by confronting Peter. The Lord's pointed question, "Do you love Me more than these [i.e., the boat, nets, and other fishing paraphernalia]?" (v. 15a) went right to the heart of the issue. Jesus challenged Peter to permanently abandon his former life and be exclusively devoted to following Him, based on his love.

Peter replied to Him, "Yes, Lord; You know that I love You" (v. 15b). There is an interesting wordplay in the Greek text. The word Jesus used for love is *agapaō*, the highest love of the will, love that implies total commitment (cf. 1 Cor. 13:4–8). Peter, painfully aware of his disobedience and failure, felt too guilty to claim that type of love. He answered by using the word *phileō*, a less lofty term that signifies affection. He also appealed to Jesus' omniscience, reminding Him, "You know that I love You."

Accepting Peter's humble acknowledgment that his love was less than he had claimed, less than Christ deserved, Jesus still recommissioned him, graciously saying to him, "Tend My lambs." "Tend" translates a term used of herdsmen pasturing and feeding their livestock. Jesus described believers as His lambs, emphasizing not only their immaturity, vulnerability, and need, but also that they belong to Him (cf. Matt. 18:5–10). He entrusted His beloved lambs to Peter's care.

ASK YOURSELF

How are you personalizing Jesus' appeal to Peter, considering it your responsibility as well to "tend" His lambs, to care for your spiritual family? What kinds of forms could this responsibility take? What would it require of you that God has already supplied?

THE MARK OF A REAL CHRISTIAN, PART 4

"Lord, You know all things; You know that I love You." —JOHN 21:17*b*

Jesus said to Peter a second time, "Simon, son of John, do you love Me?" (John 21:16*a*). Once again Jesus used the verb *agapaō*, and once again Peter was unwilling to use it in his reply. "Yes, Lord; You know that I love (*phileō*) You" (v. 16*b*). The Lord then charged him, "Shepherd My sheep" (v. 16*c*). "Tend" (v. 15) and "shepherd" express the full scope of pastoral oversight (cf. 1 Peter 5:2).

Still not through with Peter, Jesus questioned him the third time, "Simon, son of John, do you love Me?" (John 21:17*a*). Peter's grief came because, this time, Jesus challenged the level of love Peter thought he could claim. Unlike His two previous questions, Jesus now used Peter's word for love, *phileō*. He called into question even the less than total devotion Peter thought he was safe in claiming.

The implication that his life didn't support even this level of love broke Peter's heart. All he could do was appeal even more strongly to Jesus' omniscience, saying to Him, "Lord, You know all things; You know that I love You" (v. 17*b*; cf. 2:24–25; 16:30). For the third time Jesus accepted the apostle's recognized failure and imperfection (cf. Isa. 6:1–8) and graciously charged Peter to care for His flock, saying to him, "Tend My sheep" (John 21:17*c*). Peter's restoration was complete.

ASK YOURSELF

To what could the Lord specifically point in questioning the depth of your love for Him? How could you revisit these places of withheld devotion, turning your heart afresh to the Lord, discovering the awaiting possibilities in store for those who give Him everything they are?

Following Jesus

Jesus said to him, "If I want him to remain until I come, what is that to you? You follow Me!" —John 21:22

When Jesus predicted Peter's martyrdom, he immediately became concerned for his close friend John. So he asked Jesus, "Lord, and what about this man?" (John 21:21*b*). Jesus' abrupt and censuring reply didn't answer his question; the rebuke made it clear that John's future was none of Peter's business. Reiterating His command from verse 19, Jesus said emphatically, "You follow Me!" Peter's attention was not to be on anyone else but only on his own devotion and duty to Jesus Christ.

We would all do well to embrace this mind-set because the Lord has a unique plan for each one of us. Following Jesus Christ is the *sine qua non* of the Christian life, without which there is nothing else worth pursuing. In John 12:26, Jesus put it simply: "If anyone serves Me, he must follow Me." It is the mark of His sheep that they follow Him (John 10:27; cf. 8:12), no matter what the cost (Matt. 16:24; 19:27; Luke 5:11, 27–28; 9:23–25; 18:28). To follow Jesus means not only to be willing to sacrifice everything in submission to His will but also to obey His commands (Matt. 7:21; Luke 6:46) and to imitate Him (1 Thess. 1:6; 1 John 2:6; cf. 1 Cor. 11:1).

ASK YOURSELF

Do you find that you notice more things competing for your time and allegiance these days than ever before? And as you grow older and mature, are they more difficult to defend against? What does our readiness to crowd our lives with distractions tell us about the condition of our hearts? How could we better steel ourselves to resist the interruptions?

JESUS' FINAL INSTRUCTIONS

*After He had by the Holy Spirit given orders to
the apostles whom He had chosen.* —ACTS 1:2*b*

Between His resurrection and ascension, Jesus continued to teach the
truths of His kingdom. Now, as promised, He was about to end His
earthly ministry and ascend to heaven (cf. John 13:1, 3; 20:17). Jesus'
ministry in the Spirit's power during that time (cf. Matt. 4:1; Luke 4:1, 14,
18) demonstrated the pattern for believers who, like the apostles, are to
obey Him (cf. Matt. 28:19–20).

Although Christ instructed many people while on earth, the primary
targets of His in-person teachings were the apostles. Equipping them for
foundational ministry was a crucial part of His mission. "He had chosen"
them (see John 15:16) for salvation and equipped, gifted, and taught them
for unique service. They were eyewitnesses to the Son and recipients of
divine revelation; they established the message all believers must proclaim. The Lord instilled within them the organized body of truth (cf.
Acts 2:42) that established the church.

The effectiveness of every saint's ministry depends on a deep
knowledge of Scripture. As Spurgeon said, "Never a soul would be converted unless the Holy Spirit uses the Word to convert that soul. So it is
blessed to eat into the very heart of the Bible until . . . you come to talk in
scriptural language and your spirit is flavoured with the words of the
Lord."

ASK YOURSELF

You likely put great stock in the teachings of Scripture and are
devout in your study and meditation of them. But is there any way
in which you hold yourself at a distance from the Bible, not fully
engaging in the experience? How has God convicted you of late,
drawing you to a deeper love for the Word?

Jesus' Final Days, Part 1

To these He also presented Himself alive after His suffering, by many convincing proofs, appearing to them over a period of forty days and speaking of the things concerning the kingdom of God. —ACTS 1:3

Christ's appearances to the apostles, mentioned here, convinced them of His physical resurrection and emboldened them to proclaim the gospel to the Jews. That His men went from fearful doubters to powerful witnesses is strong proof of the resurrection.

A significant final activity is that Jesus was "speaking of the things concerning the kingdom of God." That theme was already a frequent one during His earthly ministry (cf. Matt. 4:23; 10:7; Luke 4:43; 9:2). He conveyed to the apostles additional truth regarding the domain of God's rule over believers' hearts. This further proved to the eleven that He was truly alive.

Jesus also wanted the disciples to understand that His crucifixion had not nullified the promised millennial kingdom (cf. Isa. 11:6–12; Zech. 14:9). The resurrection removed all doubts they might have had following His death concerning the coming, visible reign of Christ. The apostles began proclaiming their Master as King over a spiritual kingdom (cf. Acts 17:7; Col. 1:13; Rev. 11:15; 12:10). This kingdom will appear in its fullness when Christ returns to reign on earth for a thousand years.

ASK YOURSELF

How does an understanding of the kingdom of God change nearly everything about the way you live, how you orient your priorities, the importance you place on even the once insignificant parts of your day, and the way you assign value to certain activities and pursuits? How could you find yourself even more consumed with the work of Christ's kingdom, making it your principal focus?

Jesus' Final Days, Part 2

To these He also presented Himself alive after His suffering, by many
convincing proofs, appearing to them over a period of forty days and
speaking of the things concerning the kingdom of God. —Acts 1:3

The kingdom of God includes more than the millennial kingdom and has two basic aspects: the universal kingdom and the mediatorial kingdom. The first refers to God's sovereign rule over all creation: "The Lord has established His throne . . . and His sovereignty rules over all" (Ps. 103:19; cf. 59:13; 145:13; 1 Chron. 29:11–12; Dan. 4:34).

The mediatorial kingdom is God's spiritual rule over His earthly people through chosen mediators (Adam, the patriarchs, the judges, the prophets, the kings). Following Israel's monarchy, the times of the Gentiles is lasting until the second coming; and during this period God mediates His spiritual rule over believers through the church (Acts 20:25). During the final phase of this period comes the millennium, in which Christ personally exercises control over all things. Finally, the two kingdom aspects will merge (1 Cor. 15:24) and become the same.

During the present church age, then, the Lord mediates His kingdom rule through believers indwelt by the Spirit and obedient to His Word. That's why Peter calls Christians "a chosen race, a royal priesthood, a holy nation" (1 Peter 2:9; cf. 1:8).

ASK YOURSELF

What do you glean from realizing that you are part of something this very day that is more eternal and magnificent than anything your mind can imagine? What are the current worries and concerns that would fade into much clearer perspective if seen against the plans God is orchestrating around you?

PROMISED SPIRITUAL MIGHT, PART 1

"But you will receive power when the Holy Spirit has come upon you."
—ACTS 1:8a

To make sure the disciples were both motivated and divinely empowered for their ministry, Jesus promised to send the Holy Spirit (cf. Luke 11:13; John 14:16, 26; Acts 2:33). God would fulfill that pledge just ten days later at Pentecost.

The apostles had already tasted the Spirit's working, as when Jesus told them prior to a ministry venture, "For it is not you who speak, but it is the Spirit of your Father who speaks in you" (Matt. 10:20). Like other believers in the old economy, they experienced the Spirit's power for salvation and special ministry, but soon they would realize his working and indwelling in a unique, new way.

Jesus' promise also forecast the Holy Spirit's enabling for all believers (cf. Acts 8:14–16; 10:44–48). The prophet Ezekiel also recorded God's promise for all new covenant believers:

> Then I will sprinkle clean water on you, and you will be clean; I will cleanse you from all your filthiness and from all your idols. Moreover, I will give you a new heart and put a new spirit within you; and I will remove the heart of stone from your flesh and give you a heart of flesh. I will put My Spirit within you and cause you to walk in My statutes. (Ezek. 36:25–27a)

ASK YOURSELF

Even with all the misunderstandings and abuses that have occurred in connection with the Holy Spirit, what would you say are among the most noticeable things about having Him active and operational within you? How has He enabled you to accomplish feats that would have been impossible otherwise?

PROMISED SPIRITUAL MIGHT, PART 2

*"For John baptized with water, but you will be baptized
with the Holy Spirit not many days from now."* —ACTS 1:5

Jesus' words here are reminiscent of John the Baptist's statement, "He upon whom you see the Spirit descending and remaining upon Him, this is the One who baptizes in the Holy Spirit" (John 1:33). That promise would be fulfilled, as the apostles would experience it "not many days from now." And the Lord had already promised to send the Holy Spirit after He departed (16:7).

The apostles and early church received unique Spirit-enabling for special tasks, but that is not the norm for saints today. They also received the general baptism with the Holy Spirit in an uncommon way, after their conversions. Since the church's beginning, all Christians must be filled with and walk in the Spirit (Eph. 5:18; Gal. 5:25). Yet the early church was commanded to wait, demonstrating the change that occurred in the church age, during the transition associated with its birth. In this age, baptism by Christ through the Spirit happens for all believers at conversion. At that moment, the Spirit places every believer into the body of Christ (1 Cor. 12:13). At the same time, the Holy Spirit also assumes permanent residency in the believer's soul, so there is today no such thing as a Christian not yet having the Spirit (Rom. 8:9; cf. 1 Cor. 6:19–20).

ASK YOURSELF

Why does this understanding not equate in any way to minimizing the power of the Holy Spirit or downplaying His importance in the believer's life? What are the greatest dangers of limiting God's ability to empower and transform? How does the miracle of Christmas prove again what He can accomplish?

PROMISED SPIRITUAL MIGHT, PART 3

"For John baptized with water, but you will be baptized with the Holy Spirit not many days from now." —ACTS 1:5

Even as so-called Spirit baptism is not a special privilege for elite believers, neither does Scripture challenge nor exhort anyone to seek it—not by praying, pleading, waiting, or any other means. That the verb rendered "be baptized" is passive denotes that baptism by Christ with the Spirit is entirely a divine activity. Like salvation, this baptism comes through grace rather than human effort. Thus God sovereignly pours out the Holy Spirit on those He saves (Titus 3:5–6).

"Power" (Acts 1:8*a*) translates *dunamis*, from which we get the English term "dynamite." All Christians possess spiritual dynamite to activate their gifts, service, fellowship, and witness. For complete effectiveness, they must not grieve the Holy Spirit by sin (Eph. 4:30). Instead, they must be continually filled and controlled by the Spirit (5:18). This happens when they yield moment-by-moment control of their lives to Him—the same thing as yielding their minds to the Word (Col. 3:16). Paul's prayer asks for the ideal result: "that He would grant you, according to the riches of His glory, to be strengthened with power through His Spirit in the inner man . . . Now to Him who is able to do far more abundantly beyond all that we ask or think, according to the power that works within us" (Eph. 3:16, 20).

ASK YOURSELF

On this Christmas Day, celebrate not only the coming of Christ but also the power of the Holy Spirit in orchestrating the Son's birth. He is the same Spirit who lives within and animates your life on a daily basis. Worship Him today for His involvement not only in history but also in your transformed life.

MYSTERY OF THE KINGDOM, PART 1

"Lord, is it at this time You are restoring the kingdom to Israel?" —ACTS 1:6b

The earnest question the apostles ask here is perfectly understandable since Jesus had often prophesied to them about the future (Matt. 24–25; Luke 17:20–37; 21:5–36). They knew of no reason that an earthly kingdom couldn't be established immediately, inasmuch as events signaling the end of the age had arrived. The disciples heading for Emmaus had already been very disappointed that the Lord had not redeemed Israel and set up His kingdom (Luke 24:21). And since Jesus had just promised the Spirit's outpouring, which Ezekiel 36 and Joel 2 connected to the coming kingdom, it's reasonable that the eleven would expect the kingdom very soon. They hoped their roller-coaster emotions of expectation and doubt about these matters might now be over.

Christ, however, brought them right back to reality; "to know times or epochs which the Father has fixed by His own authority" (Acts 1:7) was not for them. With its many teachings about the kingdom, Scripture nevertheless does not give an exact time of its earthly establishment. As far as average people are concerned, such things remain among "the secret things" that "belong to the Lord our God" (Deut. 29:29). All followers of Jesus can be sure His kingdom will be set up at the second coming (Matt. 25:21–34). But the time of that coming remains unrevealed (Mark 13:32).

ASK YOURSELF

Perhaps you are in a situation that seems interminable, continuing to cause you pain and anxiety despite your many appeals to God for relief. If it must continue awhile longer, how will this affect your trust in God's goodness? When waiting is His answer, what might be His reason?

MYSTERY OF THE KINGDOM, PART 2

"Lord, is it at this time You are restoring the kingdom to Israel?" —ACTS 1:6*b*

Our Lord's only corrective regarding the apostles' anticipation of an earthly kingdom involving Israel was about the timing, showing that their comprehension was essentially accurate. If they were mistaken about the fundamental doctrine of a future, literal kingdom, Jesus certainly would have corrected them. Therefore it's reasonable to deduce that the disciples' kingdom expectation mirrored Christ's and the Old Testament's.

With uncertainty for Christians concerning the precise season of their Lord's coming again, and the imminent possibility of the church's rapture (1 Thess. 5:2), they must be prepared always. We need to remember Christ's words:

> Take heed, keep on the alert; for you do not know when the appointed time will come. It is like a man away on a journey, who upon leaving his house and putting his slaves in charge, assigning to each one his task, also commanded the doorkeeper to stay on the alert. Therefore, be on the alert—for you do not know when the master of the house is coming, whether in the evening, at midnight, or when the rooster crows, or in the morning—in case he should come suddenly and find you asleep. What I say to you I say to all, "Be on the alert!" (Mark 13:33–37)

Over many generations of believers, such readiness has prompted earnest expectation and diligent service.

ASK YOURSELF

How do you communicate to a child the importance of waiting, trying to help him or her understand that the end result will be worth the time spent anticipating it? What can you learn from this perspective in waiting on your own answer to prayer?

BELIEVERS' MISSION, PART 1

"You shall be My witnesses both in Jerusalem, and in all Judea and Samaria, and even to the remotest part of the earth." —ACTS 1:8b

"Witnesses" are people who see an event and tell others about it. Years ago I witnessed an attempted murder, and afterward the local court wanted to know three things: what I saw, heard, and felt. I was reminded of the apostle John's words, "What was from the beginning, what we have heard, what we have seen with our eyes, what we have looked at and touched with our hands, concerning the Word of Life . . . we proclaim to you also" (1 John 1:1, 3). A witness for the Lord Jesus is simply a person who tells the truth about Him (cf. 2 Peter 1:16).

The mission commanded in today's text was the foremost one for which the Holy Spirit's empowering arrived. And the early church so effectively fulfilled it that it "upset the world" (Acts 17:6). Christ mandates that all believers fulfill this mission through the Great Commission: "Go therefore and make disciples of all the nations, baptizing them in the name of the Father and the Son and the Holy Spirit, teaching them to observe all that I commanded you" (Matt. 28:19–20a).

So many of the early believers sealed their Christian witness with their blood that "witness" came to mean "martyr," taken from the Greek word for *witness*. Many were converted by observing how calmly and joyously those Christians faced death.

ASK YOURSELF

How seriously do you take this commission of telling your firsthand account of life with Christ? What could occur to change this responsibility from a paralyzing fear into an unqualified privilege? How have you been hesitant before? What could be different today and this coming year?

BELIEVERS' MISSION, PART 2

*"You shall be My witnesses both in Jerusalem, and in all Judea and Samaria, and even to the remotest part of the earth." —*ACTS 1:8*b*

Indisputably, Christians are witnesses, and the only question is how effective they are. If today's church is to reach a lost world with the gospel, believers must "sanctify Christ as Lord in [their] hearts, always being ready to make a defense to everyone who asks [them] to give an account for the hope that is in [them]" (1 Peter 3:15). Christians must build lives of integrity and credibility from which an effective witness can launch. Paul teaches that we should live "so that the word of God will not be dishonored" (Titus 2:5*b*), "that the opponent [of Christianity] will be put to shame, having nothing bad to say about us" (v. 8*b*), and "that [we] will adorn the doctrine of God our Savior in every respect" (v. 10*b*).

Today's verse provides a general outline for the book of Acts. Its author Luke uses it to chronicle the irresistible march of Christianity from Jerusalem, into Samaria, and on through the Roman Empire. This beginning for the church altered world history, and the gospel's spread did indeed reach to all parts of the earth. But Christians still have the responsibility for being the Lord's witnesses throughout the world. That's how extensive the evangelistic sphere is—as big as God's kingdom, and the church's mission until Jesus returns.

ASK YOURSELF

The job is much too large for any one person or church or denomination. But how might God be encouraging you to join forces with others who share your heart, uniting in Christian devotion and fellowship to obey His global vision? How does the false perception of insignificance silence our witness?

THE ASCENSION, PART 1

"This Jesus, who has been taken up from you into heaven, will come in just the same way as you have watched Him go into heaven." —ACTS 1:11b

As Jesus Christ ascended to heaven, back to His former glory, He left His apostles with a final, dramatic moment that was a powerful motivation to advance His kingdom after His departure. "He was lifted up while they were looking on, and a cloud received Him out of their sight" (Acts 1:9b). In His glorified, resurrection body, our Lord left earth for heaven, to take His seat on the divine throne, at His Father's sovereign right hand. As this astounding event unfolded, the stunned disciples "were gazing intently into the sky" (v. 10). To their further bewilderment, two angels in white clothing suddenly came alongside them.

The divine messengers asked the puzzled apostles, "Men of Galilee, why do you stand looking into the sky?" (v. 11a). This denotes more than a routine question about the men's reaction to the miracle. "Looking" refers to a long gaze; in this instance a transfixed stare as if losing someone. The question, then, was a mild rebuke to the eleven. They were not forever losing their Master, as some of them apparently feared. The angels went on to stress that Jesus would someday return to earth in the same glorious manner as the apostles had just seen him ascend (v. 11b; cf. Zech. 14:4; Rev. 14:14).

ASK YOURSELF

How much of God's power and glory do we relegate to the Sunday worship service, not totally convinced it operates quite so effectively on other days of the week? When have you experienced His enablement in rather routine moments, and why do we not experience it more often?

THE ASCENSION, PART 2

"This Jesus, who has been taken up from you into heaven, will come in just the same way as you have watched Him go into heaven." —ACTS 1:11*b*

That Christ our Lord and Savior will return just as He ascended becomes a compelling motivation to Christian service. We don't know when He'll return, but we must live in anticipation that it could be in our lifetimes (cf. 2 Peter 3:14–18). The apostle Paul writes, "For we must all appear before the judgment seat of Christ, so that each one may be recompensed for his deeds in the body, according to what he has done, whether good or bad" (2 Cor. 5:10). Looking to the near future, Christ declares, "Behold, I am coming quickly, and My reward is with Me, to render to every man according to what he has done" (Rev. 22:12). Therefore we must serve Him faithfully in view of such an imminent return (see 1 John 2:28; Rev. 16:15).

The responsibility of finishing our Lord's work on earth, of evangelizing the lost, is indeed a challenging and overwhelming one. But Christ in His mercy from the outset gave us all the spiritual resources we'd ever need to complete the mission. We must put those assets to work, as the Lord earlier admonished His apostles, "We must work the works of Him who sent Me as long as it is day; night is coming when no one can work" (John 9:4).

ASK YOURSELF

Enter the coming year with renewed hope in the power of God to do through you what you cannot, to surrender yourself fully to His lordship, and to so fully enjoy the freedom of forgiven sin that you forsake its allures completely, welcoming others to experience forgiveness as well.

MacArthur
New Testament
Commentary Series

Over a million sold

John MacArthur's explanatory, verse-by-verse approach helps you interpret and apply God's Word.
Easy to understand, yet rich in scholarly background.

For more information, visit MoodyPublishers.com

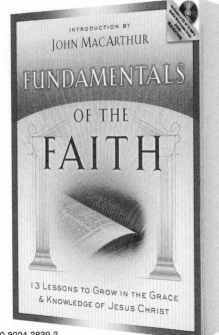

978-0-8024-3839-3

"On Sunday mornings at Grace Community Church, small groups of people gather together in Fundamentals of the Faith classes to use this manual of thirteen lessons, which blend basic biblical truths with personal obedience and service." With topics ranging from "God: His Character and Attributes" to "The Church: Fellowship and Worship," *Fundamentals of the Faith* is an ideal study to disciple new believers or realize afresh what it means to believe in Jesus.

Fundamentals of the Faith contains a CD with thirteen audio messages from John MacArthur to accompany each lesson.

Introduction by John MacArthur

www.MoodyPublishers.com

Not only is Revelation the inspired Word of God, it is also the only New Testament book that includes a promised spiritual blessing for those who heed its message. If you read and obey the words of Revelation, God promises that you will be blessed.

Is Revelation even possible to understand? Sadly, no book in Scripture has been more misunderstood or misinterpreted than Revelation. Does this mean its message is hopelessly obscure? Certainly not. God is a God of clarity. And He gave us the book of Revelation "to show to His bond-servants, the things which must soon take place." He did this in a way His people could understand. Does the End of the Story matter? Some Christians seem to think it doesn't, or at least not very much. But God certainly considers it important.

978-0-8024-7845-0

It is absolutely essential that a church perceive itself as an institution for the glory of God, and to do that, claims John MacArthur, the local church must adhere unfalteringly to biblical leadership principles. Christ never intended church leadership to be earned by seniority, purchased with money, or inherited through family ties. He never compared church leaders to governing monarchs, but rather to humble shepherds; not to slick celebrities, but to laboring servants. Drawing from some of the best-received material on church leadership, this updated edition guides the church with crucial, effective lessons in leadership. This book is valuable not only for pastors and elders, but for anyone else who wants the church to be what God intended it to be.

by John MacArthur

Find it now at your favorite local or online bookstore.

www.MoodyPublishers.com